Oracle

wisdom

Order this book online at www.trafford.com
or email orders@trafford.com

Most Trafford titles are also available at major online book retailers.

Print information available on the last page.

ISBN: 978-1-6987-1088-4 (sc)
ISBN: 978-1-6987-1089-1 (hc)

Library of Congress Control Number: 2022900937

Meet the authors at www.theoracle.ca.

Trafford rev. 01/31/2022

 www.trafford.com

North America & international
toll-free: 844-688-6899 (USA & Canada)
fax: 812 355 4082

PART ONE
Intuitive Awareness and Psychic Development

PART TWO
Personal Growth and Holistic Healing

dedication

Oracle Wisdom is dedicated to you as you travel this path to higher consciousness, creativity, and intuition. An opportunity for personal growth and spiritual development, this book is an offering for your soul.

You have been drawn to this book for a reason. Perhaps it seems to have 'magically' appeared in your life. Indeed, it is a divine invitation to expand your direct experience with the unseen world. Words have energy and the energy of Spirit is here. We wish you the immense joy that is available to you at every moment. Feel it. Breathe it. Allow it.

We are here in love and service.

HOW TO USE THIS BOOK

Each contribution in this anthology offers an intimate experience and deep connection with seventeen unique individuals who have been practicing their holistic methods for years. These pages are filled with stories and teachings in a variety of writing styles to keep you engaged and further your personal and spiritual growth.

You may read the book cover to cover, or randomly by chapter of interest; each piece being an entire topic itself. The authors share their personal experience, as well as how their psychic or holistic traits 'work'. Some modalities are complimentary while others are completely unique. You may relate to some of the authors immediately; while others engage you through the opportunity to explore something unfamiliar, new, or a completely different point of view. *Oracle Wisdom* is a tool to help you discover what works best for you.

With love and light as your guides - experiment, practice, and stretch your abilities on your journey through the world of metaphysics. Enjoy!

PART ONE

Intuitive Awareness & Psychic Development

Your Soul's Knowing

By Anne Babchuk

All humans (and animals) are born with what I call a superpower - an innate ability to sense things before they occur, or to know something without any proof or evidence to support that knowing. We all have it. It is something you are born with. This superpower is your intuition, an internal guide that offers an awareness of the unseen, unheard, intangible forces, vibrations and cues that surround you. These extrasensory signals pilot your life from your deepest intelligence. Intuition is the 'Soul's knowing'. It connects you with the Universal essence of Spirit and shows you what action or choice is best for you on a Soul level.

Why do some people recognize and utilize their intuitive awareness, while others deny it or block it out completely? It seems that childhood experiences have a profound effect on how we embrace our 'Soul's knowing'. When we are in infanthood and early childhood we still reside mainly in our spiritual essence. We are feeling beings, and intuition seems to be tied eloquently to just that. During these early years society has not yet had a chance to influence our intuition. We still cry when a person feels scary to us. We spit out food that tastes wrong. We play and learn when the Universe tells us to play and learn, and we sleep when the Universe tells us to sleep. Then, we grow a little older and physiologically we shape-shift into logical, thinking creatures and begin to file all the information we receive into tidy drawers in our left-brain. We begin to use our logical mind to help us make sense of the world. We watch the people in our life very closely and emulate them. If those people demonstrate trust of intuition we are encouraged to do the same. But if they have been pulled away from their own knowing, they will (sometimes with our best interest at heart), teach us to mistrust the signals that come so naturally.

Early peoples appear to have relied on their Soul's knowledge in equal measure to their thinking knowledge, but modern humans seem to have tipped the scale toward logic and forgotten a fundamental balance that rounded out the way we know things. We have opted for a world where what is true must be measurable, scientifically explained and driven by logic. Society, culture, religion, and family all have an impact. In today's modern model, many of us simply lose touch with the messages we are receiving from our source.

Some scientists seem to have a hard time recognizing the power of intuition because it is the only sense that cannot be proven or validated at the time it is experienced. It requires time and a reflection of one's choices and actions while under its influence in order to determine the effect it had on an outcome. It is intangible and cannot be measured or even easily described. It may be this human need to measure the immeasurable that is the very thing that pulls us away from trusting our intuition.

As I enter my fifth decade on this planet, I see the periods of my life where my connection to my Soul's knowing was so powerfully strong that the Universe directed me to places my logically driven mind could never have conceived. And I can attest that anytime I have steered myself away from my intuition - out of obligation, responsibility, self-doubt or conformity - life became conflicted, difficult, and even painful. It has taken a tremendous amount of trust, to step into a life committed to simply following my internal compass. For me, living an intuitive life feels amazing. I feel taken care of – as if I am being carried by something greater. It is not as if there are no more ups and downs, but all experiences become essential and I meet them with curiosity and fascination. There is great freedom in trusting that we are somehow connected to a higher, divine, loving, collective consciousness that guides us exactly where, when and how we need to go.

Mother's Intuition

My mother was a master of intuition. I have a childhood filled with her example and owe much of my intuitive freedom to her. Her favourite words of advice were: "If it feels right – do it. If it doesn't – don't." She taught me from a very early age that I could trust my feelings.

As a child, one of my favourite pastimes was to go to the big auction house with her. It was a huge metal building in the country where they auctioned everything from farm equipment, tools, estate items and furniture to… junk. With a bidding paddle in her hand and only a few bucks in her pocket, my mother would take us up and down the rows until we would come to the mystery boxes. These cardboard boxes were kept on a shelf and roped off so people would not make a mess rummaging through them. They could be filled with just about anything and were identified by the lot number in felt pen on the side. These boxes were left open and we could see what was on the top, but it was difficult to know what was down below. My mother would become quiet as a mouse and linger for a few moments with each box just looking at the number on the side. And then she would make her choice.

The auctioneer would start by calling the high-ticket items first, then slowly make his way down to the cheapo, mystery boxes. I would watch in amazement as my mother confidently bid on her box. Her determination was something to behold as she went head to head with other bidders. Somehow, even with such a small sum in her pocket, she would win her lot more often than not. Now, this may seem uninteresting to most people, especially when we consider that in all years we did this, not one box contained an article that had any significant monetary value. But what you may find interesting is that this was one of the ways my mother supplied our home with both our essential and our not so essential household needs.

From a bystander's point of view, they may have seen a poor, single mother of five gambling her last dollars on a box of junk. But that was not what was happening. When I asked her about it, she said "I just listen to the boxes. They tell me if they will be of value to us in some way, and I just trust that." In every box, there was something that would surprise me, something that would make so much sense to me as to why we needed it. Now I will admit that we did, in fact, need a lot of things and it may not seem so fantastic in a household of six to find new kitchenware helpful or a supply of new towels and sheets necessary, but sometimes we needed things that were not essential. Sometimes we needed things that lifted our spirits or made us feel special. Like the colourful bag of embroidery thread that came along when my older brother began embroidering jean jackets. There were the lovely pieces of 'Petit Point' china that arrived for my eldest sister who was moving into her own apartment. There was the hammock we put up in the yard that provided a quiet place to be 'alone' and read, the exotic Christmas ornaments that replaced ramshackle ones, the tackle box for my other brother and books for my mother, a transistor radio for whoever was doing dishes and canvas air mattresses for floating on the lake - which also acted as a bed for visiting guests. And then, of course, there was the infamous Ouija board for my sister and me. When we unpacked these boxes, we felt an overwhelming sense of abundance and that, in itself, was the best find of all.

When I look back on it now; the experiences that came to us through the mystery boxes were not things we would have set out to do. Not only could we have not afforded them, but it is also unlikely that we would have thought about getting them in the first place. Intuition guides us to have certain experiences because there is something creative and supportive being offered to us; something far more intricate and meaningful than we could ever have dreamed of - or orchestrated from our thinking mind.

Intuitive Openings

I have lived from an intuitive perspective for my entire life and the little story I am about to tell was not the first, and it certainly will not be the last time an opening to a higher divine consciousness appears for me. It is a moment in a lifetime of moments that has brought me here... to a place where I am convinced beyond a shadow of a doubt that we are in fact spiritual beings simply having a human experience.

I can still feel the ripple of excitement rush through my ten-year-old body as my mother and I pulled the board game from the clutter in the box of mysteries. We had won the box earlier that day at the auction. Our excitement turned to nervous intrigue as we realized the game was actually not a game at all, but an Ouija board. I had heard stories of mysterious encounters with spirits using Ouija boards and I was too curious for words. I was fascinated by the old-time graphics on the board, and my imagination went wild with stories about how the letters and numbers came to be so worn out. The wooden pointer was well used too and I was anxious to tell my teenaged sisters and our friends about it so we could try it.

There were four of us at the table. The lights were low and the candles on. We all placed our fingertips on the pointer and made sure that our pinkies were all touching in order not to break the "circuit". We were giggly and freaked out and my mother watched protectively from the kitchen. My brother's girlfriend asked the question "Will I marry Danny?" and the pointer began to move on its own accord and we all dropped our hands. We immediately began accusing each other of pushing it along and then all protested and promised we were not moving it. So we put our hands back on and just watched it move to the word NO.

Throughout the evening, we continued asking Yes/No questions and marvelled at how strong and decisive the answers came. I was strangely exhilarated by the experience and found myself thinking about the Ouija board all the time.

The next few times we brought the Ouija board out we progressively became less fearful and more curious. Each time we all swore not to interfere with the natural flow of the pointer and as kids would, we asked silly questions about boyfriends and school dramas. But then we became more serious and started requesting information about our futures and our family histories.

Magically, we began to receive words – actual answers to our questions. The pointer was quick and exact as it swiftly moved from letter to letter. It began to give us names and dates and information of past and future in long, full sentences. The pointer gave us details... details, which would later be validated (or not) in test scores and invitations to go out on dates and in the research of our historical family details.

Over time, I began to notice something. I noticed that when my friends and I sat together with the Ouija and asked a question, I would know what was going to be told to us before the pointer did its work. I would see numbers and words flash in my mind. I would see pictures that I would later realize were symbols. I would see faces in my mind's eye and feel strange sensations. I did not tell anyone at the table this was happening for fear they would accuse me of pushing the pointer – but in my heart, I knew it was not me who was making it move. I began to play around with it. A couple of times I left the room in order to take my hands off the pointer to see if I would still know what was coming. Many times my hands were nowhere near the pointer and I still knew what was about to be said.

Fascinated and immensely curious I began to let myself receive messages without the Ouija boards help. I was a very fanciful ten-year-old and it felt like I was daydreaming and making up stories.

But, little things in my daydreams were being validated. I was predicting phone calls from certain people; I knew a grandparent had taken sick, I was aware that my best friend who lived a province away was in trouble.

One afternoon, while I was in school I saw in my mind's eye an event that caused me great distress. I had 'imagined' my elder brother in a busy nightclub and then saw a flash of a bloody knife. I became very upset and decided I didn't like to do this anymore. I shut the opening and when I got home decided to put the Ouija board away for good. I did not tell a soul – assuming that if I put the board away, and put the images of the event out of my mind, it would not happen. But it did.

Late one night I was awoken by a telephone ring, my mother answered and received the news that my brother's best friend had gotten into a fight at the bar and a knife had been pulled on him and he had been stabbed. I heard my mother crying on the phone and my sister crashing through the front door. She had been at the nightclub and had seen what had happened. I was crippled with a sense of guilt because I felt I should have said something about what I saw. When my sister explained to me that the friend would soon recover I was overwhelmed with relief. My vision had come true, and I had been validated but I felt responsible. Why did I have the vision? Was I meant to stop the event? It took many years before I was ready to open up to visions like that again. I had to gain some wisdom first – intuition is about trust, trusting we are being offered messages of love and awareness. Fear blocks the flow of intuition. Perhaps if I had a calm, directed frame of mind, I would have been able to process the information in a clear and effective way to aid my brother and his friend. Instead, we were all offered amazing life lessons through that experience and were set on a different trajectory that brought us to right here, right now.

Just as animals know to run for the hills before the flood comes. This experience showed me that humans also have the ability to know things in the same extrasensory way. It showed me that my visions provide me with guidance and an opportunity of choice – "free will". What makes me see things? What makes the pointer move? I believe it is an inherent connection with all things, a collective consciousness as it were – an ever-present, loving, knowing energy that flows through everyone and everything connecting us to our Higher Self - our source.

intuition workbook
8 Steps to Bring Your Intuition Forward

If you think it would serve you to live from a more intuitive perspective, I have created these eight steps to help open the door to what is naturally within you already.

STEP 1: Notice Your Body Sensations

"Why don't you get a ride home with Jack?"
"I have a gut feeling telling me not to get in the car with him. So I think I will bus home."

Your body offers clear signals, but the trick is to notice them. Body sensations (like an ache in the gut for example) are the attention grabbers; they cause you to sit up and take notice of what is happening around you. If you are not naturally in tune with your body, it may require regular "check-ins"; moments of reflection to feel what your body is feeling until you learn to identify your personal signals. The sensations will differ for different people. Maybe you experience a tingling in your chest or a strange denseness at the back of your head or who knows – an itchy toe perhaps! Whatever is unique to you and useful to you. When you start paying attention you will see where you are consistent and that what you are feeling is a personal message for you.

Ask Yourself: *"What am I feeling? What are my body sensations trying to tell me?"*

STEP 2: Be Present and Pay Attention

"It is too crowded here. I sense there is going to be trouble!"
"How did you know I needed a shoulder to cry on today?"
"I just sensed it."

If your attention is elsewhere, if your thoughts are on 'more important' things or you are just wondering whether you have milk in the fridge or not, you will be pulled out of the present moment. Being present is essential for noticing the cues and signals that are being offered at that moment for that moment. Being calmly alert to the energies happening around you takes practice, but life becomes so interesting when you are able to hone this skill. Now I know you cannot be paying full attention all the time, but if your body first calls you to attention with a feeling – that is your first clue to start noticing what is happening around you.

If you find this task difficult, remember being intuitively aware is about being present. Often, stress and emotions like anxiety or self-consciousness can pull you out of the moment. Being disconnected is a signpost! When you notice this happening, take the opportunity to look inside yourself: What is this negative emotion I feel? Why is it here? Where does it come from? Be present with that. You do not need to get rid of it, just notice it, still your mind; listen and you will be guided on what to do next.

Ask Yourself: *"Does my mind drift? Do negative emotions interrupt my ability to be present?"*

STEP 3: Return to Nature – Your Nature

"Where did that complex mathematical equation come from?"
"It popped into my head when I was walking in the forest."
"Why did you quit that great job?"
"I had an 'a-ha' moment while playing with my kids at the beach. My stress level was too high at work – it wasn't healthy for me to stay."

Spending time in nature is one of the most valuable exercises you can do to help bring your intuition forward. Allow yourself at least ten wee, little minutes each day where you can absorb the sensations of the natural world. Allow yourself to remember that you are a part of this miraculous, intricate ecosystem where all things are connected. Take time to look at the night sky, feel the earth beneath your bare feet, watch waves at the ocean, or a spider making her web. Feel your place in it – You are nature! And don't forget to allow yourself enjoyment, because that is your nature too. I have heard it said that many great minds and creators such as Einstein and Tesla came up with their most profound discoveries while playing, not while in their studies.

Ask Yourself: *"Can I spend at least ten uninterrupted minutes in nature without needing to 'do' anything?"*

STEP 4: Still Your Mind

"What a beautiful melody! How did you think of it?"
"It came to me in a daydream."
"My deceased mother visited me today while I was meditating. She had a message for me."

Meditation not only connects us to our divine nature, but it also stills the logical, thinking mind and taps us into our Soul's knowing. It is in the stillness and silence of a quieted mind where intuition has a clear path to our psyche. Slowing down the hamster wheel of thoughts will open the gate to the higher wisdom inside you. Each day (preferably in the morning before the world comes in), sit down, slow down, and let your mind be clear for at least twenty minutes. Watch how peaceful clarity induces brand new solutions to old problems; how inspiration and guidance simply arrive without trying. Notice how your actions flow with life as opposed to going against it. Now I know, in moments where a snap decision must be made, that you may not have the presence of mind to stop and still your mind, but it is in the commitment to a daily practice of meditating that you will comfortably slip into actions that are in alignment with your intuition. Your Soul's knowing will naturally be at the helm when crises or difficulties surface.

If stilling your mind seems like an impossible task, be patient with yourself. Start slow, if you need something to occupy your mind in order to let your thoughts go, focus on something such as a lit candle, gentle music or go into nature and simply focus on the breeze on your skin. It will become easier. If you notice that some thoughts are very 'sticky' and cause you pain. It may be because a limiting, core belief or past trauma is asking for your attention. Noticing a block like this is a good thing and means your intuition has been ignited at a sub-conscious level. When negative thoughts or blocks arise in you while in meditation it means they are up for healing. Allow the feelings to arise, do not push them away, and be curious about them. Bring them out of your body, write them on a piece of paper, or tell them to the trees and just be conscious of them. If you continue to meditate regularly, over time your intuition will let you know what you need and how to heal.

Ask yourself: *"Is it possible for me to sit in stillness and silence for twenty minutes?"*

STEP 5: Recognize When Your Intuition Kicks In

"The GPS says to go right, why are you going left?"
"My instinct is telling me to."
"What made you add that splash of orange to your painting?"
"My hand was simply drawn to the colour."

There are times when we automatically and without a doubt just follow our subconscious impulses. They are so accurate and spot-on that we do not hesitate in them and in that ease do not notice that it took a certain intuitive intelligence to get there. This is intuition flowing seamlessly and effortlessly. When does this happen for you? What are you doing when it happens? Recognizing that you are already using this amazing resource is a very important part of learning how to call upon it. If you don't think you have any instances, I urge you to look closer… you do! Give yourself the intuitive credit, where credit is due, and notice how natural it feels.

Ask Yourself: *"When is my intuition spot on, accurate?"*

STEP 6: Validation: Notice When You Have Been Right – and Wrong!

"Wow, you did so well with that stock! Didn't it seem like a risky investment?"
"It just felt right."
"How did you know Jack was a dangerous person?"
"There was something in his eyes that told me so."
"Wow – I really liked that guy, he really turned out to be a jerk, how come I didn't see that coming!"

Trusting yourself is a key point in ramping up your intuition. Noticing when you have been accurate offers validation and validation creates trust in your ability to follow. It will start a momentum. Keep track, some people keep a journal, while others are fine with just a mental note; do whatever it takes for you to remember your successes. It will help you pull your intuition forward.

But what happens when you miss the mark and get it wrong? This is where it gets really interesting. Just for a moment consider, that you actually didn't get it wrong. That's right… even though it feels as if you were off the mark, or made a mistake; just consider that something more important, more complex, more valuable to you is being offered through the experience. You can't get it wrong. It may take some time to see the validation for this. I assure you, upon reflection further on down the road, you will see it went the way it did for a reason. Perhaps the mistake was the catalyst that sparked change or healing or growth. I can hear you now… "But so much is at stake!" "It was a life or death situation! I really messed up!" For these reasons it is so essential to align with your Soul's knowledge and remember we are all doing the best we can and everything happens for a reason.

Ask Yourself: *"Is there a mistake I made in the past that I now see was a gift to me?"*

STEP 7: Avoid Second Guessing

"I heard you were in a car accident."
"Yes, I knew I should have got the brakes checked, but I kept putting it off."
"My gut told me not to date her, but I went out with her anyway!"

Second-guessing yourself is different than simply making a bad choice. Second-guessing means you have been given clear guidance from your intuition and chose to ignore it. If this happens occasionally, just take note and see how you were pulled out of your Soul's knowing. Notice how it feels, and chalk it up to learning how to trust. Being aware of this choice is essential in making the decision to follow it next time.

But! If this is a consistent pattern or behaviour in your life, it might be time to investigate why you deny your intuitive guidance. Ask yourself what has caused you to be doubtful of your own power of intuition and your ability to follow the path that is most natural for you to walk on. It may be that you have had some life experiences that have caused you to doubt the Universe is a friendly place. Check yourself. Notice if your decisions and choices are being made out of obligation, conformity, poor self-worth, or just out of a need to please someone else, it is important to understand why living this way is limiting you. There is a world of opportunity and inspiration available to you when you allow intuition to guide you. It may be time to compassionately begin at Step 1 only this time with the intent to heal what needs to be healed.

Ask yourself: *"What happens when I second guess my intuition?"*

STEP 8: Free Yourself From The Need To Explain How It Works

Human beings are linear thinkers. We are mapmakers and timekeepers, we are natural mathematicians and scientists, we like to make sense of things and this is why Step 8 may be the hardest step in bringing your intuition forward. It is natural for us to want to explain how intuition works, but it seems when I try to explain it, I put up a block to it. If you think it would serve you, I suggest you free yourself from the need to explain it. Do not expect a scientific quantification or even search for a spiritual angle to explain it – just accept that it is there. All you need to do is allow it, accept it and love it.

Ask Yourself: *"Can I just accept intuition without needing to quantify it?"*

Afterthought

"At any moment, you have a choice, that either leads you closer to your Spirit or further away from it." ~ *Thich Nhat Hanh*

I use this beautiful quote by Vietnamese Buddhist monk and peace activist Tich Nhat Hanh as a sort of mantra in my morning meditation. I remind myself that each decision I will make in the upcoming day will either pull me closer to the true essence of my nature or push me away from it. And I have come to trust that it is my intuition that keeps me in authenticity and awareness. It helps me make kind choices and have loving responses to life.

When you trust and consistently use your intuition, you will be led down pathways that lead you to more choices. These are the choices that take you closer to your divinity. Intuition is like a lighthouse in the fog, a beacon providing clear direction - guiding the way to your Higher Self. Without it, you may find yourself miles off course. But don't worry! The Universe wants you to be YOU - fully activated and free. If you wake up one day and find you have lost your way, let your intuition kick in and help you make the choices that put you on the right track. No matter where you find yourself, every act of free will has the potential to reflect the truth of who you are. Your intuition is simply the access point to that truth.

With love, Anne

signs & omens

By Kelly Oswald

The man whispered, "God, speak to me"
And a meadowlark sang.
But the man did not hear.
So the man yelled "God, speak to me"
And the thunder & lightning rolled across the sky.
But the man did not listen.
The man looked around and said, "God, let me see you."
And a star shined brightly.
But the man did not see.
And, the man shouted, "God, show me a miracle"
And a life was born.
But the man did not notice.
So, the man cried out in despair,
"Touch me, God, and let me know you are here"
Whereupon, God reached down and touched the man.
But the man brushed the butterfly away and walked on.

~ Unknown

Our Universe Speaks
(are you listening?)

Sometimes life can be challenging. Maybe you don't feel confident in your decisions, or don't even know how to make your next move. The BIG questions loom; should you take the job offer? Is this Mr./Mrs. Right? Will moving prove beneficial? Is following this dream going to work? Are you living your true purpose? Or the small questions; is a particular event something you want to attend? Will a podcast be worth your time? Should you purchase that pair of pants?

The Universe invariably sends you more information the more you pay attention. When you get 'stuck', or you are not sure which way to go, you can look for signs. Any type of question can be asked for the Universal nudge that can guide you to make the best decision.

Signs can raise awareness of your connection with the world around you. They help you move towards the understanding that you are part of the infinite ebb and flow of nature just like flowers, insects, birds, animals and everything that surrounds you. You are a part of the world — not separate from it. Universal Energy connects everything. Everything is indeed energy and energy is everything. For eons, Indigenous cultures, our multitude of religions, and pagan practitioners have made use of signs; you too can tap into this beautiful and accessible tool.

When you allow your mind to relax and get out of your busy, analytical thought process, you make room for the magic to bubble up from the deeper parts of yourself. Your intuition and your subconscious can see and hear messages anytime if you let them have the space to expand. There is no limit to what signs can tell you. When you learn to go with the flow... wonderful things begin to happen! Signs and omens are constantly dished up like an all-you-can-eat buffet; your plate never goes empty and the Universe invariably sends you more information the more you pay attention.

If you are open to receive signs and omens, then you will discover them everywhere. The Universe is speaking constantly... how much you hear depends on how often you listen.

In this section you will learn:

- The difference between signs and omens.
- How to work with symbolism and your signs.
- Why coincidence is worth noticing.
- How synchronicity plays along.
- Different types of symbols.
- Different types of signs.
- How to ask for a sign in five specific steps.

The Difference Between
Signs & Omens

An omen is an occurrence or phenomenon believed to portend a future event; a warning (bad omen), or encouragement (good omen). Omens suggest an incident is imminent and it arrives unexpectedly with no solicitation or prior request. Boom! An omen shows up.

Omens have a bad rap, (thank you movie industry horrors and thrillers and scary books). But take another look and wonder why a warning would be considered a bad omen; especially if it gives you a heads-up before a difficult or dangerous happenstance. I believe 'bad' omens are opportunities to duck or get out of the way.

Because omens don't occur very often, when they do show up, they tend to be obvious and of great significance. Strangely wonderful, they can be frightening or enlightening. So yes, the movie industry is onto the mysterious and wondrous qualities of omens.

Signs are more common and therefore, not viewed to be as esoteric as an omen. A sign is something tangible or meaningful that often gives significance to something other than itself. A dragonfly may represent someone's father; 11:11 on a timepiece is the sign of a gateway to new possibilities. Signs are used for validation, affirmation or messages that pertain to any matter past, present, or guide your future path. When you are seeking the Universal thumbs up, signs can help gain confidence and provide momentum. Many people use signs as Oracles, bridging communication between the realm of Spirit and the physical world.

My Story

I have no idea when I first began 'playing' and ultimately working with signs. It seems as if I have been listening and watching forever. Falling stars, dust floating in the sunlight, and animal messages are among my favourite. Society doesn't question signs and few think it 'odd'. In fact, it's very common and even (dare I say) acceptable to talk about signs – or say "hey, it must be a sign". They are socially admissible, fun, and a wee bit magical.

They also work.

When I began to take them seriously, I was very expectant that they'd show up. Most of the time they did, but I learned that not getting a sign – is also a sign.

My first dramatic sign experience was around the age of six. Our family was driving to a summer vacation spot when a squirrel ran in front of our car causing my father to hit the brakes and stop unexpectedly. We were travelling on a particularly dangerous part of the highway; a twisting, narrow area with steep cliffs and drop-offs.

The entire event began with vultures.

They were flying around the cliffs above and below us. I had never seen real live vultures before. As my father explained what they were, one flew over the canyon – but level with my window in the car, pacing alongside us. I could see him perfectly, his shiny feathers and strange small, red, reptilian head; I felt afraid.

Suddenly, we all saw the squirrel dart out from the side of the road and cried out; my father stopped the car, which was not what he should have done (he normally wouldn't have), given the speed we were travelling. Within seconds an oncoming car barreling down the road spun around the corner towards us and its rear slid into our lane veering to the edge of the cliff; its back tires burned off the pavement and almost over the rocky edge – exactly where we would be if we had not stopped. Had we kept going, we would have been pushed over the edge of the canyon. That little squirrel saved a family of four from a nasty and most likely fatal accident.

The vultures had been an omen - the squirrel, an immediate sign to stop. We were shaken, but fine. No one in the oncoming car was hurt, but we all drove a little slower after the near-miss.

The story was made 'more real' as I listened to my parents reiterate the close call to friends. The stage had been set, and I was free to begin my dance with signs. They have filled and enriched my life ever since. Once you believe… signs are everywhere.

A later experience for me was the decision to open a New Age shop in my town of Whistler, BC, Canada. Nothing indicated that there was a 'spiritual' niche to fill, other than the fact that there was nothing like what I was planning. However; no competition is not always a good thing, it can mean a lack of interest in the subject. I was full of self-doubt, apprehension, and down-right fear.

I set out with a proposal to a landlord for leasing his space at fifty percent less than asking – my lack of confidence and anxiety obviously apparent. The landlord's office was closed, so I slid the proposal under his door and then asked for a specific sign to encourage me in my venture. I asked the Universe for validation through two bears and two rabbits on the same day; highly unlikely, but possible in a wilderness environment such as Whistler.

A few hours later, I was backing out of the driveway when two rabbits ran in front of my car. I stopped and stared. Should I go in and get my camera for the two bears I knew I was going to see next?

I didn't want to mess with Divine timing, so continued on my way. The bears I happened upon were playing by the railway tracks. I watched for about twenty minutes before they lunged away (I DID have time to get the camera).

I phoned my husband to let him know we would be opening the shop. "You heard from the landlord then?" He asked.

Me: "Nope, not yet."

Him: "Then how do you know?"

Me, with a really big smile: "I just do."

Years later, as an intuitive reader, most of the signs I am asked to help with are those related to connecting with past loved ones.

Stephanie (not her real name), wanted to be sure that a friend who had passed in a tragic accident was okay on the 'other side'. She was haunted by the thought of him never knowing how much she cared for him and how important he was to her. Stephanie sought a sign to let her know that everything was alright. She looked forward to a connection that could bring about healthy, albeit sorrowfully happy closure. Closure being the main purpose of her sign.

The specifics were decided; three deer together, within the next three days. It was out of season, so possible but not probable. She set the intention and let it go. The next day a foot of snow fell. Stephanie used her day to nurture relationships and chatted on the phone to a friend a few miles south. Her friend's dog started barking, making conversation difficult. Her friend excused herself for a second to secure the dog. Coming back to the phone the friend explained that there were deer in her backyard. Stephanie asked how many, but she already knew the answer. Of course, there were three.

Another client, Joseph, asked to connect to his fiancé who had taken her life unexpectedly. He suffered deeply and his pain was constant. He asked for a hummingbird sign within three days, even though it was late fall and the hummingbirds had migrated. He woke up on the second day, came downstairs and flicked on the TV. Instantly the screen was filled with hundreds of hummingbirds; an ad for bird feeders was shown on the commercial break. He fell to his knees; he needed nothing more than the shock and joy of the spontaneity of that brilliant moment.

Simple signs and omens can be right under your nose - cloud shapes, street names, licence plate numbers - and it is easy to miss them. My friend and I went for lunch one day before heading to our charitable foundation to give out fifteen pairs of running shoes to those in need.

We pulled up to the restaurant and parked behind a car with the license plate N91 ASS. We giggled – how often do you park behind an ass? Handing the valet our keys, he proudly told us it was his car. The random improbability of the license plate should have been enough to 'wake' us up, but in the moment of humour, we missed the deeper message. Not so funny when we later arrived at the foundation and discovered a box of runners missing from the trunk of the car - most likely scooped by the parking attendant with access to her car keys and the cheeky license plate. We hoped he needed them.

The language of energy can be quite abstract, so it's important to be as specific as possible to get the clarity and accuracy required for workable information. That being said, when the intention has been set into motion, open awareness to the reply in whatever form it takes is also required. Strict rules going in – open answer coming out. We speak the language of words, however, the Universe speaks the language of energy… it's not a perfect match, but it works.

Using time frames, numbers and things that are possible - but not probable - help qualify the request. Watching for the reply is done without active searching. Don't go to the library and look it up in picture books and searching Google isn't the Universe talking back!

Sometimes signs arrive without question and without asking, like an omen.

Together, my husband and I climbed the mountain to spread my mother-in-law's ashes with those of her husband placed there a year prior. It was a hot sunny summer day in July. We noticed little chips of bone wedged within the rock crevasses, tiny little remains of her husband that had not blown away. It felt as if he had waited for her. The weather changed abruptly, the wind came up and clouds appeared out of nowhere and it began to snow. Instantly it became bitterly cold with white flakes falling from the sky as we spread her ashes. And just as suddenly the wind ceased and the sun became hot, the weather dry. As if it had never happened.

> *When one tugs at a single thing in nature,*
> *They find it attached to the rest of the world. ~ unknown*

Universal communication can seem pretty strange when it's yelling at you. Peculiar things happen and the 'wow' factor kicks in. Sudden weather changes, animals acting out of character, a relevant song suddenly playing on the radio. It's time to pay attention; somebody is trying to tell you something. Listen up!

Spirit energy can translate through themes in the natural world. The way the light shines through trees, rainbows, patterns or shapes in clouds. A poignant message comes when an animal does something unusual and out of character for their species; take note, they may be sending you significant information. An owl may spend the day at your home, and you've never had owls before. A ladybug may land on you and stay for an unusually long visit. A bird may stare at you through a window or peck at the window, or make noises as if they're trying to speak to you. Sometimes these are signs that someone who has passed is trying to be known.

Grandma, my husband's mother, had an intense fear of birds. In the heat of the summer, she refused to open windows no more than a crack for fear of a bird entering her home. After she passed, we have had more strange bird encounters than ever before. First, we had a blue jay that parked himself at our home for about two years. Next, a robin flew madly at our bedroom window waking my husband every day while I was out of town for a week and stopped the day I returned. Then, after purchasing a new home, we arrived to find an imprisoned flicker that had flown down our chimney to become trapped in the fireplace, thank goodness we were able to set it free. A raven watched my son ready himself in the kitchen on his first day of high school and seems to appear with each significant rite of passage in his life. Our bird list continues with a chickadee who flew and hovered strangely in front of our granddaughter for an oddly long few seconds. It turns out that chickadees are totem symbols for joy, positivity, courage, cheer and love. Another chickadee spent almost half an hour at our bedroom window beginning at ten o'clock at night on our first sleep in our new house (chickadees don't usually come out at night). And I'm sure there are many more bird visits to come, it seems that Grandma is still here, engaging, watching, and playing with her family.

How to Work with Signs

Maybe this is how it works – and maybe it isn't.

But it's how it has worked for me most of my life. I hope it works for you too.

There is no scientific 'proof', but Quantum Physics has made some pretty mind-blowing inroads on the subject of energy. We know that science has discovered that our physical 'reality' consists of atoms, which are numerous vortexes of spinning and vibrating energy. Atoms are the basic building blocks of ordinary matter. They are composed of particles called protons, electrons and neutrons. Protons carry a positive electrical charge, electrons carry a negative electrical charge and neutrons carry no electrical charge at all. Therefore, human beings, according to Quantum Physics, are vibrational patterns of interactive energy, with each having its own unique signature. Everything is energy. We are made up of energy and space. It's called the 'unified field'.

If everything is energy, and everything is connected through energy, then it stands to reason that everything is sending and receiving all the time… or flowing, because that's what energy, including electricity, does. When we are paying attention or are 'tuned in' we will notice Universal messages showing up. The Universe is constantly communicating with us through messages in the form of coincidence, synchronicity, symbols, omens, and signs. Are we listening? Can we make sense of the messages we receive? It definitely takes an open mind and a receptive willingness to walk through this door. When you receive a message, you will know, because signs illuminate an underlying insight that sparks a sense of knowing from your soul.

> *"If you go off into a far, far forest and get very quiet,*
> *you'll come to understand that you're connected*
> *with everything." – Alan Watts*

Signs guide us (or our guides give us signs) in our everyday lives, whether we are aware of it or not. How many times have you said "Everything is going so well, it's all coming together" or "I'm having a bad day - if it's not one thing it's another."? Stop to think if there could be reasons why life sometimes works out so perfectly, but then at other times seems to completely fall apart. When it all comes together with perfect choreography due to the domino effect of well-placed events, magic happens. Other times, when things fall apart, a potentially worse situation might be avoided due to the events prior to the disastrous. It's so interesting that the difficult times are often leading us away from a much more challenging situation, even if it doesn't feel like it at the time. Signs are like traffic police, pointing in the direction that will make our journey safe and help us arrive at our destination in divine timing.

Signs create a bridge between the realm of Spirit and the realm of form. They connect things that may seem unrelated and they reflect our hopes and dreams. They serve as messengers about our current or future situation, act as reflections or project our hopes, fears, and desires, and send us messages from our dearly-departed. The three most common types of Universal signs are Messenger Signs and Omens, Spirit Signs, and Reflection Signs.

As you embrace your journey with signs, I highly recommend you keep a journal to make note of the unexpected and to track your expectations. In the following steps, you will lay the groundwork for asking for signs. Writing your requests on paper help make them 'real'. Solid questions asked, equal solid answers received. If your requests are vague, you'll get ambiguous answers... and you aren't looking for wishy-washy responses from something as rich, deep and fabulous as the infinite Universe. Journaling will give you insight, proof, and keep a history of your signs over time. It will also improve your connection with Universal energy and make your 'sign-system' more efficient and complete.

"Symbols are visible signs of invisible realities."
— Anonymous

Types of Signs and Symbols

UNIVERSAL SYMBOLS

Universal symbols appear everywhere and are known by most of the world. Some are ancient such as the cross, and the Egyptian Ankh and some are contemporary, like traffic lights and no-smoking signs. Stop signs, hearts, male/female washroom icons… any image within a diagonally crossed circle are symbols that almost everyone understands. The sun and the moon belong to all people and most cultures deem the sun male, yang, active and strong while the moon is feminine, yin, receptive and passive. Water can represent emotions while earth portrays the physical realm. When working with signs, it is how you associate with Universal Symbols that counts. You may find it helpful to ask yourself what a particular symbol means to you.

CULTURAL SYMBOLS

All over the world, different countries, tribes, and religions have their specific imagery and belief systems. In the western part of the world we may wear black to funerals, and use white flowers as a symbol of mourning, even though we also associate the colour white with marriage innocence, peace, and purity. In other cultures, white is associated with death and is used predominantly in funerals. Symbols such as the Evil Eye, the Celtic Claddagh and the Pride rainbow attest to cultural recognition. Your specific cultural upbringing, historical background, and your environment will have an effect on what certain symbols mean to you.

PERSONAL SYMBOLS

Personal Symbols are yours alone. They are beautifully private and belong to your world of magic signs. I have a friend who picks up feathers in unexpected places or appear to him at pivotal moments as signs from Angels. You probably already have some of your own personal symbols. Mother Nature offers us a massive menu from which to choose our symbols. The crescent moon, a particular flower, dragonflies, hummingbirds, eagles, owls… any animal totem, hearts, number patterns, coins on the ground, a certain song are a few examples; but of course, yours are yours alone.

If you don't feel you have a personal symbol yet, begin by opening your awareness to things that show up or repeat in your life. You may find that they have been there all along.

SYNCHRONICITY AND COINCIDENCE

Synchronicity and coincidence are huge demonstrators of connected energetic flow and the Unified Field (the fact that we are all connected – or as the Buddhists say, we 'inter-are').

Synchronicity and coincidence are circumstances that seem beyond serendipity or happenstance. They cause you to pause – to take stock of the situation and to reassess… but ONLY if you are open and allow them to offer the insight they are attempting to reveal. They are crazy-wonderful signposts guiding you toward wise and powerful decisions; by acting on the information presented before you, you won't miss out on the fabulous opportunities that signs and omens have to offer.

Coincidence is defined as 'a striking occurrence of two or more events at one time, apparently by mere chance'.

Coincidence is present when two or more unrelated or surprising things come together to create a perfect insightful moment. It could be as simple as a parking spot being vacated the moment you need one, or as complicated as arriving at the same restaurant as your future partner.

"Coincidence is God's way of remaining anonymous."
– Albert Einstein

Synchronicity is a series of coincidences that occur one after another. Cause and effect that seem to carry on indefinitely. The dictionary definition: 'the simultaneous occurrence of causally unrelated events and the belief that the simultaneity has meaning beyond mere coincidence.' Note that coincidence talks about mere chance, but now we are talking mere coincidence.

Synchronicity is an ongoing string of events that seem to play out on a perfect timeline, it is as if the Universe is somehow able to orchestrate events in a way you and I could never imagine.

Synchronistic events are my all-time favourite. I love to see how far back one started and note how long it seems to carry on into the future. Sometimes they can span years! At times they seem to help - other times to hinder - but always guiding in a jaw-dropping divinely energetic flow.

Whether your signs are validating and encouraging with an easy flow and smooth ride, or struggles and challenges that have inflicted a wake-up call and caused you to make changes and divert from your original plans… it is always good to take a step back for a clear view of your situation and maintain a perspective of observation. Re-assess, ask more questions and then jump back into the flow - it should be an amazing, joyful and abundant journey. Challenging? For sure! When is life not throwing you an obstacle or two? But signposts along the way are incredibly helpful, and when you are in the flow of a synchronistic pattern, anything is possible.

MESSENGER SIGNS AND OMENS

Messenger Signs may show up as validation, warning, confirmation or reassurance regarding your past, current, or future situation. They show up unexpectedly (omens) or answer your specific requests (signs).

You can ask for Messenger Signs when facing difficult decisions or need help understanding or validating a situation you are experiencing. Similar to consulting an Oracle; you ask a question and the answer presents itself. If you are open and receptive to it, you will hear the reply.

A Messenger Sign is like a note from the Universe saying something important to you. It may send you an affirmation that you are on the right track, or warn you if you are heading in the wrong direction. It can say "well done", "be careful" or "yes!" You have probably experienced them in one form or another, as animals, weather, synchronicity, or coincidence.

Often we don't even have to ask for Messenger Signs, we just need to be aware that they are happening. For instance: A book falls open to reveal a relevant page, you repeatedly see the same numbers on the clock daily, a traffic roadblock causes you to drive past the perfect apartment for rent, the same song plays everywhere you go sending a strong message, the sun shines through the trees in the forest just so, a billboard has a relevant message to your immediate thought, a license plate spells out an answer to a question, finding a similar object repeatedly gives a clue, or an unusual animal or bird encounters elicits a message.

Messenger Signs and Omens suggest you look for something deeper in the grand scheme of the moment.

Is there a time when you have experienced a Messenger Sign? It is incredibly helpful to journal and take note of your experience with signs, not only for your own validation, it also seems to 'prime the pump', opening the door for more and more messages to flow.

REFLECTIVE SIGNS

Reflective Signs increase awareness of subconscious thoughts. They can also reflect the things on which you are most focused, mirroring or validating your life path. They can also mean nothing at all – just that you have noticed the latest trend.

Reflective Signs fit into two categories; one reflects external elements and the other reflects internal issues (positive or negative).

External Reflective Signs show up when you are personally living through a 'moment'. For me, it was letting my grey hair take over before I turned forty. Slowly over the next few years, it became the 'thing'. Even young girls in their teens began to dye their hair as white as mine – adding a little purple or blue … but hey!

During or prior to pregnancy, women often begin to notice all the other pregnant women. If you like Teslas, you notice all the Teslas on the road. If you are curious about the latest Smartphone, you will begin to notice it everywhere. External reflective signs show you what you are focused on and what you desire, or are intrigued by. This is a good tool for awareness, but to me, not much more. Some folks feel that it validates where they are on their life path, however, I feel it is more a reflection of where I am at present - or where I desire to be. This doesn't make me right; it's what works for me. Your question is, "What works for YOU"?

It is important to note: What you focus on and pay attention to shows up in your life.

Internal Reflective Signs bubble up from your subconscious mind to give you a nudge, a subtle hint or a full-on wake-up call. It does this in the forms of judgment and projection. Internal reflective signs are incredibly useful for your own personal growth and spiritual development. I have a love/hate relationship with them, mainly because they are brutally challenging and make me totally vulnerable. But they work so well, I just can't ignore them.

Wayne Dyer stated that *"When you judge another, you do not define them, you define yourself."* That can be a bit of a tough nugget and hard medicine to swallow, but is also incredibly insightful.

A healthy level of discernment can help you make better choices. Listen to your vibes when you feel all 'judgy', and maybe there is a message that is trying to protect you. Maybe that isn't a safe place to go; maybe those people aren't right for you; maybe a comment made helped you see someone in a truer light. When you seem to be judging others, maybe it's a sign that you don't like that part of them and they aren't good for you. It could be an internal warning to dissociate from them and stay away. It also gives you a chance to see if you possess any of the unfavourable qualities in them that mirrors something similar in you. Reflection provides the opportunity for personal growth and self-improvement.

When you judge yourself for doing things that aren't good for you or prefer not to do (and do anyway), your subconscious will push you to do better. The Universe wants you to thrive and has no problem sending you messages, even ones you don't want to hear.

With this mindset, you will begin to embrace obstacles and delays instead of judging them as negative occurrences or bad luck. How much more fun it can be when you view a tough situation as foreshadowing or an opportunity for insight... and maybe it's nothing. Just traffic.

> *"Problems are not stop signs, they are guidelines."*
> *– Robert Schuller*

Projection offers the same sort of tool kit. Listen to the advice you give others because there is a really good chance you should take it too! The Universe will fill your life with people that enhance and complement your moments so you can learn and grow together. It is definitely easier to give advice than take it, but when you find yourself faced with the same challenge, it is very beneficial to listen to your own words as you solve your own problem inadvertently. It's pretty cool when you unintentionally inspire yourself!

People are brought together as if by magic, to help and heal each other. When you inspire yourself, you inspire others, when you heal yourself, you heal others. Illness or body pain is another type of reflective sign that comes from within. One of the biggest authors of signs in your body relating to your personal experience and spiritual journey was Louise Hay. In her books *You Can Heal Your Life*, and *Heal Your Body A-Z: The Mental Causes for Physical Illness and the Way to Overcome Them*, she demonstrates the signs and signals in your body that correlate to deeper issues and associate physical issues to spiritual and personal blocks. Other signs that come from our bodies are sensations such as timely goosebumps, tingles, or the feeling of the hairs standing up on the back of your neck.

Can you think of a time when you have experienced a Reflective Sign? Use your journal to take note of Reflective Signs as you embark on the journey of your personal and spiritual growth.

SPIRIT SIGNS (from passed loved-ones)

Connecting to departed loved-ones involves communication in both directions. You can reach out to them, but they can reach out to you too. They may attempt to show approval, share your happiness, offer guidance or connect on a level they didn't get a chance to in life.

Loved ones often use electric fields to communicate (we are all energy after all!); street lights flash, lights flicker or burn out, a clock stops at the same time - every time, the volume on your TV or device fluctuates, things beep or ring for no apparent reason, your computer acts funny.

Angelic messages can come through voices, music, room temperature changes, a fragrance or flower that relates to a loved one appears and reappears... even a feather may float from the sky.

There are times when Spirit doesn't send a sign. Please don't despair. You aren't home to answer your door all day long, and the same holds true for Spirit energy (as far as I know). Of course, I am being a bit presumptuous because I have no conscious memory of ever being on the other side or dwelling in the realm of Spirit – so what I am speculating is based on my experience from this side of the fence.

It is presumed, that when someone crosses over, that it may be a few days, even weeks before you can reach them. I still feel it's worth a try as long as you are okay without an instant reply. Some believe that no answer implies no reason to connect. Everything is fine in both the spiritual and physical realms, so there is no need to go through the orchestration of a connection. These assumptions can not be readily proven, but what is incredible, more often than not, when you feel a need to reach out, you will get a reply. It's very cool to watch a powerful 'shock-and-awe' connection unfold and it always feels very real and very hopeful.

Have you have experienced a Spirit Sign? Use your journal to take note of Spirit Signs.

"The Universe conspires to reveal your truth and to make your path easy, if you have the courage to follow the signs."
~ Lisa Unger

How to Ask for a Sign

When asking for a sign, there are a few rules that work for me.

I work with so much structure because I want a concrete no-messing-around result. I am talking about real-life questions here – I am not hanging my hopes out on loosey-goosey, maybe it's a sign - maybe it isn't. It's my life and I don't want to mess it up – I want clarity, validation, Universal support and the odd 'hello' to those I love on the other side. It's got to be loud, clear, and definite.

The 5 Steps are: **Purpose** - define the purpose of your sign, **Connection** – be specific on how the connection will appear, **Timing** – give it a deadline, **Expect** – be open to receive your sign without a shadow of a doubt, and finally, **Thank** – gratitude goes a long way in the Universal scheme of things.

The following rules are tight and controlled; they are tested over time and work very accurately for me. I hope you have the same results.

Here we go…

STEP ONE: Purpose

The first step is to be as specific as possible so it will be very clear that your sign is not a random accident, but a well-placed message. Start with the purpose of the sign.

- What do you want to accomplish?
- What question do you hope to have answered?
- Who do you wish to connect with?
- You can even ask for signs just to practice - if that is your goal.

The key point here is to be very, very clear and succinct on your purpose. Define the purpose of your sign (exactly what you want to know).

STEP TWO: Establish a Means of Communication

The next step is to ask for something possible, but not probable. Don't make it easy on the Universe, but don't make it impossible either. Get seriously clear: You are asking for total clarity beyond a shadow of a doubt. Captain Obvious is in your corner, no vague anything, totally specific. Do you want your sign once or more than once – if you need it in multiples – let the Universe know that upfront. It's best to choose things that relate to you, as long as it's very specific and tangible, such as, three deer on the trail, two peacocks in snow, one foreign coin on the road, a favourite scent, song - anything that uniquely connects you to your purpose.

Itemize and define what your specific sign should look like.

STEP THREE: Timing

Then set a time frame. Give the Universe a few days to orchestrate 'spiritual magic'. No sign within the timeline is a sign in itself. It can mean a 'no', the issue is resolved, or there is no present reason to connect.

The timeline should be long enough to give the Universe a chance to fill your order, yet short enough to keep it realistic. Letting it drag on for months is wishful thinking. You want an answer now – not next year. You may be surprised at what the Universe can pull off in just a few days!

A good timeline looks like this: Three deer within two days. Two dragonflies with blue bodies within three days. The smell of lavender and pipe smoke by this Monday. Set a short, but realistic timeline.

STEP FOUR: Expect

Then be receptive and expect your sign to show up. Just allow. No doubts and no buts. When we talk about a 'shadow of a doubt', already things begin to get harder to see. Your sign may come in a very unusual or mysterious manner, and doubt is really good at hiding subtle gifts, so if you are steeped in uncertainty, you could miss your message. You may be expecting something specific, but it may arrive as a sound, an item on a menu, or a passing comment from a stranger instead of in 'real' life. Be open to the method of delivery, it may be indirect, unexpected or slightly abstract. For example:

- What does a 'butterfly' sign look like to you?
- Does it have to be a real butterfly?
- Or can it be a representation of one? Could it be a pair of earrings, a child in a costume, the shape of a cloud, a sticker on a car, or a fly in your butter?

Allow the magic to happen without digging for it. No Googling for signs! Let them reveal themselves. Expect a reply: Watch, listen, feel.

STEP FIVE: Express Gratitude

Ultimately, offer thanks to the Universe. An attitude of gratitude wraps up a session and sets the groundwork for next time. The more you act on signs and open your heart in appreciation, it seems the more you will find signs working for you. Just expressing gratitude is enough, although I know some folks who wrap up a 'sign session' with a ritual focused on gratitude and vibrational connections. Once again, it's all up to you.

But know this for sure...

When you say "thank you", the Universe will say "You're welcome".

water dowsing
And My 'Witchy' Beginnings
By Ashala Yardley

As a Psychic Intuitive and Spiritual Channel, I've practiced in the field of metaphysical phenomena for nearly three decades. Sometimes, people are curious about how my interest and connection to the 'unseen realms' began. Looking back I can recall a defining moment when my personal perception was expanded and my Spiritual curiosity piqued. It started when I was just eighteen years old and participating in a Canadian government-sponsored national youth program.

As I recall it was late September 1980, and I was bundled off in a van with half a dozen fellow teenagers. We rattled along a dusty northern Alberta back road on our way to meet a local legend. This elderly Dutch farmer was a very renowned Water Witcher. Our program leaders thought this would be a fun excursion for us… an opportunity to experience some of the culture of the area and interact with locals. Being a somewhat irreverent and unruly bunch, most of us saw it as a chance to goof off. When we arrived at our destination we were ushered into a nearby field bordering on a forested area. There the fellow, holding an unusual set of metal rods, was waiting for us. Amidst our awkward chuckles and guffaws, he painstakingly demonstrated his craft. Many of us, including me, were not really paying attention. Then, suddenly, he asked for a volunteer from the audience. My extraverted self-responded… partly because I love the limelight and partly because I couldn't resist the challenge of likely proving to everyone this was 'a load of nonsense'. What happened next was a subtle, yet extraordinary phenomenon that marked the stirring of my curiosity of the unseen realms.

The elderly gentleman placed the two L shaped dowsing rods in my hands facing them straight ahead at a forty-five-degree angle and instructed me how to hold them gently but firmly in such a way that I would have to turn my whole wrist in order to make them move intentionally to the right or the left. He then indicated that I stand in a particular location and walk ten paces forward slowly. It was hard to take this seriously… everyone was giggling and I felt a bit foolish. After about eight paces nothing was happening and I was thinking to myself, "see I know this is silliness," when suddenly the rods began to open, rapidly swinging with a steady momentum till they faced in opposite directions. Here, he declared, was a marker of an underground water source.

I was stunned! I definitely had not moved my hands one little bit. The look of disbelief on my face was like an open invitation and next thing you know my friends were all lining up to have a turn. We spent the next couple of hours experimenting and our guide showed us how we could make our own dowsing rods out of coat hangers and even how to measure each other's auric field. Some of us had more success at working with the rods than others and indeed my first experience was likely the most dramatic example of the day. By the end of the excursion, however, we were far less skeptical and had more respect for this extraordinary phenomenon that cannot easily be scientifically measured or explained.

Up until this time I had never heard the word aura and had no idea that it referred to an atmosphere, energy or quality that surrounds and is generated by a person, thing, or place. I was raised in an old-fashioned Christian home and although we attended church regularly, I did not receive the kind of religious conditioning that made me susceptible to fear of the unknown. My family's value system was relatively tolerant; a middle of the road, live and let live sort of attitude. However, I had no exposure to anything outside our spiritual norms either, and therefore had little opinion or curiosity about other ways. Beyond religion, this new experience provided evidence of the intangible that catalyzed a very personal spiritual awakening for me. After my introduction to water dowsing, I began to consider alternative points of view. My explorations ultimately led me to become a vegetarian, to learn about crystals and astrology, and to develop and enhance my psychic sensitivities (which we all have) through practicing various styles of divination including Oracle cards, I Ching, Runes and eventually the Tarot.

It has been over thirty-five years since my unlikely 'witchy beginnings'. When invited to contribute an article for this book I found myself drawn to my long-forgotten original story and inspired to reconnect with the significance of those roots. Nowadays, more than ever, natural uncontaminated water is becoming a precious resource. Most of us walk around with little awareness or appreciation of what is beneath our feet. The massive labyrinth of underground springs and complex ecosystems of the subterranean aquifers are like a mysterious world in another dimension.

In layperson's terms, an aquifer is simply surface layers of soil consisting of sand, gravel or fractured bedrock that is porous and easily saturated with rainwater. The degree, quality, and depth of freshwater saturation are what makes a good aquifer. In some locations, further underground rivers exist where freshwater seeps between spaces of fractured rock at deeper levels. Since the dawn of time, the location of these fractures and the resulting pooling and saturation of underground water has long been of utmost importance to humans suffering surface drought conditions.

One of the oldest known examples of this is featured in the Tassili Caves of North Africa where an eight thousand-year-old image features a man holding a forked stick and dowsing for water. Four thousand-year-old etchings on temple walls in Egypt also illustrate pharaohs holding devices in their hands resembling dowsing tools. In China, there is a twenty-five hundred year old etching of Emperor Yu holding a bulky pronged dowsing device. Greek historians refer to dowsing and divining as early as 400 BC. The Oracle of Delphi is said to have employed a dowsing pendulum to answer specific questions. In his monumental work the Odyssey, Homer refers to both the art of Rhabdomancy, or divining with the rod, and also to the mystical legendary dowsing rod known as the 'Caduceus'.

By the 1400s dowsing was known in Latin as 'Virgule divine' and in German as 'Deuter' meaning to show or point. In his book, The Divining Hand, Christopher Bird speaks of English Philosopher John Locke who wrote: "by the use of the dowsing rod, one could discover water and precious minerals". Locke coined the English term 'dowsing rod' from the Cornish word 'Dewsys' meaning 'Goddess', and 'Rhod' meaning tree branch.

Sixteenth-century Lutheran theologian Phillip Melancthon attributed the phenomena of dowsing to a sympathetic relationship between the dowser and the elements of nature. His theory centres on an understanding that metals, trees, and other natural objects have subtle relationships or 'sympathize' with each other. Believers in this theory point to the fact that trees growing above mineral lodes often droop as though attracted downwards. Likewise, dowsers and their rods align with underground water or minerals through 'sensitive connection' or sympathetic attraction. Contemporary water dowser, Sharron Hope of California, often observes heavily-travelled deer trails over water veins and discovers the spot to drill a well is frequently located where two deer trails cross suggesting that wild animals, too, can pick up on the energy of underground water.

Dowsing and Divination have clearly stood the test of time. They are still employed, with a high success rate, by mining and well drilling companies in various parts of the world as an adjunct to modern scientific methods.

How and why do Dowsing and Divination work?

No one explanation to how and why dowsing works seems to suffice. Generally, historians and researchers have noticed that the approach of the individual dowser, particularly their neutrality and level of comfort and proficiency with their tools, seems to be a key feature. This neutrality is difficult to learn and cannot be faked because it stems from the subconscious and bypasses many conscious aspects of self-determination. For example, when I first picked up the rods I was very skeptical, but obviously my subconscious was at ease and very neutral so I had much success. This neutrality is, therefore, an important ingredient because subconscious resistance or attachment can alter or block effective divination and dowsing practices. Water dowsing also relies on the magnetic conduction of the rods (both metal and wooden) and of the human holding them. Locations above underground rock fractures are hot spots where the Earth's magnetism is stronger and like an upside-down lightning pole, the rods and their human diviners respond to subtle changes in this electrical current.

As with other metaphysical phenomena, it is difficult to record an unbiased scientific calculation of dowsing. In most cases, the skepticism of the researcher is, to some degree, determined to disprove any hypothesis validating affirmative results. This scientific slant creates a negative placebo (or nocebo) that affects outcomes as much as the dowser and the rod, just like it's difficult to perform an emotionally charged task with someone looking over your shoulder, especially if that someone anticipates or even prefers you to fail.

Dowsing and Divination, like most metaphysical phenomena, are sometimes discredited, even demonized by mainstream science and popular culture. In E.S. Cumbies book, *The Psychometric Pendulum and the Pendulum Board*, he suggests throughout history that "the priestly classes felt the layperson did not have the belief, knowledge or training to contact the cosmic mind for enlightenment, therefore poor people were forced to rely upon the priests to gain the guidance they sought from a higher source and the priests used dowsing devices to make this contact." Times haven't changed much. Even now, it is possible that NASA and the CIA research and utilize a variety of metaphysical practices while the masses are still fed a diluted diet of limited scientific misinformation.

Some religious communities continue to question the ethics and spiritual correctness of employing methods such as dowsing rods to access sources of pure water. However, if we allow ourselves to look deeper, there are biblical examples where Moses and his son Aron use a dowsing device referred to as 'the Rod' to locate and bring forth water and even to 'part the waters of the sea' in order to save their people. This rod and staff are described as providing life-sustaining comfort and support.

Ultimately, we are free to make our own choices regarding these matters. Personally, I think few practices are more positive and life-sustaining than employing the gentle and natural ancient technology of dowsing to seek pure water that we all need for survival on this planet. It is important in modern times to preserve these tools and skills that allow us unlimited access to clean underground water which is our birthright.

dowsing rod instructions

HOW TO MAKE YOUR OWN DOWSING RODS:

Making your own dowsing rods is very simple. All you need is a wire coat hanger and a pair of wire cutters.

- First, cut the lower part of the coat hanger in the very middle.
- Next cut the upper portion equal distance (3 to 5 inches depending on the size of the hanger) from both sides of the top hook.
- Discard the hook portion and then gently expand the bend in each of your identical rods so they change from a (7) shape to an (L) shape (the arms of the rod in a 45-degree angle from each other).

Please be aware of the rough edges. You may wish to tape the ends to prevent scratching yourself or anyone else.

THE BASICS OF USING DOWSING RODS:

To begin your dowsing practise measuring auric fields you will need an open area free of obstacles. To measure the aura of a person, stand at least eight to ten feet away from them initially to ensure you start outside the periphery of their energy field (some folks have a huge aura so it helps to practice with several individuals to get a sense of the variations). Do not get too caught up with the size of a particular aura since its size is not the only determining factor of a healthy individual. Your aim here is to familiarize yourself with the practice of dowsing connecting you and your rods to subtle variations in energy.

Begin by holding your rods with your palm, four fingers and thumb wrapped around the shorter portion of the rods. Tuck your elbows to your sides and hold both hands directly in front of your body, clasping gently yet firmly so that the rods are able to swing freely, but are also pointing horizontally straight ahead even as you walk.

Now it is time to practice humility, clarifying your intentions (for the greater good of all) and communicate them to Spirit, your subconscious, the rods and the energy fields in your vicinity in a way that feels natural and supportive. An example of what you can say, out loud or silently is, "it is my intention to familiarize myself with these dowsing rods and to practice recognizing these energy fields. I am in a neutral state of love and acceptance, aligning only with beneficial energy that supports the greater good of all."

You are not trying to do something more than to be in vibrational alignment with the surrounding benevolent energies. If your intentions are centred in love, then there is no right or wrong way of exploring. Every person is different and each dowsing session is unique. Sometimes you may feel a slight tingle (likely the rods warming up) and occasionally the rods may begin to move right away. If the energy and responsiveness of your rods ever feel overwhelming to you, then, by all means, request that they minimize to a level you are comfortable with. Like operating a vehicle, you are in the driver's seat and can press the gas or the brake simply by expressing your intention.

When you feel ready, begin to move slowly towards the person whose aura you are measuring. It may feel a bit silly and that's okay. As you get closer your rods will likely respond as they reach the outside edge of the auric field. They may swing open or closed and when this happens you will understand that the force necessary to initiate this movement was not applied by any physical means. It's an amazing feeling for everyone involved!

What happens if nothing happens? Well, that's okay too. Sometimes in our enthusiasm, we may be gripping the rods too tightly. Perhaps your test subject is not entirely comfortable with the exercise affecting the response. Perhaps you would like to switch places, or try again later, or choose a different volunteer. Please do not be discouraged. Some of the best dowsers began their journey in the exact same way; with practice, time and patience. You too will likely yield a result that you will be happy with.

I often suggest that people begin their dowsing practice indoors where life-force energies are minimal. In nature, there are so many auric fields and magnetic portals that some inexperienced dowsers may get confused in their readings. Other new dowsers find the natural world the best place to practice and only get good results practicing outside. Experiment both ways and see what feels best. As your proficiency builds you may want to explore measuring auric fields of trees or animals (if they will sit still long enough).

Some dowsers employ the rods to answer questions. It may feel appropriate (but not necessary) to ask Spirit to indicate to you different optional responses (ie. Rods opening or closing can mean a 'yes' or 'no' answer to a question) and some dowsers ask for this clarification from the rods at the beginning of each session.

Once you have practiced navigating and measuring energy with your rods and are feeling comfortable interpreting subtle variations in magnetic fields, you may decide to go the next step. Learning to dowse for water is a more complex skill than I have space to go into in this article. It is a real art form, ideally developed through training with an accomplished teacher or mentor. The dowsing part of the skill is only part of it. Professional Water Diviners understand landscape topography, the flow of existing above-ground waterways and how to take measurements on the four magnetic points that determine the exact locations of potable water. There are many good teachers all over the globe and I've provided a few links in the Resources section to get you started. It is such a worthwhile skill to learn and I predict good dowsers may be more appreciated and sought after in the years to come.

Looking back, I realize that while exploring and experimenting with metaphysics, dowsing and divination, I have never been attracted to having any sort of power over others or my environment. Instead, it has always been about connection. About feeling an undeniable link and having a meaningful personal relationship with the natural world and the cosmos. This relationship is one of devotion, deep reverence and respect. I am not trying to take from my environment, but absolving to feel a part of something that is bigger than what I can comprehend, and receive the gifts that this relationship bestows on me naturally. Each time I practice dowsing and divination, I approach my dynamic connection with the creator humbly and as a wide-eyed beginner. I navigate with love and tune in to magnetic energies, or vibrations, that are aligned with the greater good of all for the purpose of assisting the most beneficial outcomes for both nature and my fellow humans. It is always amazing… a simply beautiful and wonderfully witchy experience!

DEFINITIONS:

Astrology: The study of the movements and relative positions of celestial bodies interpreted as having an influence on human affairs and the natural world.

Auric Field: Scientific research and techniques like electrophotography have observed that all matter in existence radiates an electromagnetic (auric) field.

Caduceus: An ancient Greek or Roman herald's wand, typically one with two serpents twined around it, carried by the messenger god Hermes or Mercury. A representation of this, traditionally associated with healing.

Divining: From the Latin word 'divinus' meaning godlike, 'to see or perceive that which is unknown.'

Dowsing: A type of divination employed to locate groundwater, buried metals or ores, gemstones, oil, gravesites, and many other objects and materials without the use of scientific apparatus.

I Ching: An ancient Chinese manual of divination based on eight symbolic trigrams and sixty-four hexagrams, interpreted in terms of the principles of yin and yang. It was included as one of the 'five classics' of Confucianism.

Oracle: An oracle is a person or agency considered to provide wise and insightful counsel or prophetic predictions or precognition of the future.

Pendulum: A weight hung from a fixed point so that it can swing freely backward and forward. May be used for divination purposes.

Psychic: Relating to or denoting faculties or phenomena that are apparently inexplicable by natural laws, especially involving telepathy or clairvoyance.

Runes: Small stones, pieces of bone, or wood, bearing a letter of an ancient Germanic alphabet and used as divinatory symbols.

Tarot: A set of 78 cards displaying artistic and symbolic imagery (originating from ancient western mystical traditions), designed in the 14th century in Italy for both entertainment and divination purposes.

Water Witching: Rhabdomancy: is an ancient practice whereby a person holds a Y-shaped branch (or two L-shaped wire rods) and walks around until they feel a pull on the branch, or the wire rods cross or open, at which point water is allegedly below.

Witch: The etymology of the word witch is From Middle English wicche, from Old English wicce f. and Wicca m., deverbative from wiccian (to practice sorcery), from Proto-Germanic wikkōną West Frisian wikje, wikke (to foretell, warn), Low German wicken (to soothsay), Dutch wikken, wichelen (to dowse, divine), from Proto-Indo-European *wik-néh₂-, derivation of *weyk- (to consecrate; separate); Lithuanian viekas (life-force), Sanskrit vinákti (to set apart, separate out).

How to Read Oracle Cards without being *psychic*

By Kelly Oswald

Psychics have an innate or developed ability to access messages and information from the other side, superconscious, Spirit Guides, the unseen world, the Universe, and other sources of subtle energies. They sometimes use tools such as Tarot or Oracle Cards to access, amplify or validate the wisdom they receive.

Believe it or not, you too have natural psychic intuitive 'powers'. If you have ever said "I knew I should have done that!", then you had foresight and insight into the situation before it occurred; you predicted an outcome. As you work with Oracle Cards and begin to access your personal internal wisdom, you can't help but awaken and develop that mysterious part of yourself.

But don't worry about that now.

Reading Oracle Cards is much easier and straight-forward than the shroud of magic and mystery that psychic reading implies. You are about to read cards with confidence using a method that turns out to be based on how your brain works and patterns unfold, rather than tapping into your 'psychic' abilities.

The preface of an Oracle Deck is to provide its user with a tool for gaining insight. Most cards are designed to help you tap into your subconscious resources and inner knowing. The messages of specific cards are written in the Guide Book that accompanies each deck. The interpretation of the images on the cards is meant to reflect or give guidance to your current stage of life.

The word 'oracle' comes from the Latin verb ōrāre, 'to speak' and properly refers to the priest or priestess uttering the prediction. The most famous Oracle of all was Pythia. She held court at Pytho, the sanctuary of the Delphinians, a haven dedicated to the Greek god Apollo. Pythia was highly-regarded, for it was believed that she channeled prophecies from Apollo himself, while steeped in a dreamlike trance, seated in the Temple of Apollo in ancient Greece. The Oracle at Delphi was consulted by rulers seeking prophecies regarding war, wealth, and weather.

Delphi became so busy that several Oracular priestesses would operate at once. But seekers of esoteric knowledge had to be careful how they interpreted the answers of the Oracle.

King Croesus of Lydia (now south-western Turkey) asked the Oracle whether or not he should go to war on his neighbouring kingdom. The Oracle replied that if he went to war, a great kingdom would fall. Croesus interpreted this as being his enemy's, however; it turned out to be his own.

Oracles can be people, cards, stones, pendulums, crystal gazing balls or anything that provides communication between Universal messages (the realm of Spirit) and the person asking the questions (the physical realm). A modern-day Oracle is any type of conduit between the seen and the unseen world.

You and your cards are going to be Oracles, bridging the communication gap between your conscious and subconscious mind. You will tap into the counsel of the cards that is specifically meant for you. And no, you don't have to be psychic; just calm, relaxed, and open to recognizing your own stuff.

IN THIS SECTION YOU WILL DISCOVER:

- The difference between Oracle and Tarot Cards.
- How to choose an Oracle Deck.
- How Oracle Cards work in tune with your Symbolism Library.
- How Oracle Cards DON'T work with your emotions; hopes, fears, and desires.
- How to use signs, symbols and subtle messages to inspire, validate, and offer insight.
- How to tap into your intuitive mind during a genuine reading.
- The components of a reading.
- How to get a good, accurate reading from your favourite (or any) deck of Oracle Cards.
- How to read Oracle Cards to specifically offer insight, validation, and inspiration without being psychic.

The Difference Between Oracle and Tarot Cards

Both Oracle and Tarot decks are used for insight, perspective, validation, clarity, personal growth, inspiration, coaching, and divination.

Historically the Tarot has ancient roots, while Oracle Decks (angels, fairies, guides, fractal, animals, dragons, and others) are the new kids on the block. However, Tarot and Oracle Cards are structured quite differently. The Tarot follows its own set of rules laid out by original masters of days gone by, while the artists of Oracle Cards are free to do whatever they desire. Here is the comparison:

TAROT CARDS

- The Tarot structure is predictable. If you learn the Rider-Waite, then you will most likely be able to read any other Tarot deck.
- Tarot always has a minimum of 78 cards (Osho Zen added himself for 79, and some older traditional decks have a greater number of Court Cards)
- Major Arcana = 22 cards relating to major events, personal and spiritual growth, and life pivoting events
- Minor Arcana = 56 cards Page, Knight, Queen, and King (Ace through 10 are known as the Pip Cards, the Page, Knight, Queen and King as the Court Cards)
- The Tarot is divided into four suits representing elements; Wands (fire), Swords (air), Cups (water) and Pentacles or Coins (earth).
- The Tarot may be a descendant of an earlier version of playing cards - or vice versa (history tells it both ways); cups are the equivalent of hearts, pentacles are diamonds, wands are clubs and swords are spades. The Joker and the Fool are nowhere and everywhere and the Court Cards that remain in a modern deck of playing cards are the King, Queen, and Jack.

ORACLE CARDS

- Oracle Decks are structured independently and each follows its own set of rules created by the author of the deck.
- They may have any number of cards, usually between 36 and 64.
- Rarely have suits, although they are often numbered for Guide Book reference.

- Each Oracle Deck follows a different structure, rules, and meanings found in the Guide Book that is written specifically for that particular deck.
- Some have a bit of a Tarot theme, while others do not.
- Some have the meaning of the card printed on them.

Because each Oracle Deck is different, a specific Guide Book accompanies most decks. It is acceptable for both novices and professional readers to refer to Guide Books for the author's interpretation of the cards for greater detail.

Is one better than the other?

No – they are different. It is the deck you love that will work the best for you.

Oracle Cards tend to be easier to learn, while Tarot takes a level of practice and mastery to become proficient and offers an expanse of detail at a depth that most Oracle Cards do not reach. Oracle Decks are more free-flowing and open to many levels of interpretation that the stricter rules of the Tarot do not historically allow.

Nowadays, it is common practice for professional readers to add an Oracle spread to their Tarot sessions to validate or amplify messages received.

The perceived underlying similarity is the belief that when working with the cards, one must have some level of psychic ability. While it may be helpful, useful, and even a way to tune into ones developing psychic ability; one is not required to be psychic to read the cards.

SUMMARY:
- You have some level of psychic intuitive capability already.
- You don't need to use psychic abilities to read Oracle Cards.
- Oracles are a method of communication between the seen and unseen or the known and unknown.
- Tarot Cards are structured and follow a historical set of rules while Oracle Cards are more open to interpretation.

How to Choose a Deck

I love, love, love this part of the journey.!

There are an abundance of Oracle Decks available these days, and the artwork is incredibly diverse; shockingly beautiful, pleasantly quirky and even spooky and macabre. They incorporate people, animals, items and a broad range of worldly and other-worldly images.

Although there are no rules when choosing a deck, I prefer decks with more pictures than words. I don't feel the author of the deck knows me well enough to suggest my next move. One or two words that embrace the essence of the cards – yes – but a card that tells me what to do or how to do it doesn't work for me. However, if the deck you fall in love with has epic stories and volumes of text on both sides… trust that it's the right one for you!

The best way to choose your deck is to browse until you find one you absolutely love. The perfect deck sings to your soul and you are intrigued and enthralled with everything about it.

An outdated myth has re-circulated; it suggests that buying your personal deck is bad luck. Not true. To feel the magic, appreciate the beauty and understand your new deck's specialness – no one could choose the right deck except you. If someone gifts you a deck and you LOVE it, then YAY! I have a huge collection of decks and have found that I use different decks for different reasons. You may feel a collection coming on! One thing to note: once the deck has been opened, most stores will not take them back, so choose wisely before you walk away from the cashier and the point of no return.

A note of caution; consulting cards before your every decision and allowing the cards to make your choices for you is NOT what they are meant to do. You are still ultimately responsible for your actions. Oracle Cards offer insight, validation, and inspiration; they are not meant to be tools for dependency or disempowering at any level.

SUMMARY:
- Choose a deck you LOVE!
- You can assign different decks for various purposes.
- Avoid becoming dependent on your cards.

Your Symbolism Library

Your Oracle Deck is host to a plethora of symbols designed to bring out messages and communicate with your subconscious. A dictionary of symbols is not required because by learning to associate specific symbols to unfamiliar meanings, you would be training your mind to look for things that don't pre-exist in your personal Symbolism Library. Here you will learn what symbols are, but it is your association to the images that really counts.

IMAGES AND INKBLOTS

Rorschach Inkblots are strange images that appear to be splatters of black ink smooshed out on white paper. They were created by Hermann Rorschach and were used to determine the perceptions of different mindsets. Beginning in 1921 the tests produced compelling data, gaining popularity in the '60s before becoming controversial and falling out of favour.

In the original Rorschach tests, patients and subjects were asked to articulate the first thing that came to mind when looking at the inkblot. Dr. Rorschach fine-tuned his method on a large cross-sections of people; those suffering from mental health issues, those considered 'normal', and folks from various stations in life. The tests demonstrated that people pick up on specific images according to how their brains work and how their thought patterns flow.

The practice (now pretty much obsolete) followed the theory that the individual's association with the images would reveal inner mysteries and pick up on patterns working deep within their mind. The subjects perceived concepts would reflect their true nature or underlying issues.

What does this have to do with reading Oracle Cards? The images and patterns on each card will evoke meaning to you in the same manner as the first impression of an inkblot. Your perception of the Oracle's images will be based on how your brain works and will reflect your current thoughts, emotions, and circumstances.

PATTERNS AND PERCEPTIONS

When you see a sweet puppy, a soft curve of paint, or a beautiful landscape, your thoughts, and emotions may be peaceful, and pleasant. A bloody hand, sharply drawn lines, and falling volcanic ash create a whole different vibe.

While it seems as if shapes, patterns, and images have some effect on your thoughts and emotions; the truth is, that your thoughts and emotions react to all shapes patterns and images due to your belief system, cultural upbringing, and current circumstances.

Corporations know this. They create company logos and base their marketing and advertising on consumers thought patterns. Creating a household name and developing instant recognition is part of the plan. You can see it loud and clear with the Macintosh Apple, Nike Swoosh and LEGO. If you are a Mac fan, the Apple evokes a good vibe; however, if you have boycotted the brand, you will feel negative.

What does that have to do with reading Oracle Cards?

The symbology and images on the cards are going to give you messages using the same method: nothing psychic about it. You just need to know that it is occurring. You must be aware that this is happening as you look for the messages. If you know it is happening, you can understand why, and then move on to look a little deeper. Your first impressions may hardly surprise you, but as you sit with it, you will be amazed at what comes to mind.

DIFFERENT TYPES OF SYMBOLS

A symbol is something that references something other than itself. It can be a mark, sign or word that indicates, signifies, or is understood as representing an idea, object, or relationship. Symbols allow people to go beyond what is known or seen by creating bridges between otherwise very different concepts and experiences. They can be a tangible sign of something intangible. Symbols are used daily to quickly convey information (e.g. danger symbols, stop signs, no-smoking), or to deliver complex messages in art and literature… and of course, Oracle Cards.

UNIVERSAL SYMBOLS

Universal symbols are symbols that most people can relate to regardless of their culture, age, gender, race, ethnicity or religious background. We relate to these symbols because we automatically make connections between the object and the concept or idea that it represents. The symbol of a skull and crossbones on a label is a Universal symbol warning for poison, a heart is an emblem of love, a dove represents peace, a dollar sign signifies currency, and a four-leaf clover offers the concept of good luck. During a reading, it is how you associate with Universal Symbols that counts.

CULTURAL SYMBOLS

All over the world, different countries, tribes, and religions have their own imagery and belief systems that signify the ideology of a particular culture or that merely has meaning within that culture. Canadians associate the Maple Leaf with their country, the lotus is a symbol for Hindus and Buddhists, a long neck is culturally beautiful to the Karen Tribe in Thailand, the floral lei is a well-known Hawaiian symbol, and elephants are often symbolic of India and Africa.

Your cultural upbringing, beliefs, traditions, historical background, language, values, and environment will have an effect on what certain symbols mean for you.

PERSONAL SYMBOLS

Tapping into the messages of personal symbolism is the art of using an object or an image to represent an abstract idea. Personal Symbols are yours alone. They are beautifully private and belong to your world of magic signs; they have deep personal significance and they seem to show up when you need them.

If you don't have anything that you feel is a personal symbol, start looking for things that show up or repeat in your life. Your symbols may develop through the connection to colours, weather patterns, animals, objects, moon phases, or anything that shows up specifically for you. Notice your environment or watch the stories play out in your dreams to find elements to relate to and inspire.

SUMMARY:

- Your perception of the Oracle's images will be based on how your brain works and will reflect your current thoughts, emotions, and circumstances.
- Your thoughts and emotions react to all shapes patterns and images due to your belief system, cultural upbringing, and current circumstances.
- The symbology and images on the cards are going to give you messages.
- Universal symbols appear everywhere and are known by most of the world.
- Cultural Symbols are specific to the historical background from which they originate.
- Personal Symbols are yours alone and often show up at pivotal moments.
- During a reading, it is how you associate with Symbols that counts.

It's all in Your Head

YOUR BRAIN AND ALTERED STATES OF CONSCIOUSNESS

I'd like to introduce you to the four major brainwaves; Beta, Alpha, Theta and Delta. These guys are the 'magic' that promote communication between your levels of subtle knowing and conscious awareness. Your brainwaves play like a symphony. They create harmony for the mental state that suits your situation beautifully. But think about this; do brainwaves create your state of mind - or does your state of mind create the brainwaves? Any meditator will tell you that you can control your state of mind. But first, let's see how these brain waves operate.

While awake, your Beta waves play like a loud fiddle, but it's not a solo, the other brain waves are cycling in the background. Whether you are reading this book or having a conversation with someone, you are in a normal wakeful state and your brainwaves are firing at all levels, but your Beta Waves are taking up the most space. In Beta, you are awake and maintain rational, concrete and strongly engaged thought. The rapid pace of this alert and busy mind (15-40 cycles and up)* is great for getting things done but interferes with the ability to pick up subtle, hidden or forgotten messages in a reading. At this level, we reason, rationalize and perform the necessary chores and activities we need to do.

It's a busy brain.

Beta waves interfere with your access to fully appreciate what you can pull up from our subconscious mind. It is challenging to tune-in to the messages in the cards with our over-active Beta Waves firing. Alpha brainwaves are slower and lower in frequency but higher amplitude… cycling about 8-14 cycles per second. Alpha waves are home to creative moments and getting in the 'flow'. A sense of time seems to disappear and we are lost in gardening, painting, daydreams, fantasies, visualization. Creative energy bubbles up, new ideas pop in, and flashes of insight appear. This is the optimal frame of mind to read cards and to be open to symbolic and other types of messages.

The Alpha state is the bridge between the unconscious and conscious mind. The brain is in a relaxed and resting present-moment state. It is a place of calm and mind/body integration. Without access to Alpha, it is impossible to access the deeper states of consciousness. The Alpha state improves memory and creative insight. Some psychic experiences occur at this level, and because this is a great state to be in while reading Oracle Cards, you may find yourself having moments of psychic or intuitive insight. It will come.

If you are painting alone in a studio, playing a video game, or out for a jog then your Alpha waves become predominant. Cycling like a melodic piano, the other brainwaves are barely noticed in the background. In this state, you may lose track of time, come up with great ideas or remember things you had forgotten. But as soon as someone calls you, the phone rings, or you are otherwise interrupted - the Beta waves kick up a notch and overtake the flow.

Within our brainwave orchestra, Theta is the instrument you can't quite pinpoint. You know it's playing but don't know exactly what it sounds like. We don't even know when we are predominantly cycling in Theta state because it is quite unconscious. Theta offers understanding from deep within as it is completely withdrawn from your eternal world and therefore easily taps into internal signals. Firing around 3-8 Hertz, Theta aids in learning, memory enhancement, and amplifies intuition. Theta holds your subconscious hopes and fears, shows you Technicolor dreams while you sleep, opens the door to information beyond your normal conscious awareness and provides a direct route to your intuition.

Finally, Delta is the bass cello. It is a deep and restorative state that provides access to intuitive knowing. When you are vibing someone's energy as good or bad; you are picking up those vibes via your Delta brain waves. When you walk into a room where moments ago smiling people were having an argument and you can still feel it hanging in the air, even though there is no evidence.

That's Delta.

Delta brainwaves cycle very slowly, 1-4 cycles per second (or less.) They have the lowest frequency, but the highest amplitude (loudest). Delta brainwaves are generated during dreamless, restorative sleep and from the unconscious mind. Because they suspend external awareness they are a source of knowingness, strong intuition, empathy and developing one's 'spidey senses'. Healing and regeneration are the bonus assets of the Delta state of mind.

As you sleep, they are all playing.

During the sleep cycle, your brain cycles out of Beta and into Alpha, then Theta to Delta, in about thirty minutes (this varies between people as well as the same person, different night). You may remain in Delta anywhere from half an hour to ninety minutes, then cycle up to Theta, then to Alpha where you may dream for a while, then cycle back down to Delta. These cycles continue throughout the night.

But when you are awake, you can be the maestro.

Our brainwaves change according to what we are doing and feeling. That means that what you are doing and feeling can, in turn, change your brainwaves. You have that kind of control.

What do your brainwaves have to do with card reading?

Your Theta/Alpha/Beta waves provide access to your subconscious mind, which stores everything you have ever done or thought. I digress as I provide you with the stereotypical image of the psychologist who wags his pocket watch in front of your eyes and says 'you are getting sleepy'.

He is attempting to increase your Alpha and Theta brainwaves and decrease your Beta brainwaves so you can access material not available to your awake and conscious mind. He is putting you into the hypnagogic state. Not psychic – but incredibly effective.

Hypnagogia is the experience of being half awake and half asleep. You may have experienced this crazy state full of vivid dreams and strange thoughts early in the morning – maybe your alarm went off and you hit the 'snooze' button and went for the hypnagogic ride!

Surrealist artist Salvador Dali called hypnagogia "the slumber with a key," and he used it as creative inspiration for many of his unusual dream-like and symbolic paintings. Thomas Edison gave hypnagogia credit for many of his inventions including the light bulb. The sewing machine needle (which has its eye on the point instead of the back end of a hand-held needle) became a reality after the dream of Walter Hunt (It was later re-invented and patented by Elias Howe).

During the hypnagogic state, your mind cycles through thoughts, memories, and emotions, building associations between diverse concepts; and because you are half awake, you're conscious enough to be at least partially aware of what's going on.

The hypnagogic state is optimal – but you certainly don't have to go that far to increase Alpha/Theta and access information through Beta.

Using the knowledge of how your brain works will help you do an accurate reading without worrying about psychic ability and intuition – although once you begin reading cards, those skills will begin to develop rapidly (if you let them).

When you read your Oracle Cards, you will want to control the state of your mind so you are as relaxed as possible for the most accurate reading. If you are stressed or agitated at any level, hold off until you are feeling mellow again.

To prepare your brain for a reading, reduce outside influences such as racing thoughts, opinions, anxiety, and sensory interference such as sudden sounds and significant smells. Close your eyes to increase your Alpha brainwaves, breathe easily, relax and enjoy an open mind.

Simply and deliberately cause your brain to go into an altered state (without falling asleep). In 1929, Hans Berger discovered that the brain automatically starts generating more Alpha waves as soon as one closes one's eyes. That's a pretty straight-forward, non-psychic way to float into a reading!

Be like Pythia, while steeped in a dreamlike trance, seated in the Temple of Apollo in ancient Greece. Close your eyes, breathe and relax… Then, when you feel ready, open your eyes and pull your cards allowing the symbols to form messages and gather insight from beyond your conscious mind!

SUMMARY:

- The four major brainwaves; Beta, Alpha, Theta, and Delta. These guys are the 'magic' that promote communication between your levels of subtle knowingness and conscious awareness.
- Brainwave speed is measured in Hertz (cycles per second).
- When Beta waves rule, you are awake and maintain rational, concrete and strongly engaged thought. It's a busy brain.
- The Alpha state is the bridge between the unconscious and conscious mind. It is a relaxed state and associated with 'flow'.
- The Theta state holds your subconscious hopes and fears, shows you Technicolor dreams while you sleep, and opens the door to information beyond your normal conscious awareness providing you a direct route to your intuition.

- Delta brainwaves are a source of knowingness, strong intuition, empathy and instrumental to using your 'spidey senses'.
- Increasing your Alpha and Theta brainwaves and decreasing your Beta brainwaves promotes access to clues not available to your awake and conscious mind.
- Hypnagogia is the experience of being half awake and half asleep during which time your mind shifts through thoughts, memories, and emotions, building associations between diverse concepts; and because you are half awake, you are conscious enough to be at least partially aware of what is going on.
- Using the knowledge of how your brain works will help you do an accurate reading without worrying about psychic ability and intuition.
- To prepare your brain for a reading, let yourself relax by reducing outside influences such as racing thoughts, opinions, anxiety, and sensory interference such as sudden sounds and significant smells. Close your eyes to increase your Alpha brainwaves, breathe easily, relax and enjoy an open mind.
- If you are stressed or agitated at any level, hold off until you are feeling mellow again.

Get out of Your Own Way

Reading Oracle Cards accurately relies on starting with a blank slate. If you have pre-conceptions or are overflowing with wishful thinking, or possibly even skepticism, then your reading is not going to work. Emotions and logic are the Kryptonite to a good reading; they will weaken your session or possibly sabotage it completely. Since you can't stop your mind from thinking and you can't stop yourself from feeling, here are some suggestions for getting out of your own way and finding a smooth entry point to your own internal wisdom – your inner knowing.

EMOTIONS

When we speak of reading from the 'heart', it is more about coming from a place of love, caring, and compassion than it is about the emotions we carry such as excitement, fear, desire or loneliness which can confuse a reading.

Emotions can cause you to look for things that aren't there – or pretend situations are different than they are. Wishful thinking, hopes, and fears, all bring out a plethora of feelings that are a far cry from intuitive knowing. Being in an emotional state, whether it is excitement, happiness, depression, sorrow, fear, or anxiety, is not a good time to make any kind of decision, let alone consult the cards. You can't think straight – let alone access subtle information. A highly emotional state is NOT a good time to do a reading.

- When you are excited, joyful and happy – you may jump into something regardless of any doubt or warning.
- When you are sad and depressed, full of sorrow – you may miss out on hope and something offered.
- When you are afraid and anxious – you may find yourself paralyzed and unable to see your alternative choices.

The perfect time to consult your cards is when you are relaxed, curious and open to receive. If you have already made up your mind (logic) or you are an emotional mess… it is not a good time to give yourself a reading - or anyone else for that matter!

LOGIC: NOW THERE'S A THOUGHT

A big problem with logic pushing its way into a reading is that it brings out all those Beta brainwaves and interferes with picking up on the messages floating up from your subconscious that the Alpha brainwaves allow. It takes us into our busy, thinking brain and you may as well put those cards away because you won't get a true message. Logic wants to create patterns and put pieces of puzzles together. It also jumps to conclusions without taking subconscious messages into consideration.

How do you know when logic is ruling and Beta waves are predominant? You will be thinking, and your language is a BIG clue. When you hear yourself saying "I think this means that" then your logic has taken over and you are trying to analyze. (The key word here is 'think'.) Thinking is not allowing a subtle realization to appear or something to pop into your conscious mind.

Thoughts can take our emotions on a grand adventure and lead us right out of an accurate reading. Thoughts create and amplify your emotions. Thinking of a wounded relationship makes you sad, and dwelling on it sadder. Focusing on a new financial prospect may cause excitement and motivation. Health issues create concern, a social get-together may stimulate excitement or anxiety. The more you think about your states of being the stronger you feel about them. When sitting down for a reading, allow yourself to find the neutral place of Alpha and lessen the thoughts that drive your emotions. Of course, you can't eliminate your thoughts and emotions entirely, but being aware of what you are thinking and feeling will help you be more open to what the cards will show you.

Again, be like the Oracle at Delphi, while steeped in a dreamlike trance, seated in the Temple of Apollo in ancient Greece. Close your eyes, breathe and relax. You are ready…

SUMMARY:
- Emotions and logic are the Kryptonite to a good reading.
- A highly emotional state is NOT a good time to do a reading.
- Logic brings out all those Beta brainwaves and interferes with picking up on the messages floating up from your subconscious that the Alpha brainwaves allow.

How to Read Oracle Cards
(without being psychic)

THE SECRET TO ACCURACY WHEN READING FOR YOURSELF

Even the BEST psychics aren't one hundred percent accurate. Human beings aren't one hundred percent at anything. If you turn your thoughts to everything we do - driving cars, dancing, accounting, hair cutting… even making a pot of coffee - we can be pretty darn good – but not one hundred percent. So, be gentle on yourself as you humbly practice and become proficient at reading the cards.

The focus on this section is on reading *any* deck, regardless of the stories within the pages of the deck's accompanying Guide Book. Once you have mastered your personal method of reading, you can use the Guide Book to supplement and enhance the information you have innately received. Remember the Guide Book is based on the author's story and experience. A true reading taps into your own.

Have you had the experience when someone's name slips your mind? It's right on the tip of your tongue, but no matter how hard you try to think about it, you just can't remember their name.

That is your prefrontal cortex doing its best, but you are in a Beta brainwave state which is pretty useless at digging up forgotten and buried knowledge. So you carry on the conversation and are talking about something else - when all of a sudden the forgotten name 'pops' into your head and you remember. You KNOW.

How did that just happen? Your subconscious (your memory storehouse) was rooting around solving the problem for you after you had given up thinking about it. Your Alpha/Theta brainwaves cycling in the background offered your conscious mind a message from your subconscious. Wow.

And THAT is what you want your mind to do for you while reading Oracle Cards. Not remember forgotten names, but root around and pull up stuff that matters; the kind of things that can help you at any stage of life.

READING OUTCOMES

You know you've had a good reading when the cards have offered up something that you didn't already consciously know.

A good *inspirational reading* will leave you feeling wowed, jazzed and motivated, ready to take action and willing to view challenges as opportunity and obstacles as stepping stones.

A good *validation reading* will mirror where you are and reflect back to you what you already know to be true for you. It will help you be decisive and confident.

A good *insight reading* will show you things you may not have thought about before. It will help you think outside the box and provide solutions to problems or show ways to help yourself or assist others.

What if you don't like the outcome? Once you know what's coming, you can deal with it; nothing is set in stone, you always have choices and can take a different course of action. If you know the future, you can change it.

SUMMARY:

- You can read Oracle Cards with or without the accompanying Guide Book.
- While reading Oracle Cards your subconscious mind can root around and pull up underlying important and relevant information.
- A good reading offers something that you didn't already consciously know.

The Components of a Reading

TIMING

I believe that readings are most accurate when given a specific timeline. Because we are working with our brain more than intuition and psychic ability, then doing anything longer than our memory is capable of consciously retaining seems irresponsible.

Personally, the greatest length of time I look to the past is one year and the furthest into the future is the same. One year. Why only one year? Can you remember a previous Christmas, or your birthday over a year ago? How detailed? What did you eat? Who was there and what was said? That's at least a year ago – now try remembering two years, or three. It's hard work recalling all that information. Your subconscious is already rooting around trying to find answers to these questions, and there is a good chance, in a few hours from now, you will remember more about your last birthday than you do right now. But the point is, if you can't remember back much more than a year, how can you 'remember' forward more than that? How can you predict or validate or have insight into anything more than a year into the future?

Sticking to a tight timeline will increase the accuracy of your readings significantly. There is far too much interference that blurs the facts the further ahead you try to go. Other events occur and your trajectory changes.

Before you do a spread – set the intention that the reading you are about to do encompasses a specific timeline; three months, or a week or maybe only today. Many people choose one card readings for daily inspiration. Ultimately, it is up to you, and you can change the timing for each reading if you so choose.

HOW TO SHUFFLE YOUR DECK

Handling your deck and shuffling the cards pulls you into a relationship with the deck. You are sharing space and connecting, thinking about your question and planning on working together to understand the outcome. You are beginning a conversation between you and your Oracle. It is better if you are friends with your cards and have 'touched'.

I find that shuffling is part of my ritual. As I shuffle the cards (there is no wrong way to mix your cards), I contemplate my intentions for the readings and allow the deck to 'hear' me, even though this is unspoken. If by chance, a card falls from the deck in the process of shuffling, I always read it as a message that wants to be noticed. When the cards feel adequately mixed, I fan them out on a table face down to begin selecting the card or cards for my spread.

Cutting the cards in piles offers another method to mixing your deck. Shuffle, then stack and cut the deck in two, three, or four piles, re-stacking in a different order. If you feel like developing a traditional ritual, use your left hand to cut the piles and move them to the left. What is the reasoning behind the left-hand use? Some say the left hand is closer to the heart, therefore it is easier to reach a level of empathy, while others believe that it is not the left hand so much, as using the non-dominant hand, the hand the brain isn't used to using, therefore, has greater ties to your intuition. The kinetic process of picking cards is thought to be lead by an intuitive pull or the interconnectedness of energy patterns.

There is no wrong way to mix your cards. The more you use your cards, the more your shuffling technique will become your personal signature.

SUMMARY:
- Sticking to a tight timeline will increase the accuracy of your readings significantly.
- You can change the timing for each reading if you so choose.
- Shuffling begins the communication between you and your Oracle.
- There is no wrong way to mix your cards.

Spreads

AN INSPIRATIONAL ONE CARD READING

Use a one-card reading for inspiration. It's fun to pick a card in the morning to jumpstart your day. An inspirational message can be the boost that makes a difference in your outlook all day long. Keep in mind that the card may not signify motivation but may be cautionary. Either way, it's good to know.

1. Let yourself relax and breathe easily, not thinking, not doing, just being... maybe close your eyes and allow your Beta brain to slow a bit while your Alpha waves have a chance to expand and access that place of knowing connecting to Theta.

2. Shuffle the deck until it feels 'right' to stop.

3. Place the cards on a surface and fan them out so all the backs of the cards are visible. Use your left hand (if you'd like to follow tradition) and choose just one card.

4. Take your impressions from the card before you look up the meaning in the book that comes with the deck. Gently look for something that surprises you or reflects where you are at in your current stage of life in this exact present moment.

5. Indulge in the Guide Book that accompanies your deck. You can't help but interpret the message to fit your circumstance. Your brain will find a way to mirror your situation and uncover hidden wisdom.

Allow the message to be a reminder throughout the day and have fun with it... play is just as magical as card reading!

A VALIDATION THREE CARD SPREAD

A three-card spread can be used for validation. You will want to pick up on a pattern that is playing out to be sure your reading is on track. The three cards you choose will represent a time in your past, your current situation and a future moment. If the past and present cards are on task, then the future card is probably going to follow suit. (Note 'probably'. It is rarely one hundred percent, however 'probably' is stronger than 'possibly', and if the past and present cards are bang on, then your pattern is headed for a pretty strong probably.)

1. Let yourself relax and breathe easily, not thinking, just being, and allow your Beta brain to slow a bit, increasing access to an Alpha state.

2. Shuffle the deck until it feels 'right' to stop.

3. Place the cards on a surface and cut them into three piles to the left (use your left hand if you'd like to follow tradition). Pile them back into one stack right to left. Fan the cards out on the table and choose three.

4. Place the cards upright in front of you. Turn the first card you chose face up on your left, the second card in the center and the third card you chose on your right.

5. The first card represents your past, the middle card signifies your current situation and the third card peeks into the days ahead.

6. Take your impressions from each of the cards before you look up the meaning in the Guide Book that comes with the deck. Your innate wisdom is at work here.

7. Look for the things that reflect or mirror your situation in the first two cards. You are seeking a pattern that demonstrates where you are coming from (past) and where you are at (present) that will propel you forward to where you are going (future).
8. Finally, read the story written in the Guide Book for each card and see how it relates to the time period that the cards represent.

AN INSIGHTFUL THREE CARD SPREAD

An insight reading is mainly used for gaining information regarding a specific issue. It is meant to help answer a question. Form the question as thoroughly and specifically as you can. Also, ask yourself:

Am I hoping for a specific answer?
Am I afraid of what the card may suggest?
Have I already answered the question in my head before looking at the card?

When you turn the cards over, you are going to look for an instant association you sense with the card (ink-blot method). Next, you will look at the imagery, shapes, and pictures and allow them to make suggestions. If you are hoping for a specific answer, don't want to see the answer or have already made up your mind; then you may first see these things that you already know. That's not the important focus. None of it matters because you are looking for something you don't already consciously know; a message or impression from the card that will offer insight, validate or inspire.

It will be right on the tip of your tongue. Just wait for it.

STEP BY STEP INSIGHT READING:

1. Let yourself relax and breathe easily, not thinking, just being, and allowing your Beta brain to slow a bit, allowing Alpha waves to expand.
2. When you are feeling calm and relaxed, ask your question and let your mind stir it around in your pre-frontal cortex for a moment. Feel into the question and discern what thoughts and emotions are coming up for you regarding the question. (I usually shuffle the cards for the whole time I am thinking about the question.)
3. Shuffle the deck until it feels 'right' to stop.
4. Place the cards on a surface and cut them into three piles to the left (use your left hand if you'd like to follow tradition). Pile them back into one stack right to left. Fan the cards out on a table. Choose three.

5. Turn the first card you chose face up on your left, the second card in the center and the third card you chose on your right.

6. The first card represents hopes and fears (emotions that can motivate or freeze you = movement or no movement), the middle card signifies your current situation and is your motion card, (yes/no or stay/go) and the third card demonstrates outside influences (things possibly beyond your control that may help or hinder as well as other people's opinions).

7. Look for something that may surprise you, reflects an issue, or answers a question in all three cards.

8. Take your impressions from each of the cards before you look up the meaning in the Guide Book that comes with the deck.

9. Additionally, read the story written in the Guide Book for each card and relate it to each of the cards. Interpret the message to fit your situation, ask yourself what fits perfectly and why? Then let the questions rest while you wait for the answers to bubble up with further insight. If nothing seems to immediately correlate, just wait and see.

How will you know if your reading is bang-on?

When your reading is good (really good), it will 'click'. It will resonate with you, and you KNOW.

Your answer will have found its way to your conscious mind and arrives fully loaded. It may take a day or two to slowly develop into full bloom or it will drop smack dab into your reading.

You nailed it.

And you're not even psychic.

(Yet.)

stepping out

Of The Spiritual Closet

By Anita Pettersen

"Love is my religion…
you can take it or leave it, and you don't have to believe it."
~Ziggy Marley

Do you have a coming out story? A time when you have declared a difference from your family, peer group or community? A moment when you have risked not belonging because part of you was screaming that you just could not stay quiet for one more second? Becoming our true selves is a perpetual coming out journey, and there can be gut-punching moments of revealing ourselves that shift the course of our lives forever. These are acts of bravery. While sometimes taken as declarations of war, our challenge is to maintain our inner peace, strength and resolve, even if our coming out creates discomfort for others. As we walk the path of spiritual growth, our belief systems are ever-evolving and push us to live our truth. And keep pushing us to step out of the spiritual closet.

THE BEGINNING OF MY STORY

"Every life has its challenge. Every heart has an answer."
(HeartMath® Institute)

I come out of the closet every day. Sometimes I just stick out a toe to test the waters…Always wondering, is it safe? But each little 'test' is worth it because I get to become a little more 'me' with each rotation of the Earth. Parts of myself are out there, but so much more has yet to be revealed. It is scary. There is the fear of judgement and rejection with each proclamation I make. But those voices of fear are getting quieter as my connection to my Higher Self and with Spirit grows. So I reflect back and think— was I always like this? No way! As a child I was outspoken, chatting with everyone and telling them our family history. It was embarrassing for my big sisters. It was troublesome for my mother because she would lose me everywhere as I wandered spreading my news and seeking to quench my curiosities. And they all wondered what planet I had beamed in from! I had no fear. Fear had to be created for me so that I would stay 'safe' and stay close.

In my early years, I was free-spirited and open as I shared my thoughts with everyone. I also enjoyed listening to people's stories. In particular, I revelled in the magical stories that my mother would tell. One of my favourites was the *Miracle of the Roses* that originates from her birthplace of Thuringia in Germany. I asked to hear that one again and again, each time elated when the bread would mysteriously turn into roses and save Elisabeth's life! We were not rooted in religion, but rather in the spiritual. And in the mystical. My mother would talk about many faiths and provide interesting discussions and books to go along with our conversations. She would take us to Satsang as a holistic way of connecting with spiritual practice and be with thoughtful people promoting one love. Instead of having to choose one set of religious or spiritual teachings, our Satsang embraced all teachings and the common spiritual love in them. This evolved into formal metaphysical studies by the time I was eleven years old. These were engagements with a spiritual community without the fear of being judged. It was an opportunity to ponder the mysteries of life while nurturing personal growth.

As a child, my inner life was terribly important to me. As well as my outer connections. Even back then I knew there was no distinction between inner and outer - it is all one. I could read the energy of people, animals, plants and places, which was both fascinating and wearying. I would feel ill every morning before school with the foreboding of the empathic challenges ahead. But once at school, I was adept at transmuting the energy coming my way. I was a social butterfly, and friendly with everyone - always looking for more meaningful ways to connect with people. As an example of my efforts, when I was about seven years old I set up two stools in the garden and booked one-on-one meetings with everyone I could. My big sisters were resistant to partake, but my mother insisted. I would sit on the stool opposite my invited guest and tell them that we were going to have a heart-to-heart conversation, and I would touch my heart and then their heart. I would look deeply into their eyes — even if they were rolling their eyes with impatience — and philosophize about our connection to our world, to one another and our feelings about it all. Then at night, my mom would make sure that my sisters received the hugs that I wanted to give them before going to bed.

As we grew up, my mother kept providing such interesting and varied information to us, but always with the warning to be careful who we talked to about the mystical. She said that not everyone would understand and that people have their own belief systems. If I started talking about working with energy, reincarnation and miracles, then some people might be afraid, and that it was not up to us to decide who was ready to explore the supernatural. The vexing child that I was, returned the favour to my mom by telling everyone that she was a witch. A good witch, mind you, who would heal us with plants from our garden and potions she would create. I wrote papers about energy and vibrations in elementary school and the teacher called my mom to tell her that she could not do my homework for me anymore. Bewildered by this suggestion, my mom had to explain to the teacher that she did not even understand what I was writing about so she could not have possibly written my papers for me. My exasperated mother would have many talks with me about how I was choosing to move through the world. And I rebelled against stepping into that spiritual closet for so long.

MY MOM'S HISTORY: Weaving our histories together

"Our beliefs control our bodies,
our minds, and thus our lives…" ~ Bruce Lipton

My mother would worry. She often wondered, could she continue to nurture her own spiritual growth, and that of her three daughters, and still keep us 'safe'? You see, my mother had been firmly planted in her spiritual closet and wanted to plant each of her children safely in our own spiritual closets as well. Fear. It was so very hard for my mother to do anything without fear. Fear was a sombre figure that had accompanied her for as long as she could remember. All of her early life had been a covert operation. She grew up during the oppressive Nazi rule of Germany, and any intuitive gifts she expressed were quickly shut down by her astute and protective father. It was a very dangerous time to expose one's true self. But her father, my grandfather, understood only too well as he studied the esoteric with a non-sectarian group that prioritized the study of metaphysics and nature's universal laws. My grandfather also had the courage to be an active member of an underground anti-Nazi movement. And one day he was found out. This put the family on the run, moving them from their small town in Thuringia to hide in the big city of Hamburg. Here they faced the onslaught of frequent terrifying air raids. And eventually, the Nazi Gestapo caught up with my grandfather and he was sent to a concentration camp. My mother learned deep secrecy and fear as a result of up-close direct experience. It permeated her early years and shaped her outlook on the world.

Somewhere in all of our lineages, we each have oppressive histories. And possibly blurred yet viscerally potent past life memories of persecution. Stored and passed on through our DNA. The stories vary, but the effects are similar. These shadowy challenges create fear and keep us living small. And through her efforts to leave the past behind, my mother was torn. Unable to shake the deep programming and hurtful experiences. My mom had the yearnings of a spiritual seeker, and the fear of a child of war on the run.

Cautiously, my mother found ways to extend her spiritual knowledge and to bring us kids along for the ride. Our formal metaphysical studies started in a similar vein to my grandfather's. Our spiritual mentor began his journey as a chiropractor and then branched out into energy theory and work as well as chanelling. It was white light work. The pure white light of Spirit that sometimes becomes visible energy, creating halos around living things, as well as around paranormal phenomena such as angels. We called it 'taking a class'. We had an adult class and a kids' class where we studied metaphysics. Our little mystery school. Everyone else in the kids' group were teenagers, and my mom had to advocate for me to be permitted to join. At age eleven I was determined to show everyone that I could keep up. The lessons we studied were practical and magical, heart-centred, philosophical and exploratory of our inner lives, as well as the world around us. Not about strict rules, nor about the judgement of right or wrong ways to think, but about endeavouring to understand ourselves and each other. We discussed our ideas, our dreams and our visions. We talked, wrote, drew and painted. We listened to music and spent time in nature together. There was a sense of oneness in our group, but also with everything in our world and beyond it. It was what I was searching for, and I never wanted our studies together to end.

But our short mystery school sessions would whisk by — we did not get to live there. And the majority of our lives were spent out in a world that seemed to see things so differently than our spiritual study discussions. We are shaped by our experiences, and even our best intentions to live otherwise can be derailed. Eventually, I stopped asking my sisters for hugs. I no longer booked heart-to-heart conversations in the garden. I allowed a distance to grow between my inner and outer self. I picked up the materials that my mom had passed me and constructed my spiritual closet and put most of me inside it. I had heard about fear often enough to make the fear my own. For a long while, my spiritual side would only come out of the closet in increasingly briefer family conversations and during our formal metaphysical studies (after the first decade or so, the adult and kids class had become one group). My childhood visions of limitlessness became shackled in something called 'reality'. I was not very familiar with this thing called reality, but I gave it a try. A long try. But the confines of our 'realities' are crowded with limiting belief systems that we have each created and are attempting to coexist within.

Yet, this is what I came here for. To get the experience my Higher Self ordered so that I could learn self-reliance and resilience. And as a rite of passage, it is in the distancing from family and community where new kinds of growth can happen. Like a rebelling teenager getting insight by investigating other ways of doing things in the world, reaching for more, even if they circle back to how they have been raised. Family and community shape us on a daily basis, providing us with the right challenges and circumstances for the journey we came here to experience. It has been part of my life experience to learn to honour peoples' boundaries and belief systems. And to learn to assert mine. But, as so often is the case, learning others' boundaries happens at the expense of our own. Sometimes we relax a boundary to connect with someone or with a group, but then we stop being who we really are. And it is so much harder to declare our boundaries later. As I stopped honouring my instinctual inclinations, I was also stepping further into my spiritual closet. My strong personal resolve faded into doubt and questioning.

DO WE REALLY WANT SPIRITUAL GROWTH? AKA: We may think it feels more comfortable swaddled in the closet!

"Human beings have a great capacity
for sticking to false beliefs
with great passion and tenacity." ~ Bruce Lipton

As an intuitive reader, I have read for countless people who are on a path of seeking spiritual growth. And when we have a block in life, so often it comes down to what we are not letting ourselves see. As I grew up, I learned to play the game of ignorance that adults were teaching children.

Ignore your intuition and follow the rules. Ignore that nudge of precognition and listen to your teachers. Let institutions be your moral compass. Do not question the system or the system will question you! An ongoing challenge of the human experience is to negotiate our passion for ignorance. We become so invested in our belief systems, that when new information enters our awareness and challenges our beliefs, we may pretend that we have not noticed it, or proclaim it to be wrong information. The issue is, that as we evolve, we outgrow our belief systems.

Known in Buddhism as one of the kleshas — or mind poisons — 'ignorance' is a hindrance to our spiritual growth. Psychoanalyst and post-structuralist, Jacques Lacan worked with Buddhist thinking and explained that there are three fundamental and blinding passions — love, hate and, what he felt was the greatest passion of all, ignorance. This appears to be an extension of Lacan's field of psychoanalysis where purposefully ignoring something is known as a disavowal, which is the outright denial of something you know to be true. It is an old phenomenon. Along with Buddhism, Ancient Greek philosophers also toiled to understand our longstanding human characteristic of choosing to be ignorant. Choosing to follow customs over following senses to maintain belonging to a group. Often doing so to avoid persecution for contradicting those in power. Today, those same power dynamics continue to socially construct society and guide behaviour. It is part of our attempt to live in harmony with one another, but it can put us at war with ourselves when we feel forced to follow guidelines that do not match our personal belief systems. And when we find that we are holding two or more contradictory beliefs or values, modern psychology describes this as the stress of cognitive dissonance – where we choose to ignore the information that makes us feel uncomfortable. At least at first.

BELIEF SYSTEMS AND RESPONSIBILITY

"We can disagree and still love each other, unless your disagreement is rooted in my oppression and denial of my humanity and right to exist."
(@SonofBaldwin Social Media Community founded by Robert Jones Jr.)

Did you ever think of yourself as passionately not wanting to know something? For some, it may initially seem counter-intuitive. But upon reflection, we may remember moments where we could sense that something was off, but we hoped it would balance itself out without us having to face the discomfort of learning an unwanted truth. And when we do not want to change our behaviours – we choose to ignore or disbelieve the evidence. All those anxious little persistent thoughts that come up when we experience the duality that this cognitive dissonance generates.

But ignoring something does not keep it from existing. Wayne Dyer's last solo publication is fittingly titled, *I Can See Clearly Now,* and in it, he weaves through the challenges from his life. Looking back he shows why each event needed to happen to give him the experiences he required, for his personal growth and his successes. Dyer shows that sometimes it is only in hindsight that we can see what we have been unable to see, or even ignored. We can also look back at human history and see the passion for not accepting information as true. A passion for holding on to what is viewed as safe and comfortable, or at least not disrupting the status quo. A passion to hold everyone in place and behaving according to a plan or shared belief systems. A passion for turning a blind eye to things that we think would make our lives harder: such as eating healthy, exercising, meditating, and caring for the spaces around you. A passion to block change or progress. Yet part of the journey in our current era is that the spiritual veil is being lifted, which has allowed humans to reach a critical mass of new awareness. A couple of decades ago, my spiritual mentor would describe this approaching era of the veil lifting as a time when all will be seen and there will be nowhere left to hide. This includes matters in our personal lives, as well as those big institutional paradigm strongholds created for purposeful misguidance to try to keep the general public in ignorance.

So how can we see through our blind-spots in the heat of the moment? How do we remain present and out of the paralyzing hold of overwhelm? While it seems an impossible task for humans to be free of all ignorance, since we as humans may never know everything there is to know and we all know different things in different ways, we can still counteract the human passion for ignorance. Meditation helps us integrate knowledge, fine-tune our intuition and can ease our resistance to knowing something. At some point we each experience a form of incongruity as our old beliefs do not completely disappear — they are layered in with our new beliefs and experiences. This is perpetually in action as new information is received each day and our belief systems are shaped accordingly. And this is also why expanding our perception can be so powerful; it allows us to bring clarity to our own views while beginning to understand someone else's outlook.

What can be even harder to accept than the belief systems of others that we have been indoctrinated into, is the realization that we have outright chosen to ignore information. As the ancient Hawaiian art of practicing Ho'oponopono shows us, now is the time of taking responsibility for all that is us – the things we are conscious of, and things we are not. It is when we take full responsibility for our lives that we open our eyes to new perspectives. Our past experiences shape us, but we are still responsible for who we become. And we are responsible for how we treat others. We are responsible for our thoughts. If we do not like our thoughts, then we can change them. And seek support for those thought patterns that are hard to break. If we stay in the place of pain it is hard to see a different perspective. When we bring our heart into coherence with our mind, as is taught in HeartMath® studies[1], we can find a peace that allows us to see other viewpoints. In helping ourselves do our inner work and self-care, we really are doing the best for everyone.

However, if you keep dismissing the nudges from the Universe to be your true self, those nudges become shouts. Ignored still and they become pushes. Like getting fired from a job that you continually complained about. Realize when it is time for action or action will be taken for you. And when you have stepped out of the driver's seat of your life, the action taken may be harsh. Staying in ignorance can be a form of avoidance that we might choose because we feel it will 'keep the peace'. But your soul wants you to stay on purpose; notice the signs early and take steps that may require courage, but are really kinder and gentler for all involved.

BE BRAVE, BUT BE UNDERSTANDING TOO

Hannah Gadsby, on her time in the closet regarding her sexual orientation: *"I sat soaking in shame, in the closet, for ten years. Because the closet can only stop you from being seen. It is not shame-proof. When you soak a child in shame, they cannot develop the neurological pathways that carry thought, you know, carry thoughts of self-worth… It took me ten years to understand I was allowed to take up space in the world."*

---

1. *The HeartMath® Institute is founded upon the scientific research of creating coherency between the mind and the heart, and ultimately creating holistic and healthy balance between all of our mind, body and Spirit systems. Finding this balance allows us to reduce stress and anxiety, and access our heart's guiding intuition. It is where science meets spirituality, with the science measuring our physiological responses and the practicing of HeartMath® techniques brings about a calm yet alert state that is optimal for our health and spiritual growth.*

It does not matter who you are, or what type of closet of oppression that you are in; if you are closeting your truth or your True Self, your self-esteem is going to tumble. There are numerous types of closets to be concealed in, such as the addict closet, the mental health issue closet, the sexual orientation closet, the gender identity closet, and, of course, the spiritual closet. Needless to say, there are differences in what that entails for each person, but there are also overlapping similarities. Fear of being oneself, fear of oppression and fear of not fitting in or belonging. These are powerful fears that may impede someone's coming out. Yet, not coming out can be painful and disempowering. We are all meant to be our true selves, and not be living someone else's idea of who we should be.

I walk the line of both worlds, while aiming for them to merge together. Trying to completely step out of the closet that I have felt forced into so I can fully be my true, holistic and spiritual self. Yet as time goes on, one begins to realize the intricacies and complexities of responsibility for our choices that have kept us cloistered. There comes a time for us all to question everything. This is how we find out what is really ours and what is not. Over the years we collect information and guidance from others, and it may all be 'ours' in the sense of we were given the energetic exchange we were looking for at the time we received the input: Everything is energy, and we connect with things that are vibrating at our frequency. But we begin to realize that not all of our parents' beliefs work for us. Not all of the guidance or feedback that a friend, teacher or mentor has given us works for us.

All the comments and criticism given to us, we tend to take it all in and to take it all on – especially as children. Even if we consciously reject the notion that we are not good at math or sports or science, if everyone keeps telling us we are not good at math, often we take it on as our story. As our truth. When all that was true was that there was a time when we struggled with a concept, that a teacher said we were not good at and we took it to heart. It was not a good idea for the teacher to speak in absolutes like that, saying that we were not good at something. Maybe we just had not slept well the night before. Maybe our parents were in the middle of a divorce and our ability to process information was a little hampered at that time. And the same is true for the teacher; they might not have slept well or they might have been going through a divorce. Or they were speaking the way that their teachers and other adults spoke to them. But since everything shapes our beliefs, there comes a time when we need to purge our systems. *Tabula rasa* (absence of preconceived ideas; a clean slate). And then add back in the things that make our hearts sing. Such as, loving flowers and dancing in the rain, and allowing ourselves to cry when we feel moved to do so. That maybe, some of us do not like the taste of watermelon and we are not sure why everyone thinks we should. That we can figure out math. That one might not believe in God in the churchgoing way their parents do, but instead believe in a higher power that created life and the Universe. Being open to allowing our beliefs to expand. All we have is this moment, right here and now, and this moment is filled with opportunities for growth and change that further our evolution.

How to Unlock The
spiritual door

WHAT DO YOU ALLOW FOR YOURSELF?

"Belonging is belonging to yourself first. Speaking your truth, telling your story and never betraying yourself for other people. True belonging doesn't require you to change who you are; it requires you to be who you are. And that's vulnerable."
– Brené Brown (2019)

At my work, I hold energetic space for fellow seekers. My clients are esteemed guests that I am honoured to collaborate with. We sit together and triangulate with Spirit. People share some of the most intimate private moments of their lives, and I hold them sacred. In my paper, *Angels: a bridge to a spiritual pedagogy? (2015)*, I held space and discussed with young children about their experiences with the mystic realm. Once opening up the conversation, children are often only too happy to share their mysterious stories and encounters. This was also made clear to me through my experience of raising my own kids. Young children are some of the most honest people on the planet as they have not yet been completely programmed by the social constructs of the world around them – as illustrated above in the recounting of my own emboldened early years.

When you create 'allowing spaces' for such existential conversations, many children open up and let their stories flow out. Upon hearing about my work, their parents, like so many adults I meet, would take me aside and speak to me in hushed voices, like we were spies on a secret mission. Initially, I would be nervous that they were upset by the work I was doing with the children. Then they would say things to me like, "Don't you dare tell anyone…but this is what I have experienced…", and would go on to divulge that they too have encountered angels or spirits of some kind, or have experienced some type of mysterious paranormal phenomena. If those people were ready to step out of their spiritual closets, I could have published an intriguing book of those stories alone. But those private and sacred sharings will remain that way. Because the timing that we reveal ourselves to others in is also sacred. And only we have the right to 'out' ourselves.

Like the receptive culture we created during my research, we all need allowing spaces to express ourselves without worry or judgement. Education researchers Affrica Taylor and Miriam Giugni wrote about creating common worlds, and to "take up the ethical and political challenge of learning how to live well together and to flourish with difference". How beautiful and straightforwardly brilliant to propose this ideal of our differences actually benefitting one another in this world we know to be dichotomous. To realize it is not about getting someone else to think like you, but rather about respectfully listening to one another and creating the paths of allowing spaces. This is what I endeavour to provide during the supportive sessions that I offer. Ideally, through a reading session we are able to gather strength and feel encouraged to be our authentic selves. To try stepping out of our spiritual closets. It is freeing! Even if some days, you just stick out a toe…

STARTING STEPS

"Authenticity is a collection of choices
that we have to make every day.
It's about the choice to show up and be real.
The choice to be honest.
The choice to let our true selves be seen."
– Brené Brown (2010)

Find the spiritual circles and safe places to tell your story, so that you hear yourself saying it and start to understand yourself better. And those respectful people hearing it have the opportunity to reflect back to you with their perspectives and understandings and with their own similar experiences. This is what those uncomfortable conversations of stepping out of the spiritual closet do for us; they are forward action on our path of purpose. But it is risky. Even when you open up in what you perceive to be a safe and allowing space, you cannot control the responses of your listeners. And your listeners may be reactive if they are triggered. They may feel threatened. Your stepping out of your spiritual closet may set off the alarm systems in the spiritual closets of those that feel vulnerable. Stay calm. Their reaction is part of their journey.

And after a while, you will realize that your closet has a leak! Again, you need not worry. No repair crew is necessary. All spiritual closets have leaks.

Because while we might deny our prophetic dreams and encounters with angels while out in the 'real' world, we can never really cut ourselves off from Spirit. We still go outside and feel our heartbeat and see trees or feel the breeze or hear birds chirping. As per my ethic of body-mind-Spirit that refers to our indivisible enmeshment of ourselves and with our world, there is no "separating out of Spirit" (Pettersen 2015 p.2). This we all know, but sometimes let ourselves forget. When I have studied and written about the knowledge of Indigenous peoples (Pettersen 2016), I have found beautiful reminders that describe our oneness on Earth and with the beyond. This is Indigenous wisdom that has been passed down through time immemorial. While western world thinking has embraced Newtonian laws that separate out the body and mind for examination, Indigenous peoples bring a holistic approach to our human existence. And the rest of the world is starting to catch up with Indigenous wisdom, if not through how it resonates with our hearts, then through the modern science of quantum physics -- which confirms that everything is connected and we are all one. Even when we are in the spiritual closet, our spirituality seeps out everywhere. And as we find our courage, we can step out to show the world who we really are.

SELF-CARE ACTION STEPS:
Because we need to fill our own tanks first!

"Takes tremendous discipline, takes tremendous courage to think for yourself, to examine yourself. The Socratic imperative of examining yourself requires courage.
William Butler Yeats used to say, it takes more courage to examine the dark corners of your own soul than it does for a soldier to fight on the battlefield. Courage to think critically. Courage is the enabling virtue for any philosopher, for any human being, I think in the end.
Courage to think. Courage to love. Courage to hope."
~ Cornel West (The Examined Life)

And I would add, the courage to step out of the spiritual closet.

HOW TO GIVE YOURSELF A SPIRITUAL READING SESSION:

We often look to the healing guidance of a reading session during challenging times. If that is the case for you, then taking the first step of deciding to take action may be the hardest part. Please know that you can do it!

Before you start, decide what kind of reading you would like to give yourself — an Oracle card reading, a Tarot card reading, throwing and reading Runes, reflective writing, journaling, envisioning, drawing, painting, or whatever tools you have to work with and are drawn to explore. A self-reading can be as short or as long as you can manage.

I am going to explain how I was taught, and have evolved into giving, a Spirit card reading – which is a reading with any kind of spiritual deck, such as Oracle or Tarot cards. If you choose another medium for your reading, then adapt the steps accordingly.

1. Create Peace: If possible, find a quiet space where you are not likely to be interrupted. We can all learn to meditate in the middle of a crowded room, but if you can arrange your time and find a little peaceful spot, then create it. When I have needed to, I have even created space in a literal closet for myself while my young children were noisily playing in their rooms.

Lay out an altar of the tools you are going to use, in this case, Spirit cards — and enhance with other items that bring you a joyful feeling of connection with your heart and with Spirit. I like to light candles and bring out some of my many treasured crystals, especially my smooth selenite and my clear quartz point.

2. Create a Mindset: In your peaceful space, do an opening meditation. As a HeartMath® Mentor myself, I often start my readings with a heart-focused breathing meditation. It is simple and powerful:

*Gather all the busyness of your mind and let it
funnel down into your heart. Your heart is a gentle place,
yet it is more powerful than your mind. Your heart knows.
Let your heart hold all of your thoughts and feelings.
Now see your breath going in and out through your heart,
while holding your question or intention.*

Hold this peaceful space for as long as you feel you need to or have time for. Notice the messages that may already be coming to you.

3. Connect with Your Cards: Many of us like to clear the deck before starting — I do a swift chop with the side of my hand, others like to knock on the deck. Whatever method you choose, set the intention and go for it. Then give your deck a shuffle, again for as short or as long as you feel into doing. Then hold the cards and set your intention for the guidance you are looking for. Word your intention, or new agreement with the Universe, towards positive and empowering action, such as, "Spirit, please provide guidance through these cards on how I could make my stepping out of the spiritual closet as smooth as possible. Please guide me to the peace, joy and happiness that I seek. In the greatest interest and highest good for all involved. Thank you!"

4. A Simple Spread: How you lay out your cards is all about your agreement with the Universe, and my favourite simple Spirit card spread is three cards laid in a row starting with past, then present and finally, future. Or another way to put it, where you are coming from, where you are and where you are heading. This spread brings guidance that fits our linear human existence. If more than one card comes out with your pull, allow it to come. And if one card 'jumps out' while handling the deck, then that could be considered a key card that offers you an overarching theme to your reading. I like to keep the cards face down and read each one as I turn it over. Then look at the whole spread together when all the cards are up.

5. Interpret the Messages: Notice how your question asked, intention set or new agreement with Spirit, connects with the cards. Notice if the cards take you completely away from the question, possibly pointing to another area in your life to make a priority. Now look for your first next step. Remember there are no mistakes! Just mysteries at various stages of revelation.

6. Reflect Upon Your Reading: Wrap up your reading by reflecting on one or two main takeaway points that you feel are most pertinent. Write this guidance down in your journal or wherever you like to take life notes. I also like to photograph my spreads. A little later, as the meanings of the messages starts to land within you, it can be helpful to return to a visual so you can see how some new understandings have been formed. Deeper reflection and investigation allow you to discover the things that you did not initially notice as relevant; like revisiting a dream.

Allow your reading to help evolve and expand your personal belief system, that is unique to you, to your journey and to your experiences.

IN CLOSING, BE ENCOURAGED

"The privilege of a lifetime is to become who you truly are."
~ Carl Jung

If you are having a hard time being your true spiritual self, I wish I had all the answers for you on how to step out of your spiritual closet to let your light shine. But each of our journeys are exceedingly unique. The best I can do is tell you my story. And my story is not over. There is so much more for me to learn. And so much of myself that I have not yet chosen to reveal. What we can take from sharing the stories of our ongoing journeys is the diverse and rich ways we can each fortify our spiritual lives. And while we are doing that, we find those moments where we can step out of our spiritual closets and feel the joy of doing so. Each of us travels our path in our own way, but here are ten ideas to guide you:

1. Remember that our journeys are not formulaic, yet as we connect with the oneness of the Universe, there may be some patterns and similarities in the steps we go through.
2. Know your truths and act from them, but also be flexible with your ever-changing path. Like on page eight of the wise ancient text of the Tao Te Ching says, "be like water" and continue to flow with the changes of your own personal evolution.
3. Recognize that when your heart is open, and your intuition is guiding you with peace and joy, then you are on your path.
4. Choose the places that you feel safe to take your steps out of the closet. You have probably already been doing so. But our journeys are never over. Keep stepping out. Keep embracing who you are meant to be. If you are not finding those safe spaces, then try creating them.
5. Stay calm and find your neutrality. If you experience criticism when speaking your truth, try to remain neutral. Appreciating that we each have our own belief systems also means holding allowing space for all of us to have our own beliefs. But, if someone is being hateful or oppressive then walk away. It is not your job to 'condemn' or 'convert', as musical poet Ziggy Marley reminds us.

6. Let your light shine for the world to see.

7. Trust that you are divinely guided.

8. Have faith that you, your Higher Self and Spirit are working together. You are part of your own trinity. Not on the outside of it all, but rather engaged and agentic in each step of your life. Each thought you have, each feeling you experience and each action you take are all part of the path you are creating for yourself.

9. As you go deeper, surrender to Spirit. Let go of your need to be right, because things are always shifting, and we are human and we are fallible. Trust in your divine timing, and have faith that the Universe is with you, working for the greatest good and highest interest for all.

10. Change is only a perspective shift away. While breaking old patterns and trying new things -- like stepping out of our spiritual closets -- can be hard, through the self care of things like journaling and meditating, we create new neural pathways in our brain that help shift our perspectives. And magically, somehow the things around us start to shift. Whether we see it is our perspective that has shifted, or the behaviour of people around us changing, or both, energy has been moved and we can experience things in a way we could not before.

Always be looking for your next step of action, whatever that might be for you. Giving yourself a reading. Going for a reading. Making time for self-care and meditation. Being in nature. Writing down your thoughts to gain mental clarity. Speaking your truth when someone has crossed your boundary. Allowing your belief systems to evolve. Finding moments to have heart-to-heart conversations that nurture your soul, and that help you find peaceful balance while you weather the storms of change. And again, please be brave and find the moments to step out of your spiritual closet!

Epilogue

"Whatever your challenge is now, look at it.
Face it, do not avoid it. Bravery is called for.
Breathe deep, and leap in.
As a wise elder once said, 'the only way out…is through.'
You got this. You're not alone. Ask for advice.
Keep an eye on the horizon, and an eye on the steps ahead."
~Waylon H. Lewis

My mother passed away at the beginning of 2019, and one of my sisters and I sat talking about our mom with a consultant in preparation for her memorial service. The consultant had her mouth open and her eyes wide, listening to the journey of our mother. After a while she said to us, do you know how lucky you are? My sister and I looked at each other as we sniffled and wiped our eyes. Then we nodded. We know that we are pretty lucky indeed, that despite all the challenges we faced together, our mom still made sure that our spiritual lives were rich. She may have taught us to be cautious about stepping out of our spiritual closets, but she made sure our closets were stuffed full of spiritual potential!

Even if my mom wanted me to be tucked safely in my spiritual closet, I am grateful that her cautiousness gave me the awareness to respectfully step out of my spiritual closet in a world full of diverse beliefs. Whatever your spiritual journey has looked like so far -- whether you are just starting out on the spiritual path, or feel that you have not had spiritual support, or the support you have had so far has not resonated with your heart and you have expertly crafted a deluxe spiritual closet for yourself and filled it to the brim -- you will discover that you are journeying alongside many others on a similar road to freedom to be their true selves. Find your kindred spirits! If you have been working on stepping out of the spiritual closet, then I am sending you all the best with your own unique journey. And right here on this page is the energetic support for you to continue doing so. Stepping out of the spiritual closet allows you to shine and for the whole world to benefit from the energy that you were born to contribute.

References

- Brown, Brené. "The Call to Courage." Netflix. 2019.

- Brown, Brené. *The Gifts of Imperfection: Let Go of Who You Think You're Supposed to Be and Embrace Who You Are.* Hazelden, 2010.

- Dyer, Wayne. *I Can See Clearly Now.* Hay House, 2014.

- Fink, Bruce. *A Clinical Introduction to Lacanian Psychoanalysis: Theory and Technique.* (on Jacques Lacan). Harvard University Press, 1997.

- Gadsby, Hannah. "Nanette." Netflix. 2018.

- HeartMath® Institute. *Science of the Heart: Exploring the Role of the Heart in Human Performance.* (vol. 2) HeartMath® Institute, 2015.

- Lewis, Waylon H. *Elephant Journal.* Instagram, 2019, https://www.instagram.com/p/Bxm7n1Rn-nv/?utm_source=ig_embed

- Lipton, Bruce H. *The Biology of Belief: Unleashing the Power of Consciousness, Matter & Miracles.* 2nd ed., Hay House, 2008.

- Jung, Carl. In Tatiana Bachkirova, et al. *The SAGE Handbook of Coaching.* 2017.

- Marley, Ziggy. "Love Is My Religion." 2006.

- Pettersen, Anita. "Angels: A Bridge to a Spiritual Pedagogy?" International Journal of Children's Spirituality, vol. 20, no. 3–4, Oct. 2015, pp. 204–17. DOI.org (Crossref), doi:10.1080/1364436X.2015.1115233.

- Pettersen, Anita. "Pedagogical Relationship with Land through Poetry and Prose: Wénaxws (Respect) for Indigenous Knowledges." Journal of Childhoods and Pedagogies, vol. 1, no. 1, 2016, pp. 1–19.

- SonofBaldwin. @SonofBaldwin: Social Media Community founded by Robert Jones Jr. 2019.

- Taylor, Affrica, and Miriam Giugni. "Common Worlds: Reconceptualising Inclusion in Early Childhood Communities." Contemporary Issues in Early Childhood, vol. 13, no. 2, June 2012, pp. 108–19. DOI.org (Crossref), doi:10.2304/ciec.2012.13.2.108.

- Taylor, Astra. *The Examined Life.* Zeitgeist Films, 2008.

- Tzu, Lao. *The Tao Te Ching.* 2001. 2nd ed., Penguin Group, 2008.

- Wise Secrets of Aloha, Harry Uhane Jim "Learn and Live the Sacred Art of Lomilomi." On Ho'oponopono, http://harryjimlomilomi.com/209926.html. Accessed 5 Oct. 2019

Journey into mediumship

By Nicole Newman

My Journey

I was born a psychic intuitive, with the ability to communicate with other realms, the Spirit world, discarnate people and other etheric beings. This was a trying experience during my childhood because Spirit energy was constantly coming and going in my awareness and it was not always the easiest thing to understand or deal with. As time went on, I became much more grounded and able to shut it out, which seemed like the right thing to do, because in many ways, it was stressful and confusing. In hindsight, it would have been better to have had guidance to help me develop it then and stay open, as opposed to shutting it down and restarting later in life.

Although I had closed the door to Spirit communication, my intuitive nature stayed with me and over time I learned to understand myself more.

At the age of eleven, I was drawn to attend Camp Firwood; a Christian camp at Whatcom Lake, Washington. There, I had an amazing spiritual experience where I connected deeply to God and higher realms and remembered much about my true Self, my destiny, and the work I would do in life to serve God and humankind. This experience helped carry me through many difficult experiences and gave me the faith I needed to persevere when the 'going got rough'. I believe all of our life experiences serve to create more understanding of our being and give us the tools to be of help to others.

As time passed, I suffered personal losses - people dying, illness, and other dramatic changes and sorrowful life events and I was called to re-establish my communication link to the worlds unseen.

In 2013 when one of my sons passed unexpectedly, I threw in the towel on 'regular normal life' and endeavoured to reach into the afterlife realms, to commune with my beautiful son, who I have a wonderful relationship, even now, and explore what it is to be 'me'. I became fully immersed in the teachings, the meditations, sitting for long extended periods; any and all modalities required to go into the different spiritual parts of myself and my energetic being. During that time, I developed a strong connection to my Soul and inner being, my intuitive guidance, and my ability to project my energy into other aspects of our Universe or existence. In these places, I discovered that we can find communion with those who have passed, with guides and angels, other etheric, non-physical beings, who are all a part of our world and our everlasting existence. A connection with our true Selves, our own Higher Power.

Remembering my many astral projection experiences as a child, I realized that we exist more fully, outside of our bodies. That we have a rich life that is not as limited as we are here in this physical incarnation and that we have much to do as we progress on our evolutionary path. I know there is so much more than what we see here, and that when this life is getting us down, we only need to gain the perspective of our immense, limitless nature to realize how much focus we place on relatively unimportant things. This knowledge helps hold us high through life's trials.

In this exploration of self and consciousness, I have learned many ways to help others get closer to their own essence, their True Self and Soul, and in that, their personal divine path that is truly an important purpose. I feel this is my path in life. To help others connect more fully to themselves and their own God source, to help them heal from their grief and the injuries that life can bestow upon us… and to empower people to live in the true nature of their Soul, to be connected to who they truly are and what they really want out of their life.

Your Journey

As you explore your Self and energetic being, you will discover such a vast beautiful internal world, that you may wander through many various feelings, states, places, experiences, and depths of deep meditation or consciousness.

These experiences strengthen the connection with the divine Self as well as your ability to commune with energetic beings (non-physical) and to learn the languages of Spirit and consciousness, as it doesn't always come in clearly at the beginning.

I have experienced many forms of meditation, guided and non-guided, to deepen my Spiritual connection, expand my energy field, and strengthen my internal connection. The BEST meditation is the one that works for you.

There are many ways to attain these states of connection and expansion and you may already slip into them easily on your own. If not, find a few guided methods that appeal to you and stick with what works, changing it up to another when you hit a plateau. Or choose non-guided when the guided go-to meditation of your choice seems to lose its effectiveness.

Many things can affect your level of connection on any given day, week, or season, so don't expect things to always progress linearly.. A strong connection tends to have many influencing factors, therefore it is important to keep your faith, openness and beliefs expanding into the process as you surrender to what and where you are being led. One thing is for sure; it will keep changing and evolving, sometimes seemingly backwards, but it is only another way of propelling you forward into deeper learning and greater understanding.

Things that are consistent in any method to create and stimulate your connection to Self and Spirit are:

1. BREATH

Get yourself into a rhythmic breath that works for you. It is not necessary to follow a guided breath method, because everyone breathes at their own pace. Some meditations will lead you to 'breathe in for five seconds, hold it for five seconds and exhale for five seconds'. While this may work for some, it may cause others to start to feel they need more air or feel light-headed. This is not the goal and should not be continued if you are experiencing any discomfort in breathing.

Simply breathe in a way that is deep down into your belly and feels soothing to you. Breathe at a pace and depth that relaxes you and allows you to enter a state of surrender. It may take a bit of practice to get into the right 'groove', but trust and listen to your body. Your body will guide you into a comfortable breathing state that allows you to unwind. To relax and begin to drift away from your conscious mind is the goal with this type of breathing.

2. RELAXATION

As you relax, the 'monkey mind' (a term for an unfocused and busy conscious mind) begins to drift inward. For some, this may seem foreign and can be difficult. One method is to pull your consciousness away from your left brain and away from your frontal lobe. Your left brain and the frontal lobe tend to hold more thinking and process your busy, 'regular physical life'. It can be helpful to visualize your consciousness (the part of you that is aware of yourself, aware of your thinking mind, and aware of your inner self), to move into the back of your head between your ears and even more to the right side of your head if things are busy-busy inside. I know this may sound odd, however; it is easier to let go of physical-life thoughts and patterns if you can move your consciousness away from your left brain and frontal lobe. It isn't necessary to do this, to reach an altered state, however it is a method I have found helpful when I can't slow my thinking down or find myself being pulled back into the thought process. The goal is to go within, identify with your inner Self, your Soul Self and let go of the regular thought processes that often occupy our time and mind. Keep breathing; find your way into a calm, detached and level state. Your breath should be slow by now, your thoughts quieter and in the background - not important to you at this point. Your body will start to slip away and you won't feel your physical structure much. It is almost like falling asleep but not… you are fully aware and in a slowed down and relaxed state.

3. ASK FOR GUIDANCE

In this relaxed state, ask your 'Soul Self', or 'Medium Self', even 'Higher Self', to please come forward and guide you; to lead your body and mind, and to be in charge of your physical being. To take charge and step forward fully. Allow your smaller mind, or conscious mind to back up even more still, even visualizing that part of yourself behind your body or resting at the back of the mind/neck/body. Ask your Soul to fill your body, expand your energy and surrender fully to the ethereal YOU. What is 'surrender' in this context? You can access surrender by opening your heart as much as you can, perhaps connecting to a feeling of someone you love deeply (that feeling) or to your feeling of God, or the Spirit of yourself. It can almost hurt sometimes for some people…almost like pleading with the Self to please let me live my life through you. To please let me live my life through love, fully committed to Love and Service. Love and Service are the gateways to the soul. Sometimes the heart-opening can have a bit of pain attached to it, especially if you have experienced loss, which most people have in some form or another. Feel yourself surrender. Feel your Soul in its stillness, or perhaps in its movement. It is not uncommon as you surrender to feel an internal stirring… a feeling of the Soul literally MOVING inside of your physical form. You may feel your Soul energy pull out of your body to one side or another. You may feel your Soul turn its head sideways, left and right, pulling, moving, expanding, making you aware of Soul presence, the individual energy that is separate from the physical body! Your Soul can get up and out! Revel in this beautiful experience and feel and allow your Soul strength to build and become freer as you build this connection to yourself. Ask your Soul to guide your life, to help you find your way to mediumship and self-realization. Be firm in your convictions on this. If you really WANT mediumship. Your strong intention encourages your Soul energy to guide the way. Your Soul IS YOU… I don't mean to confuse the situation by talking about your Soul as if it is different than you… but it is. We are divine, multi-dimensional beings and we have many moving parts! Externally and internally. Many eastern philosophies described us as having multiple energy bodies. Imagine, all of this is a part of our selves… our physical body, our Soul, our Spirit… and perhaps many energetic bodies or levels/aspects of our own being. Don't overthink it… let it be and let it reveal itself to you as needed. Just focus on your project of developing mediumship … the love project. Your Spirit Love Project. Love yourself and your Soul and ask yourself to bring forward your ability to serve the Souls of others. Your Soul will respond although it is not always instant. It may take time and practice but your love and dedication to the project of your mediumship practice will prevail. Your natural mediumistic ability will begin to surface.

4. FEEL ENERGY MOVE

At some point, if you sit long enough, you will feel energy movement, and often pure ecstatic joy will begin to expand inside of you. You may also experience a bit of dizziness or liquid-like feeling in your mind as if you are in water or floating through a 'liquid-y' type field. Other people experience it differently than 'liquid-y' but this is the best description I have at this time.

Allow that joy to expand and evolve as much as you can in each experience. Sometimes this can tucker you out a bit, so go at your own pace with what seems comfortable for you. Do not judge each experience as good or bad, or less or greater than the last one. Accept and surrender to your experience and have faith that you are on the right track, that you are being guided by your soul and that you are also being guided by other energies or beings that can help you progress when the time is right.

5. EXPAND YOUR ENERGY OUTSIDE OF YOUR BODY.

Some people may want to do this on one side of the brain or the other side. Many will simply breathe into the expansion and reach to the heavens... upwards and outwards. Depending on who or what you would like to commune with; you may change how far you want to reach. The discarnate Spirit world is accessed very close to us. We do not necessarily need to reach HIGH UP for this, and in fact, if we reach TOO HIGH we are more likely to connect with guides and inspirers, as opposed to our discarnate relatives of the person we are reading for. Ask your Soul to be the guide; ask for assistance to go be a medium for the discarnate world, if that is what you are intending to tap into. Or go to the angels, guides, inspirers, if that is your intention. You will begin to understand the subtle differences over time.

Enjoy!

As time goes on you will find it quicker and easier to enter into these states without as much preparation. At some point, you will even be able to just call upon mediumship without entering into an altered state. Or at least that state is so close and accessible that you can operate in it while still keeping your conscious mind well functioning, alert and thinking. It is practice, practice, practice, at that point. Time, speed and state of surrender will vary, grow, ebb and flow in their depth and necessity as you develop your 'mediumship muscle'. It is a muscle. It needs exercise. It is a pathway in the mind that will always be there once activated but will perform in varying degrees, depending on how you nurture your connection at any given time in your life.

HOW TO CONNECT :

Now you are in a great state, you feel marvellous and open. You have a sitter (someone who would like to connect with a loved one) in front of you perhaps? Hopefully you have had a conversation with the sitter before getting them into an open allowing state. You may want to lead them through a small guided meditation before the reading or play a piece of relaxing music. You require their cooperation and openness, their ability to surrender to the process and to connect to their loved one. 'Sitters' or clients, don't necessarily show up relaxed and ready. They don't always fully believe in Spirit connection, or feel comfortable with what they are doing. They may be protective, afraid, stubborn, blocked, mentally stressed or even difficult and doubtful, looking for a reason NOT to believe. Hopefully not, but if this is the case, your reading will suffer and you would do yourself and them a big favour, to correct that 'state of the sitter' before you get going. Sometimes they can take quite a while to become relaxed and in these cases; calming music or guided meditations and prayers can help. Many readers choose to say a prayer silently before they begin a sitting, or even out loud with the client to open the energy. These things are very helpful and recommended.

I always ask; "May I serve this person in the way they need the most? Please help me give them what they need".

Do not worry whether you have your eyes open or not. Closed is fine and sometimes helps. It is common for it to take a bit for the connection to become noticeable or to be sure it is happening.

Now you are ready to connect and you ask the Spirit communicator, the passed love-one, to come forward. Ask your Soul to step into mediumship and make this happen. It is okay to almost demand this from yourself, and by this I mean your intention needs to be strong. Don't be passive. At this stage, you are in a surrendered passive state, but you need to STEP UP into a more mentally active state where you absolutely intend to make a connection. You REACH your energy into the person in front of you if you don't make the Spirit connection immediately, you will at least begin the connection there. At that point, you may begin to receive information about the sitter. This is fine. Voice it. Speak it. As the energy starts flowing, reach to the Spirit World with determination. Sometimes you can connect immediately or directly to the Spirit World without connecting too much to the sitter. Often in the beginning stages, it is an easier path THROUGH the sitter, it is great if you can connect directly to the Spirit communicator (passed love-one), without connecting to the sitter (client), although many times throughout the reading, your connection will be moving back and forth between all three (or more) people. This is natural, let it unfold and flow, keeping your intention pure and strong. Simply know: *in your pure and open loving heart that you want to serve this person to the best of your ability and bring them what they need today.* Your mediumship will happen naturally with an intention like that.

THE FIRST THINGS TO NOTICE:

As you are sitting there in your relaxed consciousness, you may start to notice something different than yourself. This is why it is vitally important to know yourself, to know your 'baseline' of how you feel, how your Soul feels and what is YOU and your CONSCIOUSNESS and what ISN'T. You will find that this is your best clue that you are experiencing a mediumship connection. Either you are in your own mind and you feel at home there, or there are thoughts, feelings, emotions, sensations that don't seem to necessarily be originating FROM YOU. That doesn't mean they feel outside of you. They usually don't. They feel INSIDE you, inside your mind, heart and consciousness; the Spirit World uses our own mind and references to communicate with you, especially in the beginning, to bridge the gap between them and us.

What do you notice? Do you feel a subtle presence that may not be you? Do you get a sensation of female or male? For me, that is usually the first thing I notice. Male or female. It is as if I am feeling in my mind MALE or FEMALE. This is not always the first thing to come for everyone, but it is an easily distinguishable characteristic that seems to happen for many people. If you sense someone may be in your consciousness, that is not you, ask for them to blend deeper, come closer into your awareness, expand themselves. It can be 'asked' through a thought process but it is also attainable by reaching your energy into theirs. You can REACH into them the same as they are reaching into you. We are trying to mutually create a blending of energy between ourselves and them. This is done as we raise our vibration and they lower theirs. Let's just say, we are 'bringing our energies into harmony with each other' so that we can commune. I don't want to put a specific parameter around your connection as we are all unique and your connection is yours and yours alone and should, therefore, be nurtured energetically by you, through your Soul, as opposed to following a written or word-based description to the letter.

Now that you have a connection, and you know if the Spirit was male or female during their life here, ask them to tell you their story. Ask them to show you memories or information that will help the sitter know who they are and that it is truly them who has come to communicate today.

This can be the hard part. Your ability to hold your 'power or connection' as well as the spirits ability to communicate, and your sitter's ability to openly participate in the reading, will determine how much information you can relay to your sitter. You will know you are blending your energy with the Spirit communicator, when you glean certain things about them, perhaps their relationship with the sitter, their physical appearance, or mood in life, but you may struggle with more specific information. Trust that more will come with time.

Once you know you are connected and blending, open your mind and begin to speak. As you speak, even when you don't know what you are about to say other than the first couple of words, trust that more will start to flow. And it does! Speaking opens the channel for the energy to stream. It shows the Spirit communicator that you are trying to speak for them, and they will take advantage of their opportunity. Sometimes you will say things that are so specific and accurate that it even surprises you. This occurs because the communicator is literally speaking through your mind and out of your mouth. They are not taking over your body or mouth - they are simply blended with you and able to speak through you because you are open and in surrender to the process. You have harmonized your energy with them!

You may find your conscious mind wants to keep butting into the flow and trying to 'think'. Your mind may try to make associations or interpret something in a specific way. This can be where you go wrong with the information. This can be your mind, interrupting the pure flow of energy. Simply let it go, don't worry about it, and go back into the state of mind that allows the flow to continue. This back and forth between the states can be something that takes a while to get right, and it will always be different with each reading, so accept it, know you are doing your best and keep pulling your consciousness back to where you know it needs to be. Relax. Breathe. Ask their story to unfold. You may 'feel' the information. In this case, simply describe what you are feeling as best you can. PLEASE NOTE: it is normal for the communicator (passed love one) to give you feelings of how they were in life, however, this is not how they are now. It is given to you so that you can show the sitter that you are in fact, describing their loved one, because the feelings or personality are those of the discarnate loved one. So do not be afraid to describe them accurately. Trust yourself; do not doubt yourself or your information. Self doubt is the number one reason we slow down and inhibit our progress and learning. When I finally began to trust myself and the information, I discovered I had been holding it all in for far too long. The information had always been there. My self-doubt inhibited me from sharing it and saying it out loud. Do your best to trust what you receive from the start.

Usually, you will receive personality information and feelings. Maybe even emotions about the passed loved one's way of thinking or feeling throughout their life. Don't elaborate, just 'give what you get'. Do not try to interpret it, make sense of it or make it run through your logical conscious mind. Just spit it out! Say it! It doesn't need to make sense to you and the best information generally comes from you not even understanding what it is about. If you try to understand it or make sense of it, you will inevitably start to go wrong with the information. You may also be pulling yourself out of your power or connection with each conscious thought that tries to make sense of what you are receiving.

Just say it! Is the Nike slogan of mediumship!

Once you have been able to accurately describe the discarnate person's physical life personality or relationship or moods, or other details about them, you will start to receive even more information. Just let it flow. If you feel stuck or that nothing more is coming, you may stimulate the connection by asking them questions. They know your aim is true, they know you are coming at this from a place of love and desire to serve them and their sitter - they will trust you by now - they will respond with answers to your questions. These answers may come in feelings, or visions, (pictures), words - or maybe even smells or tastes. Sometimes just pure 'knowing'. You will simply know them or know the answer to the questions.

I suggest staying relaxed and asking one question at a time. It is easier in my opinion. Easier for the answer to be clear. Their energy comes in quick and fast... it can be easy to miss or not fully comprehend, so keep it simple. You may receive your answers easily or they may not come easily or at all. Do not beat yourself up over this. This is an ever-evolving, non-linear process. One day you will give incredible information, the next day you will think nothing came together. It is the way of the world of mediumship and happens for many reasons. Move past it and keep going. Do not dwell and do not allow it to ruffle your feathers or damage your connection. Stay calm and carry on!

When you feel it is okay to just receive what they will offer, you may emote to them that you want them to help you deliver whatever the sitter (their loved one) needs right now. Often your mind will fill with something that relates to your own life! Gulp! You may think, "oh no, I'm on my soapbox about my own stuff... ! Why am I thinking about this? Stop it!" But the funny thing is... it is often what is supposed to be happening - the Spirit world is using your own experiences to show you what the sitter needs. The sitter is likely going through a current experience that mirrors your own life experiences. Initially, I thought this was some kind of bad joke: A. I don't want to think about that while I am focusing on someone else's needs! And, **B.** I am afraid I will impose my own opinions on the sitter!

Trust. Know that the Spirit and your Soul trust you. They all know that your personal experiences and lessons are valid and helpful and are what the sitter currently needs to hear.

Be careful that you are at peace with your own issues and experiences and that you can deliver unbiased, clean information that is uplifting to the sitter. And yes, this is the tricky part.

This is the reason that mediums need to know themselves and understand themselves deeply. We need to be at peace with our life experiences, no matter how bad they have been. If we aren't, we will deliver biased information that is not always the most helpful to our sitter. We can also unbalance our minds if we are not able to come to terms with our own life experiences. We can make quite a mess for ourselves if we are not diligent about our self-realization and discovery.

Of course, this is a whole other story but it is important.

CONNECTING THROUGH PICTURES

Now that you have experienced 'feeling' Spirit information and have begun to understand what those feelings are saying, we will explore how you may also see something in your mind's eye. A picture, a vision. You may even 'feel' as well as 'see' a picture. In these altered states, we gain information through many faculties of our being and they often blend together. This is wonderful, though you may find it helpful to focus on one way or another at specific times to strengthen those methods within yourself.

If you are fortunate enough to see or feel a picture, you can glean an entire reading from this one picture or vision. It is because it opens and expands into the rest of the information. It is a marvellous experience and truly amazing that the Spirit World can access your visual mind and then unfold stories, experiences, and memories through this picture. Open your mind, surrender to the vision and allow it to unfold into a story.

Do not try to interpret the picture. Simply say what you see. Inevitably, if we try to interpret what we are seeing, our conscious mind makes it mean something that it doesn't. Simply, give what you get such as, "I see trees, I see a path in the forest." However, if you say "I feel like you may be walking on this path" it is an interpretation - you may be right - or you may be wrong. If you want to be right, simply say what you see. If you are compelled to say something about the path and what you logically think it means, you will learn through trial and error, but realize your chances of getting it correct all of the time are much lower. Time will help with your interpretations, but interpreting, in general, isn't always productive, as it is discouraging if you are wrong, and when you are beginning you may not want your confidence to be rocked. Of course this is your personal choice, as is much of mediumship, and you will end up doing it 'your way'.

I have taken many courses from a wide variety of different professional tutors. None of them explain mediumship or teach it in the same way. That in itself has been confusing. But all information and various approaches or modalities are helpful and give me more tools. Even in this book, there are several different approaches to the same subject. In the end, I make my own choice on what to do and not do, based on what feels right for me, and what maintains my connection the best. Stretching your comfort zone is fantastic and educational, but strengthening your connection to Self, to the Soul and the Spirit world are by far the most important factors in becoming a good medium. And practice. Not to the point of wearing yourself out, as this certainly does use your spiritual energy and can tire you out if you overdo it without proper balance in lifestyle, and self-care. But practice is very important and you want to practice with people who are willing to help you and let you be wrong. Do not practice a with folks who really need you to be right. This will put pressure on your learning that is not helpful in the beginning stages.

Ask your Soul for guidance; ask God, or your version of Source Energy, for a union that you may serve as best you can. Ask yourself to take care of and love every part of you as best you can. These things will help open you to the beauty of your abilities and nurturing capacity.

Your success comes with trust, faith, belief, and perseverance. If your aim is true and your heart is open, you will unfold the medium within you.

Mediumship is not the end of the road. It is a process and a part of our own development. It is the higher abilities of the Soul, during a physical life experience, and it takes on hundred's of variations, though most people think of it only as 'talking to dead people'. While that is part of the experience, mediumship is the ability to connect with, and bring forth energy in multiple forms and ways to bridge the world of the physical with the many dimensions of non-physical and to do this in endless beautiful ways.

It is the evolution of consciousness, and consciousness exploration is the new frontier of modern humans. Be in love with mediumship and yourself and with humanity, this will give you the motive to never cease to learn on this endless journey.

You ARE a MEDIUM.

Interview with an

intuitve

Akiva Maas

Akiva is an Empathetic Healer and Channel. His direction comes from Spirit Guides and a deep connection through empathy which provides the information to bring body, mind and spirit into balance, harmony and joy.

When did you discover you could connect to Spirit?

Akiva: Officially it came at fourteen years of age, but I have a feeling that Spirit has been actively involved in my life since age two. Because I was able to read letters and words when I was only two and it was as if Spirit decided, "We're gonna give you a little upgrade here and get you reading real quick". It was also the first time that I began having an imaginary friend named Penelope, who has since become one of my 'by my side guides'. She's like the bouncer guide, so she's the type that doesn't say much, but makes sure that everybody is falling in line so that they are not harming or hurting me or anything like that. So she's kind of like my guardian angel.

When you say 'everybody is falling in line', do you mean people in the physical plane or the spiritual plane?

Akiva: I would say both. But I'm healthy and solid in both worlds at any given moment. It's how I've been, "You know, Akiva, his head is up in the clouds", but no, I'm right here, but my head is also in the clouds.

What was the first trigger that confirmed that you were undoubtedly connected to the Spirit world?

Akiva: This is a really easy story. I was part of a world leadership camp at age fourteen. I was sponsored by the city because I was working with kids leading summer camps and volunteer work at Camp Rainbow in Osoyoos, which I believe is now called Camp Yes. It was a leadership program and it was the first time that I was introduced to Maslow's Hierarchy of Needs. I was triggered by his phrase 'self-actualization'. I hadn't realized till that point that I was self-actualized in my ability to, what I would now call 'read psychically', but back then I just considered it helping people -- helping people with the connection to Spirit as a source of wisdom.

I was on the bus going to this camp and 'accidentally' psychically connected to the girl sitting beside me. For some reason, I was compelled to ask if her stomach hurt, because I could feel that my stomach hurt and it wasn't my stomach. That was weird for me (probably for her too), and so as I'm such a talker I'm always going to broach the subject by speech. She said, "Yeah my stomach is hurting". I thought 'interesting', and said "Yeah mine too", even though mine wasn't hurting. I knew that it was me feeling her stomach.

After that, it flowed. I just started reading people at the camp, and when I got home I started reading my friends and family. The next thing I knew I was reading for adults at only age fourteen. I was helping them or supporting them with the help of Spirit, so this happened early for me. 1987. No surprise that it was the time of the Harmonic Convergence. That's when I blasted open, at fourteen years old.

What kind of psychic would you classify yourself as?

Akiva: I would say multi-purpose because Spirit says, "We're going to send you various types of people. You have to be able to hold space for those diverse types of people; we're not going to send you one type. We're going to send you a whole bunch because we know you; the diversity will keep you interested."

I want to connect with everybody who needs me and Spirit knows. I want to be accessible to everybody. So if I say for example that I am a fortune teller, I only read the future, then that's pigeonholing me. Then that prevents access to all other people that need me for other reasons, such as spiritual connections, holistic healing, personal empowerment, grief, forgiveness and sometimes, just holding space while a client processes.

What type of psychic am I? If we are talking labels; then I'm definitely an intuitive, and most definitely an empath. Those two words have to be a part of the package; intuitive, empathic, energetic, Spirit connection... even mediumship comes in and out. My guides don't guarantee mediumship and they always preface it with me when they say, "You will never be able to prove it Akiva, that you are doing mediumship". Okay! I feel this helps because then I don't get hung up on the pressure of trying to get a name, date of birth, hair colour or all that stuff – no – when someone says I want to connect with my brother sister, mother, father, grandfather do you think the person on the other end is going to say this is my hair colour? Not in my experience. In my experience they are going to relay the messages that they want to give to their loved ones. Right? This is why I don't get hung up with the word 'psychic'. There's branding to it. I'm not a brand; I'm Akiva. The people who come to me aren't brands either. They aren't 'the relationship problem', 'the health issue', 'the career seeker' ... there is a person there. Junie, Francis, Sam, Jeremy. They are people.

That's what my purpose is. 'Healer and helper' would be the label that Spirit is guiding me towards in this next phase of my life.

Being myself. Then it's real. I'm happy that I can be in a place where I can do all of that and not have to play a role, or do an act, or pretend that there are facets of me that aren't realistic or true because the people that come to me, the people I know that Spirit sends to me, will see through that. I want to have a genuine experience, a true connection with people; something really real. That's the long-winded answer.

You held a previous career as a professional wrestler, that's a far cry from a psychic intuitive. How did you go from wrestling to psychic reading?

Akiva: Here's the thing, you know I do channelling work, therefore a lot of the aspects of wrestling that I brought in from the Spirit world were actually channelling. I channelled the character, I channelled the energy that was necessary for me to portray that character because he was a far cry from me - and also exactly like me. The character was this demonic, crazy, animalistic character. I channelled a lot of my anger into that character not only to have an imposing presence, but to rid myself of built-up anger in my body. He was a vessel for healing release. I speak in the third person simply because I don't identify with that character anymore.

Wrestling for me was catharsis, so when I did it for twelve years it was like I was banging out all of the supposed evil that was in my body and my brain – like saying, 'Third-dimensional reality I challenge you to a duel! And I want to see how long I can last with this physical body'. I lasted a long time and I came out relatively unscathed, which says a lot. The aspect I bring from wrestling into the work that I do now is my ability to be in front of somebody and be who I need to be for that moment. To channel the energy for what they require right here and now. I feel like it's the channeling, being able to open up and be something that you're not in that moment, allowing something else important to show through all the while, still being authentic and real. The only difference between the Akiva in session and Akiva beyond the reading room – is that I swear. No kidding, I swear a lot. It's my third-dimensional spiritual emphasis.

When you began this work what was it like? Were you scared, excited, confused?

Akiva: Scared. I've been scared for a lot of my life in general. The thing I worry about the most is -- is all this channelled information really coming from Spirit? Because it's not as if sitting here next to me is Archangel Michael -- really, truly, physically sitting here with his flaming sword right beside me in the flesh so that everyone else can see. It's not like they come in third-dimensional form on a regular basis and be like, "Hey, this is me, this is what I'm saying to you". No. I have to feel it, intuit it and there's no 3D quality to it. The fear occurs when my 3D brain questions, 'is this real?'. But that's the fear... and I'm now able to navigate that fear like a boss. Because the whole point is not to have it in third-dimensional reality, because it's not from our 3D world so why would Spirit transmute it into something and spend all of that energy just to prove a point? No, that's not the way that it works. I navigate those fears regularly and it does take a lot of energy out of me. Although, over time, it's become simpler.

Navigating the fear allows me to have more energy and more clarity into whatever a person is presenting in front of me so that I can help them the best that I can. That's what I'm here to do - help people and navigate my fear so that I have the right flow of energy as and when needed.

Of course, fear dissipates when people validate. Whenever someone says to me, "Oh, you know that thing that you said to me?" (and I quickly correct to say what Spirit said – because it came through me, but was not me), and they continue, "It came true" or "This worked out". That validation gives me confidence and trust. It doesn't happen all the time, but when it does happen it bolsters my resolve to continue. It confirms that I have the support of Spirit behind me, in front of me, around me. There's less need for proof. Also, because I've done it for so long and helped so many people that the feedback confirms the connection.

It seems that when I've needed the most support, more profound guides show up. The current guide who I'm working with is extremely visceral, as far as I'm concerned, regarding the answers that I get from her, she is the most intuitive guide that I've ever had and I feel like she's the one that understands of a lot of my fears. Her name is The Morrigan, she's a Celtic Goddess. I know I have English blood, but I'm not sure if I have Irish blood and I asked her if I was part of her lineage. She said no. When I asked her why she chose me, she said it was because I was a nice person and was a good representation. She said I'd been a warrior at one time, but was no longer practicing. She knows I was a wrestler and have the warrior inside me, but I have no desire to fight.

She's very unique because she brings her experience as a battle goddess. This experience is so important in navigating our world right now as we learn new strategies for communicating with Self and others. She supports this through her strengths in divination and foresight. But to me, what is interesting, is she's a hard-ass. She keeps me in line, which is good because I need discipline and she knows that. It's one of the things missing in my life, a little bit more discipline. Other than that, I think I'm pretty good, but I'm better off with The Morrigan on my side.

Are there certain tools, so to speak, that you use to implement your work?

Akiva: I used to use a lot of different things, such as dice, dominos, Oracle cards and pendulums, but I realized I was getting hung up on the toys and not fully present in the reading. So then I learned Tarot, however, I don't use the Tarot in a traditional manner, with varied elaborate spreads. I do the same thing every time. I either pull three or nine cards and that's it. That's the only way for me to keep the message clear. The messages can't be marred with 'bells and whistles and flash' because I feel I can get hung up on the flash. When I started working with The Morrigan she started whittling the tools away. She doesn't feel I need them.

For me, Tarot cards have changed my life in such a positive way that I use them as my primary tool, but I only use them bluntly. I don't use them sharply, so for example I don't go into a lot of detail as to what the cards traditionally mean. I go into what they mean for that person in that moment, so I use them really as a snapshot and then they intertwine with channelling. The Tarot is a key that I use to open the door to the energy of a person and when the channelling comes through it's almost like my brain needs those pictures to believe what the heck is going on and then it gets out of the way so I'm able to channel better.

When I first sit with a client, I want them to have a good reading, I want them to be happy in their life, if they are anxious I want them to feel calm. My head gets wrapped up in all these concepts. Tarot takes me out of my thinking brain and puts me in the abstract, and then from the abstract,

I'm able to get out of my head. This allows Spirit to come through and figure out the puzzle.

What is the best part of your job?

Akiva: The best part is the connections that I have with each person. Each encounter is so unique and so varied. I love the smiles on people's faces, but it's much, much more than that. The mutual gratitude, for them and from them. There is something beautiful about people when they are in gratitude. Although it may fall short on us sometimes because it's a viewpoint that is in short supply; awareness of ourselves while we are in gratitude.

Connections are number one. It doesn't matter whether they're happy connections, sad connections, angry connections, frustrating connections, it's making the conscious connection first and then being able to provide relief or validation.

The relief aspect can come in so many forms. It can be that it was exactly what someone needed to hear, or maybe the relief comes as someone realizes that I listened to everything they said. Sometimes Spirit asks me to pass on information, other times, Spirit gives me the energy to just hold space. I've had sessions where I've barely said anything while the client just goes and goes and goes, and then Spirit says one or two things that verifies everything that they've intimated to me, and the client leaves happy with new insight. I say to Spirit, "But I didn't do anything", and Spirit is like, "Yeah, that's the whole point. You're not supposed to be doing anything. You're supposed to be there as a vessel so that people can do what it is that they need to do in front of you, on behalf of Spirit, and then they continue on their journey".

I enjoy all the various ways a reading may unfold. But what I love the most is the connections because they're so varied and they're so unique and I haven't been bored yet.

What is the worst part of your job?

Akiva: This is an easy one. I can navigate through it – but the worst part is that Spirit does not show up in a tactile, physical form and give me the information and messages in a third-dimensional way. I want to see, touch and be with Spirit 'in person' - real time - real life. I hear Spirit in my ear, so there is a voice part, but it's not like a voice that is sitting in front of me coming right out of someone's mouth. The worst part of my job is not having third-dimensional proof. I have fourth-dimensional or fifth-dimensional proof, but I don't have Spirit in the third-dimension. That's just me and my brain, total logic – nothing to do with intuition and the rest of what we know. Even though I over-think like this, my thoughts also allow me to bring the information from Spirit down. I am with Spirit and in the material world, and one is 3D and the other is not. One foot in each world. That's me.

If you mention that you are a psychic to people you meet socially, do they want to know if you are getting anything on them on the spot?

Akiva: Every time! When I'm personally attending a social function, other guests may not necessarily be people that Spirit wants me to work with. But if their guides are leading them to me then maybe, but it's not the time. A more sacred time is needed. Some people get excited and want to have a reading right then and there, so I take the opportunity to briefly educate people on how a reading connection works. For me, we have to sit down in a sacred space, then there has to be an exchange of energy. Many things need to happen for it to be genuine and comfortable.

I don't mind discomfort to a certain extent, but I need to be somewhere comfortable to extend my antenna, to connect with Spirit, to be sure it's right, sharp and clear. I read best in a sacred space or environment designed for the type of work I do. An accountant needs their computer, a painter needs their canvas, a surgeon needs an operating room. It's not that different. So if someone comes to me and randomly wants a reading saying, "Oh, I heard that you're a psychic. So-and-so said that you're a psychic - can you tell me what my future is?" I say, "Oh my gosh, I'm so sorry it doesn't work that way. I would love for it to work that way, but no, it just doesn't. This is how it works…", and then I explain to them how a reading unfolds and I see if their eyes roll. If their eyes roll, then I stop. I don't mind that.

What do you hope people will take away from a session with you?

Akiva: Connection. Connection is the most important part for me because without that we are not going to have clarity of the intended message. Clarity of information. Clarity of resolution. The connections co-create the session, and that is what I love about reading. When a client comes to see me, we create a triangle with Spirit and without that client it would be just a straight line between me and Spirit, so we need that third person. We need to bring something into form so we create a triangle with each of us at a point; Spirit, me and you. Then we co-create something beautiful, an amazing healing connection that holds space in loving-kindness and resolves issues.

The crazy thing is, after each session, Spirit takes the details out and I get to forget, so I don't carry worry and client concerns. I feel this is another gift from Spirit; the ability to forget everything, so I don't take on other people's energy. So don't be surprised if you come for another session and I don't remember anything that we said previously, because I don't remember. The gift that I get is a mindwipe, like in "Men in Black" - you know the neuralyzer thing - that's my gift from Spirit. I don't remember most of the things that clients tell me. Spirit knows I will take everything to heart, and overthink things, so they do this mindwipe. This began when I started working professionally and reading for folks I didn't know. Before that, I could remember everything and carried a heavy load of thoughts and worry for others, which doesn't help anyone.

Do you go for readings yourself?

Akiva: Yes. Definitely, it's part of my self-care. I have two people that I see who I trust the most with my information and it's a necessary component, it's reassurance.

Can you help others connect with their personal guide?

Akiva: Yes and no. If you seek a particular guide, maybe they aren't ready for you yet. And just because you want to connect with a chosen guide, doesn't necessarily mean that they are the right guide for you. It can't be forced. Just because there's a desire to want to have a connection with the guide doesn't necessarily mean it will happen. For example, you may be wanting to connect with Archangel Michael and you may or may not make that connection. It's the hardest part, trying to help people to connect with their guides because I feel like there are specific guides for specific people and if a person is not a vibrational match, it's a miss.

We have to remember that the guides also have their own personality and purpose. That they connect with the people they choose, or who they already had agreements before incarnation. Free will doesn't necessarily dictate who it is that we get to connect with as Spirit Guides, so it's a little bit trickier than saying, "I will connect you with Archangel Michael now". If your intuition is on point and you are doing personal and spiritual work, there's more of a chance that you will connect with the guide.

Yet in a different way, some people have a connection to their guide right away. I met mine at two years of age. Some people are just meant to have that connection earlier, while others are meant to have that connection later and some aren't meant to have that connection at all; they may have other reasons for being here. It's not necessary to know your guides, they are present and guiding you on your life path whether you connect with them in real-time or not.

I can think of a few people who really, truly want to connect with their Spirit Guides, but are having a hard time doing so. Maybe the timing is off, or they are supposed to focus on other things, or perhaps it will happen, just not on their agenda. I feel the frustration. But maybe they need to be more present in the physical world of form. Maybe they are supposed to help other people in the third-dimensional reality and less in the esoteric. Many people needing help are fearful and may not understand that they are meant to connect with other 3D physical people who will guide them in their life.

Whether you know your guides or not, you can trust that they are there for you. There have been multiple times I've come close to death, and Spirit comes in, whether it's been Penelope my guardian angel, or one of the other guides that I've had in my life that have kept me alive, saved me from death.

If you have been immersed in personal growth and spiritual development for a long time, and still haven't met your guide, know their name or have an image of them, then I believe that your guides are purposely in the background.

I know everybody has guides; everybody has at least one presence watching over and guiding them. Of course, you may not see them, but we're all connected to them at some level. Your guides are orchestrating in the background. Helping you find parking spots, avoiding life's potholes and stirring life purpose in your heart, whether you realize it or not.

I would love to show people what they can't see, or offer them an experience with their guide that validates the invisible because it's wonderful to have a connection like mine with The Morrigan Goddess. I feel so blessed that she chose me. Thank Goddess!... because it is wonderful having her as a companion, as a guide, as a goddess, as a queen! I want people to have that experience too, and so even though I have been successful to an extent, it's not a perfect science.

How can people attempt to meet their guides on their own?

Akiva: Meditation is the key, and preferably in water. Meditate while you are in the bath, in a lake, a river, or even better -- the ocean, or a float tank ... even just a foot bath. Water is an amazing conductor of spiritual energy and so if you're in the ocean, if your feet are in the river, or if you put your feet in a bucket of water,. My Spirit guides tell me that water is phenomenal when it comes to increasing the connection to Spirit. They're showing me that water has been a medium to connect with Spirit forever. People go to the ocean, worship the ocean. Water, and especially salt water, is the best amplifier of a signal that you can get. It is so great for those of us living by the ocean.

If you are not seeking connection with a particular guide, such as Archangel Michael, I can get most people connected with at least one of their personal Spirit Guides. But those folks who are mostly in their head or are new to spiritual concepts, that's tough. I know that there are people wanting to connect with their guides, so when I look for the key on my spiritual keyring and I can't find the key for the people that are too in their heads or are not willing to take the time to do their personal and spiritual work, it isn't instant. As much as we both want that key to make it so.

How do you advise someone in starting their meditation practice?

Akiva: As I mentioned, meditate in water. You will be using your imagination (imaging), and bringing the idea of white light into your body. White light holds the most important frequency for opening up to Spirit. Imagine a white pillar of light coming gently from above, yet powerfully down through your head, down your spine, all the way down to the centre of the Earth. Expand that light so that the diameter of the pillar becomes bigger so that it encompasses your entire body. We're not picturing the egg or circle of light format that encompasses the auric field; we're picturing a long straight pillar of light energy that goes from source, through you and down to the earth, and vice versa. You hold and expand that light frequency through your entire system to facilitate plugging into your connection.

Water meditation combined with a visualization of a white pillar of light will help you start to fine-tune your antenna to boost your carrier frequency on your own. It will help develop your straight line to Spirit.

You don't have to say mantras unless of course you feel compelled to.

But it's the simplicity and directness of this practice that strengthens the probability of connecting, and then ultimately powers up your actual connection when it comes.

We use white light to make Spirit real in our third-dimensional reality. It is the best transmitter; the key to unlocking the door to Spirit. As you actively meditate connecting with white light will increase the carrier frequency and as a result will increase the possibility of connection. And that's what we're trying to do here, which is opening up to connect to Spirit. It's not guaranteed, but we are in a position for it if it's meant to be.

We can increase the chances by doing our spiritual work and setting the stage with meditation to a certain extent, to bring ourselves in alignment to connect with our Spirit Guides. It doesn't necessarily mean that you will connect with your Spirit Guide, you could even connect to something even greater. When we get too specific with what we want, we can limit ourselves. Try letting go to a larger framework, then who knows – you may connect with another source – even a Supreme intelligence, so don't think too small. Let go of the outcome, it's not up to you.

Another important part is you have to connect with yourself.

To be a person of integrity that will represent Spirit you have to do the personal and spiritual work and part of the work is bringing light into your system and relaxing your physical body. The light brings a sense of peace. You may know people who channel Spirit Guides. Are they agitated, angry individuals? No, they are usually calm and do the work, which is the reason why they *can* channel Spirit Guides. Again, we're at a triangle, bringing all aspects together in a healthy body-mind-Spirit connection. We have to take care of the body and mind as well.

When meditating, should I be asking a question or just allowing something to come?

Akiva: Both. Begin meditation by stating your intention to connect with a Spirit Guide who is meant for you, or whatever Spirit sees fit. Then be open to receive, sitting in the expanded light. If nothing happens during a good half hour, then say thank you so much for the connection, thank you so much for the Universal Light and then shut everything down. Then try again tomorrow. Go to your float tank, the bath or your meditation cushion or whatever - and open up again. Open up the light and set the same intention and be open to a response. Repeat daily.

Something will happen, maybe you'll hear a little ding in your ear; log that, write it down, "I heard a ding in my left year" and if that's all you got that day then that's all you got. Shut it down and try again tomorrow. Keep showing up for Spirit, because it's persistence that is going to give you more of a chance. It's like playing the lottery or going fishing, you've got to buy the ticket or put the hook down or you won't get anything. It's about consistency... or sometimes it's just blind luck.

In summary, this is my practice to connect with Spirit:
- Meditate in or at least near water (the conductor).
- Bring in a pillar of light from Heaven to Earth (the connector and protector).
- Relax, smile.
- Set your intention.
- Relax, allow.
- Wait and be open to what feels like it may not be 'you'.
- If nothing happens. Try again tomorrow.
- If something happens, journal it and try again tomorrow.

Eventually, you will connect with Spirit.

Or not.

I Just Want to Talk to

dead people

By Geoff Millar

In December of 1996, I was fortunate or unfortunate, as the case may be, to be involved in a high-speed collision with a five-ton truck. I was driving an older minivan with no airbags, on icy mountain roads in Rogers Pass, BC. I was traveling downhill at over one-hundred kilometers per hour nearing a flat spot at the bottom of a hill. The truck was coming down a similar hill in the opposite direction at a similar speed. Near the bottom, he hit a patch of ice and lost control, drifting into my lane and hitting me head-on.

I have no memory of the actual crash. What I know I've pieced together from police and ambulance reports and eye witness accounts. My body was shattered. I sustained multiple fractures in both arms and legs and a serious open gash on my head. It was only the extreme cold that prevented me from bleeding out.

The next thing I remember is floating upward above the van. I was being lifted with great tenderness and care by what I can only describe as angelic presences. Then I found myself traveling forward through the magnificent tunnel of light.

I was passing through a brilliant energetic array of individual soul lights belonging to millions of people. There was an amazing display of colours and feelings that are impossible to describe from an earthly perspective. I felt a sense of wonder and peace at the same time. Beyond the euphoria of the moment, I thought to myself, "If I am in the tunnel of light then I must have 'bought it' somehow". That's when I realized that my human body must have expired.

At that moment I surrendered. My eyes gently closed, as I transformed from a feeling of density to a wispy lightness of Spirit. I remember thinking, "This can't be real". I was dumbfounded because I sensed I still had a structure as if in a body. I could move and I had absolutely no pain. At one point I made the effort to reach over and touch my arm to see if it was real. It definitely had the feel of a body, but not the same as an earth body. I was perplexed because there were no actual bones, but somehow there was some form to it. "This doesn't make any sense." I thought. "Am I dead or alive?"

Voices broke through my reverie and confusion. "Welcome!" "Congratulations, you have graduated." "You've made it!" I was being greeted and welcomed by many as I moved farther into the tunnel. I recognized the raspy and annoying voices of my Uncle Jack and Auntie Ellie. Then the more familiar warmth and closeness I felt with my paternal grandparents was unmistakable. I could hear their voices, but I also felt, sensed, or perhaps tasted the bloodline of my family lineage. The mood was celebratory as if I had just completed my earthly tasks for good and would now be working full time on the other side. I should have been delighted, but somehow it just didn't seem right to me. I had an awareness of the celestial plan and my participation in bringing it to fruition had been cut short. I was not done yet.

It dawned on me, that if I was really in the tunnel of light, then I was about to pass the point of no return. Immersed in that place of all-knowing and all-loving energy, I was intrinsically aware that I still had work to do. A strong resolve came over me at that moment. I put out my foot and made a Flintstone-type of braking action. "NO," I thought, "I have to go back". Being in that sublime overwhelming feeling and place of all awareness, I could see and sense what I had yet to do in the world. I started to struggle, argue, and fight to come back to my earthly body.

The angelic beings who were gently moving me upward and forward through the tunnel were somewhat stunned. "But your mission is complete and going back was not part of the plan". Being a rather tenacious type, however, I kept insisting. They responded that it was beyond their power to send me back. I would have to an audience with the decision-makers of more authority and have a life review.

A portal appeared in the side of the tunnel of light. We passed through it and entered into a grand semi-circular amphitheatre. Immediately, it felt familiar. I was centre-stage, surrounded by artifacts and regalia commemorating my past lives and missions accomplished. As I gazed around, I became aware of energetic forms that did not seem human at all coming in from far, far away. They were entering from another dimension, or somewhere beyond light-years of space and time.

As they came forward, I seemed to recognize them from long ago when we had shared consciousness during great epics or travails. As they entered the theatre and floated to their seats, they morphed from their unrecognizable selves and took on more of a body shape. Perhaps done to allow me to remember them more. I felt a genuine wonder and excitement about recognizing dear, dear, long-lost comrades. They were here to vouch for me as character witnesses.

All at once, there appeared three grander beings of about ten to twelve feet, in light flowing robes in muted colours. Their appearance commanded a presence among all as the ones in charge. Information started emitting from them, opening the proceedings. As they were broadcasting, I continued to vehemently argue for my return. The group consensus seemed to be unfaltering. In their eyes, I was done.

To prove their point, they materialized an enormous Book of Life with massive golden buckles and inscriptions. It took up the whole stage. The book opened on its own to about a quarter of the way. Within this history of humanity, I recognized some of the parts which I had played. It was like watching a holographic movie of knowingness and it all seemed very familiar. Undaunted, I kept maintaining that I had to return.

My persistence prevailed and to humour me, they decided to show me a portion of the future timeline. They were sure this would prove their point. Immediately the vibration of the proceedings changed. It was palpable. There was a pause, as unbeknownst to them, a frequency shift had taken place in the unfolding future. Unexpectedly, the consciousness of humanity had shifted and there was a profound change. It was so dramatic, that it felt as if everyone present was holding their breath.

Suddenly, these all-knowing, all-loving beings had been put off balance. The unforeseen circumstances they were being presented with, caused them to reconsider the plan they had previously thought was set to unfold. The situation was strange for all of us.

The new information made them start to reconsider my request. However, I was made aware, that my physical body was broken beyond repair. Confidently, I responded, "I am a healer and I can work with that". They also conveyed that most of this information I was now privy to would be lost or forgotten as I went back through the veil. Again, I said, "I am a healer and visionary and will work tirelessly to awaken my consciousness, so it doesn't matter". They cautioned that if I were to truly surrender and be of service, many on the earth plane would simply not understand. They would simply consider me crazy and foolish and this would be challenging for me.

Their efforts to discourage me, however, had no effect.

What followed could only be described as a distinguishing moment of pause beyond silence within the group. I even stopped arguing my position. An eerie stillness was palpable as if all time stood still and yet eternity was present. It was an experience beyond words.

All at once strange metallic-looking energy tubes floated in front of me, emanating a harmonic-like sound. Each time they morphed their shape, the pitch and octave of the tones seemed to change. They were singing vibrationally encoded information directly into my DNA structure. I felt like I was being repaired and upgraded on a cellular level. Beyond that, there was also a sense of being given new orders. I quieted and received the information with pride and humility. It felt as if my personal mission was now being folded into a larger scale galactic plan.

As the scene faded away, I became aware that I was descending. I found myself floating over my smashed up vehicle. Slowly, I came down through the roof of my minivan and reentered my body. Loud noises ruptured the sense of peace that I had been in. It was so jarring for my body to have to interpret the earthly sensations.

The crash happened near the top of a mountain pass and it took the fire department almost an hour to get there. The van I was in was so crumpled the Jaws of Life had to be used to cut me out. What I was hearing, but not yet fully cognizant of, was the whining of the compressor and the tearing sound as the jaws bit into the metal to stretch and pull it apart. I opened one eye, not yet feeling pain. I wondered why there were 'gumboots',my name for firemen, in turnout gear all around my vehicle when I was just having a nap on the side of the road.

The volume was being turned up on the horrendous noise. It was becoming more and more difficult to endure. Then the vehicle bumped and popped and I felt a very strange discomfort come over me. It was a feeling that I did not have in the heavenly, all-knowing place of peace and love. The feeling was getting stronger and stronger. I started to recognize it as overwhelming pain.

Another bump of the car and my arm shifted. It was then I saw the two bloodied bones of my forearm sticking out beyond the skin. Calmly and casually, I thought to myself, "Oh, I must have been involved in a wreck", hence the tunnel of light. With that, I relaxed as a sense of trust washed over me.

Twenty-four hours and multiple operations later, I drifted in and out of consciousness. I felt disoriented and confused as I started to come around. There was a mass pounding in my head as if I had been on a terrible all-night drinking bender. I thought somebody must be playing a cruel joke on me. I was wrapped in an array of casts in colours like a lit-up Christmas tree. There was a green cast on one leg, and a purple one on the other. My arms were each red and yellow, respectively, and I couldn't speak. I had multiple fractures and a head injury. I could see the mouths of the nurses moving, but I could not seem to understand what they were saying.

As I began a slow and arduous recovery, I found that I possessed a high degree of new and strange insights. I seemed to know what would happen in people's lives even before they did. It was as if I could read their timeline like a comic book. The head injury had taken away my filters, so I shared whatever I was sensing. What I found though was that all too often I was talking about things that the person was either in denial about or only just beginning to consider. Saying it out loud before they were ready was really disturbing to them. The feedback I was getting from those close to me was that it was scary and I should stop. So I gradually had to shut it down.

Many years passed during which learning to walk and talk again was my focus. True to my word, nose to the grindstone, I worked hard to heal myself. I also had to figure out what I wanted to be when I grew up, so to speak. What would I do after I retrained myself to function in the world? I was eager to be of service and fulfill my mission.

Enigmatic feelings told me that I would be working with Spirit, but I did not know exactly how. There was a hesitation in me. I was somewhat fearful about appearing weird or strange. It became so overwhelming, that I decided to become 'normal'. I took some business courses and eventually opened a printing and sign franchise. As time passed, however, I found it to be more and more unfulfilling. I was haunted by my resolve to fulfill my mission, but I didn't seem to be able to find the right people or the right energy to make it happen. I just didn't know what it should look like.

It seems like a lifetime later, which also entailed children, the answer began to make itself known. I went through a dark time during which I was hospitalized and ended up with pneumonia. I was not well for many months and I found myself getting more and more depressed. Gradually, I lost the will to live. I gave up. I couldn't figure things out and it was too painful to be here. I kept saying that I wanted to be taken to the other side. I was miserable and I just wanted to 'go home'. Then one day, in the depths of my despair I heard a voice say, "What do you really want to do with your life?" "What do you want to be when you grow up?" Over several days, which turned into weeks, I heard it say again and again, "If you could choose to do anything, and what others thought did not matter, what would it be?"

I had a sense that the three tall beings from the life review were around me a lot during this time. It felt like the questions were coming from them. It was almost as if they were testing me. The only answer that welled up from inside of me over and over again was, "I want to talk to dead people."

Over the next few months, I found myself saying the same thing in answer to their persistent questioning. "I want to talk to dead people".

Finally one day I heard clearly and profoundly, "Well then, get on with it." The clarity of the response took me by surprise, but I also found it motivating. I didn't know how to talk to people on the other side then. I wasn't even aware that I could, but something about that idea resonated with me. The doorway had opened and it felt like new energy was starting to pour in. With that, I began to get out of bed and take a few steps.

While in recovery, I enthusiastically started taking mediumship courses, one after another. I studied with some of the most renowned people in the field: Eileen Davies, Tony Stockwell, Liz Probert, and Gordon Smith. I couldn't get enough of it! This along with much time spent sitting in silence laid the foundation for the work that I was destined to do.

Today, I feel I am on the path towards fulfilling my mission. I am in service, which was very important to me. I am also connecting people with their friends and family beyond the veil. I am still fine-tuning my craft, and learn nuances all the time. I feel like I am just beginning and Spirit is training me. The work is an extension of the biggest knowing that the crash left me with and that is that we do not die. Of that, I am certain.

How to Embrace the
gateway

THE GATEWAY OF CONNECTION IS STILLNESS

Mediumship is really all about the energy and feeling of Love; Love of Service, Love of Spirit, Love of Self. It is the frequency of love that carries the information and facilitates the connection from the other side. It is the resonance of love that allows you to tune in to the feelings. In short, if your heart is shut down, your receiver is not going to work. The heart is the key, but it does not work alone.

We all have three processing centres that work in concert. There is the mind, which is just an antenna or receiver. It is connected to the ego and thinks it's driving the bus, but in reality, it only accesses about two percent of awareness. It is limited in its function, and yet most people are trying to use it to determine all aspects of their lives. The result is that they get caught in their mental constructs which keep them trapped and limited because they are not accessing the wisdom of Source. The intuitive receiving part of the brain is found in the pineal gland and is 'separate' from the analytical mind, which is not useful for intuitive functioning.

The antenna alerts you to an energetic message coming in. This must be brought down into the processor which is in the core of the body, behind the navel. This is where we were connected to our mother and continue to be connected to Source. The energy comes in on a wave or beam of love and moves into that localized core processor which is a transmitter. The lower body has to feel the information to be able to communicate it. It is processed into a frequency and then disseminated out through the first three chakras. It is important to have the chakras spinning and open, the front and the back, to give, receive, and interpret. The frequency is then available for the heart.

At the core of the heart, deep within the sino-atrial node, which is separate from our actual heart, is a sensor. It is connected to the Universe and is the place of origin for the electrical spark of life. The stillness of the Universe resides right here. It's the spark of energy that initiates the heartbeat. If we go deep into the empty space before the heartbeats, we find silence. This is our connection to our consciousness and Oneness with all things. It is where the I Am Source lives. Connecting with the Oneness is the gateway.

It is the electrical frequency via the heart's node which is carried through into the auric field. All our extra-sensory perceptions are felt through this ever-fluctuating field. This is our creator brain, so to speak. Arriving at this point, we then must surrender into radical trust where the greater truth resides. It is only then that we realize the value of the silence.

It is essential to sit in silence for at least an hour every day to cultivate your connection. Finding stillness and letting go of the mind and ego takes time. I believe anyone can choose to master this skill. However, it takes daily practice and dedication to expand your auric field and cultivate the state of love which increases your vibration.

Stillness is the key because otherwise, it is your ego and your busy mind that are keeping you in distraction. In the stillness, images or communications appear very subtle at first, and if your mind is unsettled, you will not be able to perceive and acknowledge them.

Many people believe that they have been meditating for years, however, it is my opinion that often they are stuck in the controlled phase and not allowing themselves to let go of the emptiness. They fear relinquishing control and fully surrendering. Therefore they allow for the distraction to keep them on the surface and feeling safe.

Meditation is active, whereas stillness is passive. The active part is important because it helps you let go of the day's events and go inside. It also facilitates awareness of all your chakras, each of which has a specific function, and your grounding connections. These are skills you need to develop to connect with your auric field. Once you become proficient in these disciplines, you then must surrender beyond the zone of control.

The next step will not necessarily happen automatically. There may be resistance, and this is where some people stop and hold themselves back. Your breathing can become very shallow and subtle at this point. The mind slows down and all thoughts cease. There is a level of trust and an allowing you must shift into because you leave behind your human-doing self and slip into the potentiality of your auric field where that creator mind resides. It is only experienced when you go beyond the busy mind.

The first couple of times this happens, there may be a distinct feeling of loss of control and identity, which can be scary. But the more you practice, the more you learn to trust and allow and then the adventure begins.

As the journey unfolds, we all must remember that we are everlasting souls temporarily in a human body and a constant state of development. Infinite guidance, love, and support are available at all times through our connection to Spirit. Mediumship is about continually connecting and growing. It is a work of service, reverence, and love.

Listen within and cultivate a deep sense of reverence for all that is. The strongest reflection of your higher self is trust. Know that you are never alone. You are loved and supported beyond your conscious mind and you will always receive what you need in perfect timing if you are open and doing the work. In reality, you are God; you are powerful; you are the most powerful entity in existence. You are also unique and I invite you to cultivate a profound love of self by following that divine spark within and seeing where it guides you. Remember, you are created just for this moment in time – don't just dream it.

Choose it.

Be it!

Choose Your Own Tarot

adventure

By Azra Silverstein

"If I am not for myself, who will be for me? And if I am only for myself, what am I? And if not now, when?" ~Pirkei Avot (1:14)

Many people are blessed with hearing their spiritual calling at a young age. Some people hear messages or have prophetic visions, and some come from a long line of psychics. I have always encountered these stories with fascination and envy. My metaphysical journey was not peppered with voices from Spirit as a young child, although I longed for an entry point into the magical realm.

I admit though that I did have a little Tarot deck at one point in my childhood. It was an original Rider-Waite-Smith deck that came with the little white guidebook, but even after reading it the cards felt cryptic and distant. I also had no idea how to use them, let alone how to interpret the cards. This was of course before the internet and the bouquet of excellent Tarot books available today. I left the cards in a drawer and slowly abandoned my Tarot dream.

Being an avid reader as a youth, I spent hours at the library trying to find more accessible metaphysical gateways. I remember pouring over a book about the I Ching in my room for hours, trying to create my own pendulums using whatever I could find around the house. I loved the idea that my body could be a vessel for communication with transcendent energy. I tried divining for lost objects and asking the kind of questions typical of a yearning teenage heart, but the answers never came, and I had no one around to ask if I was doing it right.

One of my most disappointing teenage spiritual moments was a failed journey into witchcraft. With books as my only portal into otherworldly modalities, my heart raced as I turned the pages of a borrowed book on Wicca as I looked for secrets on how to cast spells and practice magic. But as I read on I was shocked to learn that spells and magic were not just tools for receiving divine messages - what I was reading about was actually rooted in a

115

deep and ancient religion! Now religion was something I knew about; I am Jewish on both sides of my family and I had always felt a strong connection to Judaism. We belonged to a small reform synagogue in a predominantly Christian suburb in Ontario, and I had an active Jewish life in our community and at home. When I thought about the years spent studying and deepening my connection to my religion - including becoming a bat mitzvah, which at the time was still a recent accomplishment - the idea of taking on a new religion was overwhelming. I had felt drawn to the earth-based elements of Wicca and witchery, and I was in love with the idea of goddesses and religion based almost solely on women's experience and spiritual energy, but I could not even imagine how to navigate these two religions that seemed so contrastingly different. My fantasy of casting spells with my own coven went up in smoke as I placed the library book back on its shelf.

The fantasy, as it turns out, would return again several decades later. And who knew that it would once again, start with a deck of Tarot cards.

In Judaism, turning forty years old marks a significant spiritual milestone. The number forty is often associated with a transition between worlds, and the Talmud teaches that age forty is when a person transitions to another level of wisdom, known as binah or 'insight'. Traditionally this has been interpreted as the age when a person is ready to study Kabbalah, a school of Jewish mystical thought. The truth is that I hadn't been interested in anything mystical since my teenage years, that is until exactly one week after my fortieth birthday.

My partner surprised me with a gift as we waited for our meal to arrive at a romantic table for two in a downtown Vancouver restaurant. I still remember the feeling of excitement that rushed through me when I unwrapped the rectangular package and saw what she had bought me - it was a deck of Tarot cards!

Unlike the little white book that I had read years ago in my teenage bedroom, this Tarot book came with an accessible, narrative explanation for each card, as well as suggestions for Tarot spreads and guidelines for doing a reading. The cards were beautifully illustrated with vivid, colourful images of mostly women in contemporary clothes and scenes. I read the book cover to cover over one weekend and was surprised that even after one reading, I was able to close my eyes and see each card in my mind. I spent hours lying in bed visualizing the cards and then checking the guidebook afterwards to see if I had missed anything while I contemplated the cards in my mind's eye. I was hooked.

Soon afterwards I began doing readings. First for myself, then for family, then for friends, and then eventually for anyone willing. I brought my cards to work, to parties, to virtually every occasion. I bought Tarot books, listened to podcasts, went to meetups and participated in workshops. I eventually branched out to other Tarot decks and tried designing my own spreads.

What I loved most about Tarot was how it offered a window of insight into whatever problem or issue was on your mind. But what I grew to love even more was watching other people's reactions after a reading. I saw people feel a sense of hope in times of stress, and others found something to focus on when feeling lost. I felt like I had entered into a kind of 'helping' profession. I loved the relational aspect of the Tarot.

What mystified me was how Tarot worked. I wondered what belief system it was based on. How come the insights that came to mind usually seemed to resonate with people? Although I could not find a consistent answer as to why Tarot reading worked, I learned that a key factor was intuition. Being the studious sort, I set out on a journey to improve my intuition to become a better Tarot reader.

And this is where the next chapter of my spiritual adventure began.

Tarot became my entry point into a new-found spirituality; I kept up my readings and began to read professionally, but my spiritual pursuits did not stop there. In my quest to deepen my intuition and open myself up to messages and insights, I began to explore meditation. Taking my cue from other Tarot enthusiasts and professionals in the psychic world, I started by downloading a popular meditation app on my phone and began experimenting with daily practice at just a few minutes a day. Although I had veered away from meditation for many years based on the fear of being left alone in my head with my shadows and no one to talk to or save me from the darkness, I was surprised to learn that meditation was an embodied experience. For the first time in my life, I learned to feel my body from the inside. I marvelled at how the sensation of wind on my face made me feel alive and refreshed, and how this seemed to magically melt all my anxieties away.

I longed to connect with others to discuss these revelations and to find out if others had magical experiences through intentional inward journeying. I began reading and learning about magic and intention, and it was not long before I found myself facing the portal to witchcraft once again. This time as an adult I was determined to connect with others to find out what this witchy world might have to offer a magic noob like me. I found a class taught by a local witch and priestess and for four weeks we explored what it meant to create sacred space together. I learned about calling in the elements, casting a circle and building altars. We went into trance, read each other's Tarot cards, and shared stories about close relationships in our lives. For the first time, I felt what it was like to be in a sacred space with only women and non-binary people, most of whom were queer. Our collective attuning to the Indigenous and colonized land we were on invited a socially just spiritual consciousness into our ritual space.

While this intersectional, anti-oppressive and decolonizing magical practice resonated with me deeply on multiple levels, I couldn't help but feel like an outsider in someone else's traditions. Deep inside I felt Jewish at my core. I knew that bringing myself fully into this curious witchy landscape meant bringing my Judaism with me. But how?

I launched into my program of study to find if any intersections between Judaism and magic existed. I did not anticipate, but maybe had hoped, that what I found would shift the course of my spiritual direction forever.

It began with a dive into scholarly literature on Jewish Goddess Religion and explored the Pagan roots of Judaism. I learned of modern Jewish witches who were combining Jewish and Pagan traditions, including Starhawk who famously revolutionized modern witchcraft. Thanks to the internet and the emergence of new virtual spiritual spaces, I was able to find and connect with communities of Jewitches and others who practice Jewish ritual magic. I began taking courses on topics such as Jewish dreamwork as a spiritual practice, with the Kohenet Hebrew Priestess Institute, and I felt my feet start to settle on an aspirational path towards Priestessing.

The interest in the Tarot among Jewitches should not have been surprising given the deep connections between Tarot and Kabbalah, a Jewish mystical system of the cosmos. Nonetheless, as I encountered inspirational Jewish Tarot readers and thinkers, including renowned author Rachel Pollack, I felt an increasing sense of belonging in the global mystical community.

Tarot helped me to feel a sense of grounding in my Jewish identity as I navigated a diversity of mystical practices. It was not long before I began to explore other spiritual traditions. I quickly fell in love with Vedic palmistry, or Hast Jyotish, a divine science rooted in Hinduism, and I've been doing further learning related to breathing techniques, yoga and Ayurvedic cooking. My meditation pursuits have also drawn on many traditions including Buddhism, Judaism, and even New Age spirituality. It seems every corner points to a different spiritual path that offers new gifts and inspiration. My ongoing learning in each of these areas has helped me to access my higher self, expand my consciousness, and become more energetically generous.

Recently after a meditation session, my partner who has also been engaged in their spiritual journey, found me in a bubble bath lined with candles, listening to a recording of a Hindu mantra. They glanced at the scene and commented, "When did we get to be so New Age ?" "This mantra is old age," I said, remarking that Hinduism was the oldest religion in the world. "Yes, but this is new to us," my partner pointed out, and they're right. This spiritual adventure is new to us, but I hope that we do continue to grow and find new spiritual adventures until the end of our earthly years.

As you may have gathered from these highlights of my journey, my spiritual path has felt a bit like a choose your own adventure. I am still turning the pages with anticipation and each turn reveals a new possibility. Every person, including you, has their own adventure to choose from, and I encourage you to explore and follow what interests you. For me, it all started with a deck of Tarot cards. Where does your adventure begin?

Learn to Read Tarot

Where Do I Start?

Here are some helpful steps to get you started on your Tarot journey:

1. Choose a deck: This may seem like an obvious one, but getting started with Tarot requires having your own deck. There are many to choose from so it's important to find one that resonates with you. For a starter Tarot deck, you may want to consider:

- Tarot verus Oracle: Make sure you are choosing a Tarot deck versus an Oracle deck, so when you read other resources on Tarot you'll be more familiar with the different types of cards and suits. A Tarot deck has 78 cards and is usually based on the Rider-Waite Smith deck, although there are Thoth and Marseille decks as well with slight differences. I recommend starting with a deck that is based on the Rider-Waite-Smith deck as this is the most popular deck used.

- Style: Make sure the style and colours of the images are compelling to your eye.

- Representation: You may want to consider the diversity of people depicted in the cards, particularly around racial diversity, gender and sexual orientation, body sizes and shapes, able-bodied vs. people with disabilities. Modern Witch and Next World are some examples with good diversity.

- Situational versus. Abstract: I find it is easier to start reading Tarot using a deck that has clear pictures of different situations to help remember the meaning of the card versus an abstract deck that may require more memorization. The Everyday Witch and Light Seer decks are examples of situational style images, while the Wild Unknown is more abstract.

- A Comprehensive Guidebook: Most decks come with a guidebook that describes each of the cards. This is very helpful when starting out with Tarot, and you'll want to find a guidebook that closely links the author's interpretation or intention of the card with the images, rather than a broad description loosely connected to the image.

2. Read the Guidebook: Start off by reading the author's intentions and how the cards are meant to be used. Often there will be some great tips for reading the deck and some starting spreads as well.

3. Learn the Cards: Set aside a few hours to familiarize yourself with your deck. Here is a process that I use when I am learning a new deck.

- Start with the Major Arcana cards and then move through the suits in order, going through the cards one at a time. For each card, look at it and see what words or ideas come to mind. Then read the description of the guidebook for that card. Look at the card again and try to recall some of the words or themes described in the guidebook. Then, close your eyes and visualize the card, trying to recall key words and themes. Open your eyes and look at the card to see if you got the image correct.

- After going through the Major Arcana and then again after each suit, close your eyes and try to visualize each of the cards in order. If you can't remember what the card looks like or what it means, look back at the guidebook for a reference. Repeat this as many times as you need until you can see each card in your mind and have a sense of what it means.

4. Read for Yourself: For your first reading, try reading for yourself. Treat it as special as you would treat any Tarot reading. Try these steps to get you started.

- Create a sacred space: Find a quiet space where you won't be disturbed. You will want to have a clean or special surface to lay out your cards. Remember that reading Tarot is a spiritual project, so feel free to create that sacred space using objects like candles or even just setting an intention.

- Choose a simple spread, like past/present/future, or even just a one card spread for insight.

- Think about your question: It's helpful to think of something open-ended like, "What are some insights to help me with this situation?" rather than a yes/no or "when" question.

- Relax and clear your mind: Try taking 3 cleansing breaths, meditating for a minute or two, or even saying a little blessing or special phrase.

- Put your question out to the Universe: Ask the question in your mind or even out loud

- Shuffle and choose the cards with intention: There are many ways to do this and each one is right. I usually shuffle the cards then divide the deck into three piles, stacking them on top of each other in any order. Then I fan them out on the table and choose whichever cards call to me. Some people use their left hand because it's said to be connected to the intuitive side of our brain.

- Lay the chosen cards out in front of you, face down. Then turn each of them over one at a time. Note any first impressions, feelings, thoughts that come to mind.

- For each card, try to answer the question inspired by the images you see on the card or its theme. Go with the first thing that comes to your mind. Remember, the currency of Tarot is intuition, so just relax and see what comes up.

5. Read for Others: Once you have read your cards a number of times and are comfortable with it, try reading for a close friend or relative. Let them know that you are just learning. Follow the same steps as in reading for yourself. When you are sharing your interpretation, it may be helpful to phrase things as suggestions or insights that they might want to consider, rather than stating what is or will be. Pay attention to how the person you are reading for is feeling. Ask them if what you are saying resonates. Feel free to ask them for feedback at the end. This is the best way to learn about how to give an effective and helpful reading.

6. Practice and have Fun: Learning Tarot takes time and everyone has a different journey. Some people feel comfortable for reading for others right away, and some people prefer only to read for themselves. Tarot is your spiritual practice so make it your own, take your time, and enjoy!

Came Calling For Me
(ready or not... here I come!)

By Fabia Marcelli MacNair

I dreamt that I was a trans-medium, like Whoopi Goldberg in the movie, Ghost. In my dream, I was receiving messages from a dead guy and I was reiterating his message to a live woman. I guess I didn't paraphrase it properly and the Spirit became incredibly upset. "That's not what I said" he hissed. I, in my smart ass sort of way, responded, "I guess I missed the memo on how to talk to dead guys. If you can do any better, do it yourself." I felt a jolt as he took that as an invitation to take over my body. My hands seemed thick and masculine. I felt heavier. My voice dropped and he was speaking through me to the woman. It took me a minute to realize what had happened but when I did, I objected "WTF!!! Dude, get outta here!!! I didn't permit you to do that!" I inhaled sharply, the intense feeling startled me awake.

The heavy sensation followed me out of bed and into the bathroom. I got ready for my day and walked into my home office. My design business was located in a room on the second floor at the front of my house. I had a bird's eye view of the sidewalk from where I sat. My assistant and I were going through our morning emails when I received one from a person I'd met a week prior. She sent me a link to a mediumship group that she had a sense I would be interested in. "How strange is this?," I said to my assistant, "I barely know her." I then told her about my dream.

I clicked on the link that took me to a web page of a local spiritual intuitive healer who was giving meditation and mediumship lessons. She looked like an angel with beautiful long dark-haired and kind eyes. Her name was Angela, which means 'angel' in Italian. When I looked at the address I noted that she lived directly across the park in my backyard. Seriously... right in my own backyard? I went back to work.

A few hours later still up in my office, the radio turned on from the kitchen downstairs, which was startling since we were the only ones home. The radio personalities were joking about ghosts and were asking the question."Do you believe in spirits or mediums.?" It was a rock station and not the usual subject matter. My assistant turned to me and said, "I'm nervous working in your house, there are too many strange things going on." We both laughed nervously wondering how the radio got turned on.

We were back in the office after lunch. I noticed somebody walking on the sidewalk. I glanced down and realized it was Angela. That was one too many coincidences and way too many messages to ignore. I threw my hands up in the air and said, Ok I'll go. That's when I started learning how to channel and receive messages through mediumship.

I've had many strange messages and dreams since, many 'visitations' from passed-on relatives, some that I'd met, some that I didn't know at all. I loved laughing with my grandmothers and seeing my ancestors. There was overwhelming love in those moments. In one dream, I was at a party with all of my deceased relatives. One man with bleached white hair called me a Cicia but I didn't recognize him. When he saw my puzzled look he said, "You know me, you know me, ask your Dad." I later told my mother about the dream and she confirmed that it was my uncle who held me when I was five months old. He called me Cicia which means 'chunk sausage' in Italian slang. He died when I was too young to remember him.

I couldn't believe what I was discovering. How I looked at life, interacted with it and what I believed all shifted. What started as dreams made its way into my conscious life. I practiced the skills I learned when I had a quiet moment, I would receive messages. I wouldn't always know who they were for but when I did, I would disguise it and say "I had a dream about you…" It was a lot easier for people to welcome the message and the information it held when they didn't have to make sense of how it came.

I was waking up on a lazy Sunday morning when I heard a voice "Get up! Get up now! Call Shannon! You need to do it now. She needs to know I love her, now!"

By this time I knew I could talk to Spirit so my response was, "She's going to think I'm nuts unless you can give me something she'll connect with." The curt response came, "Tell her about the red shoes. Just get up and tell her now!!!" The Spirit pushed me. I felt the urgency emotionally and physically, like when you walk into a room that someone had been arguing in. It was palpable.

Shannon is my husband's cousin. I called her to let her know. Of course, I started with, "Hey I had a dream about you last night… It was about your

Grandmother and she needed you to know in a crucial way how much she loved you and she is still with you right now. She wanted you to remember the red shoes." Shannon started to sob. I felt horrible listening on the other end of the phone. It took her a while to catch her breath then she told me how much she was missing her Grandmother and that she had received red boots for Christmas from her the year before she passed.

Through this learning process, I'd doubted myself a lot and at times I still do, but what I learnt is that there is an unmistakable, undeniable sensation of what I started calling 'truth tingles'. Every time I gave someone a message with some evidence that I would have no other way of knowing, I get the physical sensation of a massive whoosh.

It started happening in everyday conversations. I would get spiritually inspired messages talking to neighbours. It happened when I said something important, at just the right time and they were open and willing to hear it, expanding who they were. Giving these messages felt like coming home. It was like being high without ingesting a substance. It was a welcome contrast to the periodic depression I felt. That moment of connection to another soul as opposed to being disconnected from everyone. It was like the first time the sun warms your face after a long, cold, winter and it quickens your skin. I had a sense of purpose and an answer to the question, Why am I here?

I remember being at a party with a fellow my husband knew. I'd met him a few times but didn't know him very well. He was complaining about his new job and how his new young boss was an unbearable tyrant and had no people skills. At the time, I didn't know why I said it; it just came to me: "He doesn't know any better, it's what he thinks he has to do. It was the way his father ran the company and he watched and learned it from him." He pulled his head back and twisted it to the side and stared at me for a long moment. A slow crooked smile stretched across his face. "How did you know that?" he asked. "I didn't tell you he took the position over from his father." Then his eyebrows furrowed together as he thought about his boss. He started nodding his head in understanding and it helped him have empathy for his young boss and the truth tingles came again. Sometimes your life purpose comes down to a single moment just like that.

These were moments of stillness, pure connection and presence. Everything would stop as I watched the message sink in. Their eyes widened and caught my eyes. Their cheeks would pull tight in a smile of acknowledgment, and things seemed to quiet down around us. The 'ah-ha' would be absorbed into their being and mine, and I wanted to live there, in the awareness that we are all connected.

I had an intense emotional attachment to the tingles and wanted more but the more I wanted, the less they came. I felt like I needed this gift to define me, and I was grasping. I believed, if I had it, then I would be special. That thought took me out of flow and was the end of my messages. I had the impression I had lost a precious gift. What is wrong with me?

I was born with a gift that wasn't nurtured. I had intuition but was conditioned, albeit unintentionally, to deny it. Gaslit by so many authority figures, they told me, 'don't feel that way', ' how could you possibly know that?' , 'you don't know for sure.', 'why would you think that?', 'you're wrong', 'I know better', 'don't listen to yourself', 'listen to me'. These were the repetitive messages and I swallowed them in spades.

Denying my intuition came automatically and I had to retrain myself away from self-doubt.

Mindset is everything. I didn't understand that there was nothing wrong with me, I just had something happen to me, and there is a distinction. Now I believe the only thing wrong with me is the belief that there was something wrong with me. I am not defined by the ability to do this work. In retrospect, I had some growing, healing and realizing that I was a gift even without the ability to give messages. Understanding where I am will lead to where I need to be. I am connected, I am focusing on what I want to expand and it leaves me feeling charmed.

I FOUND MY SOUL AND IT SPOKE TO ME

I didn't always feel charmed. I had a very tumultuous childhood. I was raised by two Italian immigrants who were both full of insecurities, anxieties and unhealed traumas from being raised during World War II, not to mention the long list of unhealed ancestral trauma of physical abuse, alcoholism, poverty, and being imprisoned at Auschwitz. They did not have the knowledge of psychology that we do today, and they lived their lives unconsciously through their coping mechanisms and subconscious programming. They were very intuitive but they had no idea what to do with it. I believe this was a major factor in their battle with self-awareness and depression.

There was a huge stigma attached to being intuitively sensitive so that 'stuff' was left to the few women in the village who knew the craft. The ones who were sustained by the people they healed with offerings of eggs and bread. They predicted how many children you were going to have with a sewing needle and thread, and how to cure 'il malocchio' -- 'the evil eye' -- with oil and water. These were women who were pushed to the outskirts of town, repudiated by church and state. This was not the life someone would choose for themselves or their children.

Having no conscious knowledge of who they were, they were inept to teach me who I was. They believed that the materialistic outer world was more important than the emotional inner world and I inherited these beliefs. Being a highly sensitive person puts the two worlds at war with each other. I bent and contorted to the whims of the outer world which led me down a painful, convoluted path.

Now, I would like to tell you about my scandalous experiences but there are too damn many and this is not that kind of book. However, what they all had in common was a complete disregard for the voice of my Soul (my Self). In my many misguided attempts to stop the war and to have coherence between my inner and outer world, I suffered from the life-sucking symptoms of self betrayal and self abandonment better know as selling out.

It was a fire sale. I traded my authenticity for belonging, trying to feel whole, accepted and deemed worthy. This gravely underestimated the value of my life. All of the codependent patterns I adopted depleted my life energy. When the inevitable feeling of betrayal and exhaustion set in, I would blame someone else for taking advantage of me. In reality, my 'giving' in hopes of 'receiving' was the real manipulation and the true thief of my energy. Admitting this was not an easy pill to take and it took me many years to swallow it.

Desperate to save my own life, I realized my belief system was not helping me so I started seeking help. That's when Simon came into my life. He was a psychiatrist who held different spiritual beliefs than the ones I was raised with. He challenged my understanding of who I truly was and asked me what my soul wanted, but I didn't know how to respond. The only thing I knew about a soul was that we all had one, but I had never been able to locate mine. This was probably because I was searching for it in everyone else's opinion. Simon gifted me many things; not only the acceptance of past pain as a spiritual guide but of the practice of gratitude for it. He led me to the idea that your emotions create your reality so do the things you love, that 'I am' is a very powerful statement so mind what you put after it, and finally he introduced me to meditation. It was the beginning of the journey back to myself.

I was twenty-four years old when I realized I had a soul and I was on a path following the breadcrumbs it left for me. The meditation part took forever to figure out, ten years or so. I had so many voices in my head; my parents, siblings, priests, teachers, society, friends, parents of friends, neighbours, and with all these voices to listen to, how could I choose which one to follow? With practice, I did learn how to quiet my mind and put a microphone to my emotions allowing them to heal. Now being able to listening to my internal guidance that helped me hear the whispers and counsel of my soul.

DO YOU BELIEVE IN MAGIC?

I do, but some call it manifesting.

A 2006 book called, The Secret, coined the phrase "green lights and parking spots," it's a way of co-creating events in your life, but why stop there? Digging deeper to understand how the Universe was guiding me, I realized my triggers, and my emotions were key. They are road signs leading me to my next task and the work I had to do spiritually/psychologically. Believing there were no bad decisions, just the way I thought about things, and another step along my path, even when it felt like I was going backwards.

I started to get clear on the concept that your thoughts create your reality and decided I would start the practice. I sat down and meditated to create something I wanted, I understood the concept of Quantum Physics and the role it can play in Metaphysics. Here is the 'Fab's Notes' version of what was taught:

Positive feelings attract higher vibrating emotions and positive life events and our body doesn't know the difference, chemically, between an emotion you're presently in or the one you're imagining. If you train yourself to feel the higher vibrating emotions like love, joy and gratitude, using meditation or imagination, the Universe will do the work to align you with events that bring about more of the same emotion. The same is true for the opposite. What you focus on expands so if you choose to dwell in the pain (memories of past hurt) you'll cycle in that feeling, creating more situations that bring similar painful emotions.

Of course, this is an extremely oversimplified version and it does not mean doing it will be easy. It's like the process of painting. Painting is putting paint on something. Anyone can do it but what the end result looks like depends on how much time you spend mastering it. Similarly, creating your new reality is a process. You'll have to break old habits and it is natural to ebb and flow with the success of it but it can be done, and it pays great dividends.

Catch yourself in the moment and get connected to the thoughts and energy of the future you want. You'll need faith in both the Universe and yourself, focus your efforts on the 'what and the why', leaving the 'how' to the Universe. You will start to see situations in your life that will shift without you having to force them, like 'green lights and parking spots' just appearing when you need them to. Let go of micromanaging the details, pushing for them, manipulating them, fighting for them. A little side note here, it also helps when there is an element included in your desired goal that also benefits others, the Universe is more forthcoming.

It was time to put the concept to the test. I picked a problem I was experiencing and focused on what the solution would feel like. I had recently discovered a yoga studio that I liked. I started to experience that mind, body, Spirit connection and bliss buzz every time I went. Unfortunately, the studio was a half-hour drive from my home, the classes were ninety minutes and it would take me half an hour to come home. I had to choose between bedtime snuggles and stories for my two young children or tranquility for myself. I did not want to choose. I sat down and created the parameters of the 'what and the why'. The first thing I needed was to be at home to put my kids to bed. Next, I wanted yoga in my small town so I didn't have to travel. Somewhere that would be convenient for me and the women in my town, where we could experience the connection I was experiencing. I wanted to be part of the design and aesthetic. I didn't want to pay for yoga. It was expensive so I threw this one in as a test to see how far I could go.

I sat down and, using a meditation from Dr. Joe, I imagined my new future. Using all my senses, to create the new yoga studio. I pictured the location, seeing its location in the rearview mirror every time I pulled up to the take-out window at Tim Hortons. It was the perfect place, I saw the logo placed on the face of the hip-roof above the door. I walked through it as I envisioned the type of floor, the shape of the lighting, the colours on the walls. I felt proud of the design. I could smell it and feel its warmth. I believed taking classes with my friends would benefit all of us. I finished my meditation and let it all go. How this was all going to happen was not my concern. That was the Universe's job.

A few months later I was running errands in the neighbouring town. Standing in a coffee shop lineup, a woman in front of me was speaking to the barista about the yoga studio I used to attend. I haven't been there for a very long time because I was choosing bedtime stories with my children instead of going out to yoga. She was an instructor who had not been teaching because her mother was ill had recently passed away. She had been left an inheritance and she was considering opening her own studio but had no idea where to open it. That's when I opened my purse and handed her my business card and said, "I know exactly where you should open it, give me a call."

Three months went by before I received the call. She apologized for the time it took for her to reach out. There were so many things that had to happen that were now falling into place. She informed me that she just signed a lease in my town and was looking for my help designing the space. The conversation gave me my truth tingles and I told her she didn't have to tell me where it was because I already knew. Sure enough, she confirmed she had signed a lease right behind the Tim Hortons.

I began the process of estimating the renovations and my coffee shop yogi secured some more financing, but then things went weird. My spidey senses went off and raised some red flags. There was something odd about the way things were going down so I pulled away from the process. I don't know why, all I knew was that it felt wrong and I listened to the warning signs this time. Although it was going against what I wanted and listening to my gut was hard. I doubted myself and the breadcrumbs I was following, the magic was happening and then it stopped. I was truly disappointed in myself and the process, thinking it didn't work.

It was almost a full year that went by before the yoga studio opened its doors. I was away on vacation and remember emailing a bunch of friends to tell them this new place was opening and that they should go and experience yoga for themselves. It took me about a month before I walked in the doors for my first class knowing that I did not have to choose between bedtime and yoga anymore. At least some of it happened and I was grateful for it.

The owner saw me and pulled me aside. She apologized for the way things went down and thanked me for being an integral part of starting the process. It was a bittersweet feeling but I was happy to be acknowledged. Then she told me if it wasn't for me this place would not have happened and she thanked me by handing me a free lifetime pass to the club. Tingles all around! Although I doubted it through the process, this punctuated the fact that the 'how' is not up to me. The path was different from what I expected but it had happened, after all, and I had gotten just what I had asked for.

I believe that this process has been responsible for assisting me in finding my last three homes, moving to West Vancouver and being published in this book. There have been too many coincidences and incidents in my life for me not to believe that I am co-creating my existence with Spirit. Once I figured out I had a soul, I knew I had to get quiet as often as I could to hear what it had to say. I trust that it is leading me. It leaves me messages and signs and it brings me through detours I never knew I needed, but become obvious when I look back. Managing my emotions with these meditations is the key that got me to manifest my dreams. My Soul is literally my personal piece of Spirit, its connection to the Universe and all its magic.

how I connect to Spirit
And You Can Too

To connect, I have to get rid of what could get in the way. Mainly the clutter in my head, the lists of things to do, everyday noise and distractions, even expectations as to how it's going to feel this time. I create a sacred space and ceremony, these are rituals that get me quiet, clear my space and invite Spirit. I have found these necessary to connect. I do not have the ability to plug in like some of the TV mediums who can just do it when they walk in the grocery store, although that's what I really want and I keep asking for it. For now, I need to work at it.

By opening up to the way Spirit wants to work with me and not the other way around, it feels like I will learn new unexpected ways. I burn sage to clear my space, light candles and play music. I get quiet, set my intention then meditate. Part of the ritual is to try to do it in the same time and place as my body starts to react in a Pavlovian way the minute I sit there. It's like exhaling the minute you hit your yoga mat. Your body knows what's coming. Who knows, if I keep practising maybe one day it will become more automatic and I can tell my hairdresser her grandma with the limp and purple hair is saying "hi".

When I start to feel the presence of a Spirit, I open more or increase my energy or aura to merge with their energy. It feels like blowing up a massive balloon with the permeable outer layer, as my balloon gets bigger it engulfs their balloon. I asked them to draw near and merge with my energy and to complete the triad, meaning the Spirit, myself and the person the message is for. I then share any information that I get with the client and test for validation. I sometimes don't need to test as I know immediately when I have spoken I get the tingles.

CREATING SPACE AND CEREMONIES

1. **Ground:** picture roots from the bottom of your feet connecting into the earth. Then picture absorbing all the energy your roots can absorb as a green light from Mother Earth and draw it up into your body.
2. **Ascend:** Focus your attention in the middle of your eyes and just behind them. Picture the heavens opening and pouring glistening white light into the top of your head and have it fill your body from above.

3. **Suspend:** Allow the white light and the green light to merge and fill in your body. You will feel suspended between heaven and earth. Relax into where you are and trust. Let go of all judgment.

4. **Expand:** Be patient and start noting the way information comes into you. Everyone is different. You can picture a TV screen if you like and observe what comes onto it. I see waves of light undulating in different shades of grey energy until it takes shape. For me, it's usually a symbol of something that I understand. It may seem random or trivial but for example. In a recent read for someone, an image of a pillowcase came to me. As I caught the thread and followed, it morphed into a pillow being stuffed and fluffed up and put onto a bed making it comfortable. We had already established it was her grandmother, but this brought back a significant part of her childhood memories, lying in a very comfy bed, snuggling with Grandma. Her grandmother would fluff up the pillows and blankets on her bed and make it all cozy for them to cuddle on. The image of the pillow cover had no initial meaning for me, but that is the thread you pick up and trust. If you grab it, it will lead you to another and another. Ultimately this had great meaning and significance for the client. Your thread can start as a vision, sensation, a knowing, a sound or scent.

5. **Allow and Trust:** I breathe into whatever form I'm experiencing, I expand my energy. I do this using visualization and intention. I visualize my aura expanding like that permeable balloon that encompasses their energy. When that happens, I can feel their personality and intention. I can even sense physical characteristics like my dream where I felt his hands become my hands. I merge with it as much as I can and open all my senses and feel, knowing that I am in complete control and can stop it whenever I wish, then ask it questions. I ask for it to show me its shoes or what's in its pockets. Even the smallest or broadest piece of information and I allow it to take me deeper. Never underestimate how simple the beginning messages are. Just trust that it is being shown to you for a reason and follow where it leads you. The more you trust, the further down the rabbit hole you will go.

How I Divine in the Moment

Going into nature to connect helps me hear the energy communicating with me. I clear my head noise, get quiet, set my intentions and ask a question and use something around me for my answers. It's a shamanic practice. If I'm on the beach I'll pick up the stone and look at one side. I look for images and take the first thing that comes to mind. I trust the image and the message that I quickly find in it. I look for four images then I flip it over and look for four more. I write down the eight images that I have collected from the stone, then I go back to the first side and ask how these images are all related. I see different images and a clear message or answer to my intention will emerge. The trick is not to doubt what you see, and the more you can trust it the more it will work for you.

I was feeling a little lost and unsure of myself, so I set the intention and asked the question,

How can I feel like myself again?

Image 1: Upside down heart - the message it gave me was - straighten out (my thoughts of course).

Image 2: A bright golden colour and a star - shine brightly.

Image 3: A carnival mask - stop hiding and have fun.

Image 4: A cat - don't be sly, own it.

The message from this side of the rock was: *Be yourself.*

I turn the rock over:

Image 1: A volcano - don't erupt.

Image 2: Dark and light moon craters - you are the light in the dark.

Image 3: Doodle lines - draw more, be creative.

Image 4: Lion - have courage.

The message from this side of the rock was: *Be in nature more. Don't make it so heavy. Lighten up.*

When I turned the rock back to the first side I saw a rocking horse - the message, "you rock," Nice! The process made me laugh and changed my energy. It's what I needed to hear.

I can do the same with images in tree branches or clouds. The shapes will emerge. It's like a Rorschach inkblot test from the Universe but nobody is analyzing you, just helping you figure things out. Let the images talk to you and give you the messages your soul is sending you.

I was grieving and asked the question, "Why am I struggling so much?" When I looked up at the branches, I saw the shape of an incomplete heart with many scars on it. They told me, your heart has a few wounds on it, you can not be wholehearted when you are trying to mend a broken heart, be patient with yourself.

Music is also a great way to get messages. Leaving a power yoga class feeling inadequate and a song from the 70's group The Band called, "You don't know the shape I'm in," reminds me to stop berating myself.

Leaving a medium workshop, I put on my coat and as I looked in the mirror into my own eyes I asked, "what do I need to do to change my world and feel better?" I was asking for a clear sign of what my next step could be. I got into my car to meet a friend for lunch. As I start my car one of Michael Jackson's song comes on the radio and the phrase "no message could have been any clearer, if you wanna make the world a better place take a look at yourself and make the change", I don't know how many times this phrase is repeated in the song, but it was a lot so I acknowledge and show gratitude for the message. As I entered the restaurant, written on the mirror just as I walked in the door was the exact same phrase.

I now see my version of the truth, and I permit myself to have my perspective. I have more confidence in my knowing that life's performance is for me. It's a play that I'm a part of and we -- life and I -- are writing it as we go. It's not always a comedy, but I do laugh at uncovering the plot, like finding money in a coat pocket I forgot I left there. It's like a game that at first, I didn't know existed let alone what the rules were, but now I have figured it out. I can play it well and finally, I'm working on mastering it enough to teach it.

The secret to getting what you want is to listen to then elevate your emotions, catch yourself not feeling the way you want to and sit down and imagine what you really want to feel like. Remember, what you focus on expands, so choose between cycling over your negative emotions or filling yourself with how you want to feel. You can create your reality by using your imagination to level up and by feeling the emotion before it happens. Then you are creating a new future that will have a new feeling in it.

I am 'seeing' my feelings and not 'being' my feelings. I am mastering the language of emotions. It is cleverness and poignant humour that make learning quite a trip. I feel alive and energetic and I am a willing traveller on this path towards enlightenment. I do this for all those who traveled before me. I do this for the ones that follow me, so that all their paths may be more clear, but mostly I do it for me, as I deserve it. Although I know the journey continues, I can enjoy where I am. I am being led home following the breadcrumbs where my ancestors are baking bread and I will get to enjoy it right out of the oven with salted butter melting into it!

I found my Soul and it speaks to me. The better I get at listening to it, the more I hear other souls as well.

a spiritual journey

No Glasses Necessary

By Patricia Giannasi-Heshka

The beginning of the most fantastic journey of my life.

Do I need to wear glasses? This was a question that was running through my innocent and naive brain at the age of four Circa 1953, my parents probably instigated this thought. Some of the lights and shadows being brought to me after we moved into a new home, although not scary, were quite different from the normal world. I did not understand that these presences or spirits bringing the sounds, flickers, touches and floating sensations were preparing me, 'Softly and Gently' whilst sneaking into my bedroom at night. My father took me for an eye examination revealing 20/20 vision, dismissing my stories as wild imagination. Please understand that I remember from a young age seeing, feeling, and talking to my (not) imaginary friends.

Growing up in Liverpool, England my family were hardworking, middle-class, and as normal as possible recovering from tragedies bestowed from World War Two. Times were tough, although there was always love for all and hot food on the table, served with lots of discipline and laughter. At four years old my wonderful Grandmother Nellie Quayle came to live with us, she had lost her husband and two children during the turbulent, sad times in her life. Living in Britain, it was very normal for two and three generations to live together in cramped conditions. This meant that I would share a bedroom until aged seventeen with a lady that would influence my whole being; she was a Psychic Medium, tea leaf reader and friend to many. Nellie worked in the Liverpool Alder Hey Children's Hospital as a housekeeper. The nurses and staff in the hospital loved her readings and insisted that they would set up a special place in the storage closet for her to sit most of the day; during this time they would fulfil her duties and chores while they took turns having readings. I am sure this would not be accepted in this day and age, but back then, everyone knew and understood. Many had suffered great losses during the war, and they desperately wanted her to contact spirits to bring evidence that their loved ones were alright in their new life in the world unseen. Many people just wanted to know how life would be for themselves. At the top of the list was information concerning children, husbands or boyfriends or suiters in the future; quite simple requests really.

Once Nanny settled into her new home, I would revel in wonderment at the explanations of her stories, and lessons from my grandmother night after night in our own private world. The start of my journey with a deep connection to the World Unseen had started. Perhaps already instilled in all our DNA waiting to be revealed is such a beautiful gift. 'No glasses necessary'.

Today, as an adult, my journey continues in the development of Psychic and Spiritual Awareness. The following words come from Spirit through my own guides who have blessed me with a gift to share their knowledge through me as a channel.

Blending and Meditation

Have you ever noticed how successful people make decisions quickly with confidence? Some say they have a lucky star, and some say they act on their gut feelings. The fact is, we all can tap into this powerful source and create the world of our desires. Accessing the source is the catalyst that makes the Law of Attraction and Abundance work. It is the key to your intuitive development

The word intuition means 'inner teacher'. Some people call it an intuition and others call it a hunch, but we all have experienced this beyond-the-physical senses 'aha!' moment. Often referred to as E.S.P. or extrasensory perception, it is anything but 'extra'. This inner guidance is the internal GPS that is meant to guide us through the maze we call life.

Unfortunately, for most, it is a fleeting moment, here and gone, that leaves one wondering if it were just a figment of the imagination.

Have you ever known who was calling on the phone before you looked at the screen display? Have you ever been thinking about someone and, within a short time, you happen to run into them? What about a strong urge to take a different route home that you ignored, only to find yourself stuck in a traffic jam!

We receive dozens of these hunches every single day through our four psychic senses. These are the senses of the soul. I call them gifts of the Spirit. Eastern religions consider it inner guidance.

Unfortunately, most of us have trained ourselves to ignore these signals, which are the real power behind effective decision making. We shake off and rationalize these moments of pure inspiration when the wisdom of the Universe is revealed to us.

Four main spiritual senses connect us to our inner guidance; clairaudience, clairvoyance, feeling and prophecy. (There are many more 'clairs'.) Each of us has all four available to us, but one is often dominant and is our primary perception and personality type. These are how we communicate with each other and how we receive our intuitive messages and hunches.

It is interesting to note that these four perceptions closely align with the Myers-Briggs personality tests used by corporate human resource departments.

1. Clairaudience (psychic hearing) – people high in this psychic sense obtain their insights through thoughts or words that they hear within. These are the people who like to gather facts and gain an understanding before moving forward with a decision. A person with this perception is a natural leader and, when balanced, have stick-to-it-ness and a sense of fairness when dealing with others.

2. Clairvoyance (psychic vision) – people high in this psychic sense obtain their insights through visions, dreams, images and symbols. Often, they have a 'photographic mind.' They are excellent executives because they see the big picture and have empathy because they can see others' points of view. In their personal appearance they are impeccable, and like harmony and beauty in their environment.

3. Feeling (psychic feeling) – people high in this psychic sense obtain their insights through a gut feeling and sensations. This individual is extremely sensitive to the environment, the feelings of others, and does not handle criticism well. When out of balance, this type feels taken advantage of and is susceptible to skin problems; in balance, they are tremendously inspirational. They are natural healers.

4. Prophecy (psychic knowing) – people high in this psychic sense obtain their insights through inner knowing. They assess situations quickly and 'just know' how things will work out. This perception is adept at multi-tasking and keeping tabs on several projects. When out of balance they are procrastinators. In balance, they are creative and good team-builders because they know the potential in others.

Meditation:

Importance and Technique

Meditation is a technique where you can use your mind to move into your own individual space of consciousness to heal and bring calm and peace to oneself; physically, spiritually and emotionally.

For thousands of years, our ancestors have connected with their innermost feelings and ancestors for direction, wisdom, healing, and strength. Did our ancestors really understand the power that they were using could change the world and themselves? Archaeologists have unearthed evidence dating back as early as 5000 B.C. that meditation had ties to many countries and religions. Ancient Egypt, China, Judaism, Hinduism, Buddhism and Sikhism all used meditation as a powerful tool.

Bringing us into the modern world, meditation brings peace healing and harmony to all those who practice this wonderful art.

Let us explore the benefits of meditation as we attempt to understand our complex existence. There are many different types of meditation to explore. It is best to follow your own path and discover which mode of meditation feels right for you. The main nine groups of meditation currently practiced alone or in groups are:

- Mindfulness meditation.
- Spiritual and healing meditation.
- Focused meditation.
- Movement meditation.
- Mantra meditation.
- Transcendental Meditation.
- Progressive relaxation.
- Loving-kindness meditation.

Each form of meditation has a comfort-connection to those who practice this wonderful gift and benefit. All meditation modalities are connected and achieve the purpose of fulfillment.

We all have gifts we can develop at our own pace. Each one of us has some psychic ability. We can all develop our spirituality in many ways. We are all different; there is no set way, and there is no 'wrong' way. We are all open to endless possibilities. Enjoy meditation practice as a method to open to Spirit and develop your psychic abilities.

SPIRITUAL AND HEALING MEDITATION

Sit in a quiet area with low light and perhaps some gentle relaxing music of your choice. Have a candle burning in front of you; meditate alone or with other people.

Visualization is a great part of PEACE.

Be aware of your breathing, deep and slow, feel your own heart pumping.

Visualize a soft glowing light in the centre of the room, with every breath you take feel the light grow and it will eventually completely cover you. (This method may be used for healing or protection).

The light will slowly enter your body through your crown Chakra on the top of your head. Compare to liquid gold light pouring down your spine and spreading throughout your whole body from the head down to the tip of your toes. Ask the Spirit Guides to come close, blend your energy with theirs and this will assist to develop your skills. Take your time and relax.

Meditation helps us to achieve confidence by sitting in the moment. Sitting in the Power. Practice makes it easier. Try daily even for 5 minutes. If you prefer the company of others, try to find a home circle, or start one!

When you have become comfortable in your meditation practice, you may take it to the next level - 'blending' (merging with Spirit energy).

In a meditative state, sit quietly and still your mind. Empty your whole being and allow your friends and loved ones in the unseen world to fill you with their energy, expanding your vibration (energy) to link with theirs. A heart and soul connection through pure love. No fear, just peace and connection. You may feel one strong presence or a whole network of beings merging with your vibration. When you feel the deep union of souls, you will know you have blended your energy with theirs. Blending can be achieved with dedication and practise sitting in a meditation group, or alone.

Wishing you Love, Light, and Laughter on your journey of development using meditation and blending with Spirit.

By Kelly Oswald

"The only real valuable thing is intuition."
– Albert Einstein

Day One: Introduction

Why bother developing intuition?

Because it is a lifesaver! It helps you solve problems faster, gets you out of sticky situations (or prevents you from getting in one), saves you from making detrimental decisions, aids in achieving goals and smooths the road ahead. Everything is safer, faster and more effective when you tap into your intuition, listen to your inner wisdom, and then act on that wisdom.

Intuition allows you to know things spontaneously, without any rational explanation for why you know it. You simply know something, the same way you would know how to unlock your door – only without ever learning how.

Intuition can help you with your life purpose, self-confidence, relationships, finances, career, family, health, simple choices and big decisions. It can save you from difficulty, stress, anxiety, insecurity, and potentially dangerous situations.

What is intuition... really?

Intuition is the direct knowing or learning of something without the conscious use of reasoning. It is immediate understanding without thinking - sudden knowing. It sounds very mystical and magical.

Here's what the dictionary has to say...

INTUITION DEFINED
- direct perception of truth, fact, etc., independent of any reasoning process, immediate apprehension.
- a fact, truth, information, perceived in this way.
- a keen and quick insight.

- the quality or ability to have direct perception or quick insight.
- an immediate cognition of an object not inferred or determined by a previous cognition of the same object.
- any object or truth so discerned.
- pure, untaught, non-inferential knowledge.

That's great! Now we know that intuition is an immediate understanding or knowing something without reason. How do we access it, recognize it or call it on demand?

First, let's find out where you are in your intuitive development. We all have access to our intuition whether we know it or not. Answer the questions to the following quiz as best you can. Tally up your total and read your results. No matter what the outcome, journaling is the best tool to boost your 'spidey senses' even higher.

INTUITION QUIZ:

Circle the number that applies to your experience.

1=never 2=rarely 3=sometimes 4=often

You pick up on people's emotions easily.	1 2 3 4
You know who's calling on the phone before you answered.	1 2 3 4
You thought about someone and then they contacted you.	1 2 3 4
You have vivid dreams with relevant themes.	1 2 3 4
You have instantly felt a building/house/room was a happy or threatening place.	1 2 3 4
You seem to know something about an object/person by touching it.	1 2 3 4
You are very discerning; you pick up on red flag warnings as well as strong attractions.	1 2 3 4
You can help someone (who you don't know) finish a sentence.	1 2 3 4
You have felt there was someone in the room with you when there wasn't.	1 2 3 4
You wake from sleep with solutions to problems or answers to questions.	1 2 3 4
Thoughts or ideas just pop into your mind seemingly from nowhere.	1 2 3 4
You have felt that something would happen and it did.	1 2 3 4
The hairs of your neck bristled and the mood of your space suddenly changed.	1 2 3 4

You made correct decisions because they felt right - even against
popular opinion.   1 2 3 4

You have made spontaneous decisions with positive outcomes.   1 2 3 4

You experience a great number of coincidences.   1 2 3 4

You have been told you have good insight, holistic abilities,
or you're a natural psychic.   1 2 3 4

Solutions to problems 'pop' into your mind when you are not focused,
such as relaxing, driving, showering, meditating, and exercising.   1 2 3 4

Total your score and see where you are experiencing your current level
of intuition.

18-35 Your level of awareness of your intuition will grow as you are
becoming more self-aware and know what to look for on your intuitive
journey. A journal will strengthen your relationship with your innate abilities.
Keep up your practice! The more you do it – the better you will get.

36-53 You are experiencing a conscious level of claircognizance
(intuitive knowing) and recognize it before or after it happens. You may not
trust it one-hundred percent, but you notice that it is a useful tool and helps
your life flow when you follow your intuitive hits. In addition to journaling,
consider playing with Oracle Cards or divination tools to expand your
openness to infinite possibilities.

54-72 You regularly tap into your intuitive side and have the advantage
of insight. You are aligned with your life path and feel intuitively guided. You
continue to trust your intuition to keep you on track. Always learning and
growing. You journal, play with Oracle tools, explore signs in nature and
delve into the mystic. Your life flows well and you are 'lucky' ... as a result of
trusting your inner voice.

*"What I am actually saying is that we need to be willing to let
our intuition guide us, and then be willing to follow that
guidance directly and fearlessly."*
– Shakti Gawain

INTUITIVE DEVELOPMENT EXERCISES

Start or continue journaling your intuitive experiences and any time you think 'I knew it!', or have a 'feeling' about a situation, person or place, write it down and see what unfolds.

Find ways to challenge and record the following questions:

- Does it feel like the right thing to do?
- Does it seem like the right answer?
- How do you feel when you think about "_x_" situation?
- What is/was your gut reaction?
- Do/did you have a hunch about that?
- Where in your body do you notice a reaction?
- If you did know the answer, what would it be?

Put your 'hunches' to the test:

- Forecast the weather; it's calling for rain, but will it?
- Feel into the energy of a friend's new date, is it a good fit?
- Follow a stock on the market, is it a winner or loser? (you don't have to buy it!)
- Without looking, feel which key will open your front door.
- Using a deck of regular playing cards, shuffle and flip over the cards 'predicting' which colour will appear, red or black. Record your score each time and see if you can push it over fifty percent accuracy.

Find other ways to challenge your intuition and write down both the present-moment 'vibes' and the ultimate outcome.

> *"The more you trust your intuition,*
> *the more empowered you become,*
> *the stronger you become,*
> *and the happier you become."*
> *– Gisele Bundchen*

Day 2: Instinct

"Your instincts know the way." - Unknown

"Always follow your heart." - Unknown

Oops... both the above quotes are kind of wrong.

Let's start with the first one.

Intuition and instinct are NOT the same thing.

INSTINCT

Instinct is a primal resource for self-preservation, like all animals, humans have instincts, the non-learned, inherited (genetic) patterns of behaviour generally ensuring the survival of a species. Salmon swim home to spawn, birds nest, spiders spin webs, sea turtles head to the ocean, squeamish feelings prevent us from eating spoiled food, our biological clocks advise us to procreate, fear saves us from danger. Instinct is a behaviour... not a feeling.

Instinct comes from the word instinctus, or, 'impulse', it is a biological tendency that a person or animal has to behave or react in a particular way. The source of this primal knowledge is located in our primal (reptilian) brains (hindbrain and medulla). It is responsible for survival, drive, and instinct, there is not much thinking going on when this part of the brain is being triggered so it may easily be confused with intuition. Instinct is a helpful, useful and effective tool for self-preservation; however, it lacks the wisdom that comes through intuition. Instinct is a subconscious reaction to circumstance that challenges your safety - like putting your hands out to prevent a fall.

INTUITION

Intuition is a subconscious psychological process where the brain calls on patterns, past and present experience, cues from the environment, the self and those around you to help make a quick, effective - but unconscious decision.

Intuition comes from the word intuitio, or, 'consideration', meaning it's an accumulated belief. It's the ongoing collection of experiences, apropos of everything up until now.

146

Intuition is an immediate understanding of something; there's no need to think it over or get another opinion—you just know. It arises as an unemotional feeling within your body that only you experience. It allows you to know things spontaneously, without any rational explanation for why you know it. You simply know something, the same way you know how to unlock your door – the only difference is that with intuition, you would never need to learn how, you'd just 'know'. Maybe it sounds like an instinct – but the differences are the depth of wisdom, the source of knowledge and the unwavering sense of 'knowing'.

Intuition arises from the subconscious mind (a storehouse of experiential wisdom), the collective unconscious, and the superconscious. Sometimes it arrives in an "a-ha!" moment; other times it's a slower realization. It can act as your GPS and help you navigate your life path with ease and effectiveness.

"Intuition is a spiritual faculty and does not explain, but simply points the way." – Florence Scovel Shinn

We've learned that instinct is a behaviour. A motor response by the body initiated by an external stimulus. It is not a feeling, but an innate, 'hardwired' tendency toward a particular behaviour.

Meanwhile, intuition is a cognitive process whereby the subliminal processing of information that may be too complex or too vague for rational thought can solve a problem or makes sense of a situation. When neuronal pathways join even weakly associated concepts, ideas, facts, into a neuronal network it seemingly 'puts the pieces of a puzzle' together. *

SUBCONSCIOUS INFORMATION

The function of your subconscious mind is to store and retrieve data. Everything you have seen, heard, thought, or done is stored in the database which is your subconscious mind. It houses significant and insignificant moments, belief systems, skills and experience. Your subconscious knows about the first French Fry you ever ate, who came to your seventh birthday, the name of the person who cut your hair when you were fourteen years old, those, and every other experience in your life. It houses all the things that would take up too much space in your conscious day to day mind including ideas and concepts that don't even register with your conscious brain. The subconscious mind can be a valuable resource when it comes time to retrieve some of that data.

In the present moment, your subconscious is processing everything that's going on around you and within you. Your subconscious mind never stops; it is constantly re-evaluating and problem-solving. In the same way that a machine does not reason or judge, but just acts on the task it is designed to do, so does the subconscious mind. It operates behind the scene, you are unaware that it's working for you until the solutions cross into your conscious mind... like the person's name that was on the tip of your tongue, an hour later the name 'pops' in... and you remember.

Pretty cool.

COLLECTIVE UNCONSCIOUS KNOWLEDGE

Collective unconscious refers to structures of the unconscious mind that are shared among beings of the same species. It is a term coined by Carl Jung. Intuitions from the collective unconscious are - by Jung - held to be generally far more important than are intuitions from the personal unconscious. The concept that we are all innately connected may vouch for some of the mutual 'vibes' we pick up with others.

SUPERCONSCIOUS WISDOM

The superconscious mind encompasses a level of awareness that sees beyond material reality and taps into the energy and consciousness behind that reality - otherwise known as Universal wisdom, ether or a flow of electromagnetic waves that permeate all matter and space. The concept of superconscious wisdom offers the possibility to tap into Universal knowledge beyond our scope of beliefs and access information from a higher power or broader source.

ACCESSING INTUITION

First of all, it's good to know you were born intuitive. It may have been squished out of you... but it's still there, you just need to go dig for it. But how?

You've been there before. That feeling when you've lost a sense of time. Maybe you drove home and when you arrived didn't remember driving, you got creative and lost in your project, you played a video game or browse the internet for just a brief moment that turned into a lost two hours, you were walking or jogging and all of a sudden realized where you were, mid-shower you can't remember shampooing. This is known as 'flow'.

Repetitive movement or doing routine things removes the banter of the conscious brain and allows your subconscious to have a turn. Your inner wisdom searches around for the best solutions to your problems, but to 'hear' that solution, to 'get' your answers, the subconscious has to cross the bridge to your conscious mind and that only happens when you relax that part of the brain. When you stop stimulating thoughts and just allow. This is one of the reasons meditation is such an effective means to amplify your intuition.

"You have powers you never dreamed of.
You can do things you never thought you could do.
There are no limitations in what you can do except the
limitations of your own mind." ~ Darwin P. Kingsley

INTUITIVE DEVELOPMENT EXERCISES

Write down three things you'd really, really, really like your intuition to help you with. 'Feel' into the desire that rises when you focus on each of these three things. Allow yourself to honestly want those three things to come to fruition with the help of your intuition. No doubts.

Continue journaling your intuitive experiences:

- Any time you think 'I knew it!', or have a 'feeling' about a situation, person or place, write it down and see what unfolds.
- Start a meditation practice or a way of getting in the 'flow' and turning down the volume of your conscious mind. It can be actual meditation, exercise, a self-care routine, cooking, play music, paint, or anything that relaxes your mind.

Get positive:

- Become excited about the process of working with your inner wisdom.
- Work with positive affirmations and positive thinking to eliminate doubt or negative self-talk. Empowering yourself is important.

Access your subconscious consciously:

- If you can't remember someone's name – but it's on the tip of your tongue – relax and allow your subconscious to remind you. Don't think about it or chase it – in fact, think of something else. It will bubble up and you'll remember.
- If you misplace your car keys – or equivalent – instead of running around looking for them, sit quietly, breathe and relax. Let your mind

take you on a story of the last time you held your keys in your hand. Your subconscious mind knows where you put them, but you must allow it to bubble up as you relax into the story of their current location. It's much faster and more effective than tearing the house apart. (It doesn't have to be car keys; it can be anything that you have misplaced).

- Before bed, ask a question that truly resonates or can help solve a problem. Write it down and trust that your subconscious mind will come through for you, and then go to sleep. Wake up to the answer or solution.

Keep putting your 'hunches' to the test:

- Continue to 'vibe' the weather.
- How's your stock pick doing? (remember, you don't have to buy it!)
- Without looking, feel which key will open your front door or without looking, tune into an unexpected text.
- Using a deck of regular playing cards, shuffle and flip over the cards 'predicting' which colour will appear, red or black. Record your score each time and see if you can push it over fifty percent accuracy.

"Intuition is knowing without knowing." - Anonymous

See ya on the next page... we'll talk about that second quote that talked about following your heart.

Day 3: Emotion

"Your hearts calling overcomes the whisper of your intuition."

FEELINGS

Emotion is not intuition.

So many people ask me what intuition 'feels' like. It's a personal 'vibe' that is yours and yours alone. My intuition may not feel like your intuition; however, one thing is for sure, intuition is NOT an emotion... it's not that kind of a feeling. Intuition is an unwavering knowingness, sometimes it is a 'feeling' of tightness or expansion, but not an emotion.

Following your heart and following your intuitive hunches are NOT the same thing.

Emotion often wreaks havoc with intuition. We get excited or fearful and head in the direction of our emotions. It's dangerous to make decisions when emotions are running high, positive emotions or negative ones. When emotions run high, it's possible to make huge mistakes; some examples of over-excitement are marriage, starting a business, having children with the wrong person, investing, making a large purchase (home, car), and emotionally charged over-shopping. Examples of fear-based decisions are similar - running from commitment, afraid to start a business, nervous to invest, worried about making a purchase. Fear-based thinking holds you back, while excitement propels you forward – neither is intuition, both are unreliable.

Intuition is an unwavering knowingness – it doesn't have emotion; however it does feel like something. Your intuitive 'feeling' will be as unique as you are. It could be the classic gut feeling, goosebumps, an inner voice, a warmth, coldness, a tightness, unexplained discomfort, expansion, unexplained sense of peace, shiver down the spine, a hunch, hairs stand up on neck/arms, heebie-jeebies, feeling 'yes', feeling 'no'. None of these are emotional – they are sensations.

Then why all this 'follow your heart' stuff?

Maybe it should be 'explore your heart'. You take the lead; don't just follow.

Go back to the three things you'd really, really, really like your intuition to help you with. Feel the desire? Write them all down in order of importance on a small card and put them in your wallet or pocket. This is how you'd like things to unfold for you; you have set the ball in motion. When you do your meditation today, focus deeply on the one thing that feels most important to you. We will do a focused meditation in a few moments.

"Intuition tells you what you need to hear, not necessarily what you hope to hear." – Anonymous

As you go about your day, your subconscious mind is sifting and sorting and working in the background to achieve the goals that you desire. It will match choices to help you achieve those goals. To simplify; a goal of having one thousand dollars in your saving account will cause your subconscious mind to look for ways to earn or save that amount. As you go throughout your day, it will throw out intuitive hits that lead you towards your goals. You will sense that a purchase isn't necessary or that a small investment may be fruitful. Your subconscious will guide you to your desire if you listen to the cues.

"Trusting our intuition often saves us from disaster."
– Anne Wilson Schaef

Your subconscious mind is constantly working in your best interest, using your personal experiences and harvesting the wealth of information beyond - information from the common unconscious and the superconscious. If you don't have a focus for your subconscious it will still look out for you anyway, but if you have a strong focus, such as the list of three desires you've got in your pocket, then your intuition becomes your superpower.

Superpower? Really?

Yes.

Think of all the successful people you know of who claimed that their successes are due to intuitive insight ... even Albert Einstein and Tomas Edison make the list.

*"You will never follow your own inner voice until
you clear up the doubts in your mind." – Roy T. Bennet*

So let's get your 'spidey senses' fired up and working for your success.

- Find a comfortable place to sit straight – nice and aligned from the base of your tail-bone to the top of your head. Relax your shoulders and breathe easily.
- Close your eyes a let your mind focus on the number one goal on your list, and feel the emotion behind it. The excitement, fear or desire. Those are just feelings that come and go as you think about your goals.
- Imagine what it will feel like when you achieve your number one goal. Let that emotion wash over you as you explore your heart. Ask questions, stay positive, and be willing and open to the possibility that this could unfold for you.
- When you feel you have explored that number one item on your wish list, open your eyes and go about your day. Your subconscious is doing the work for you behind the scenes. You've given it instructions.
- Stay aware and watch for signs, solutions, and progress.

*"Trust your intuition – your brain can play tricks,
your heart can blind, but your gut is always right."
– Anonymous*

INTUITIVE DEVELOPMENT EXERCISES
- Continue journaling your intuitive experiences.
- Continue a meditation practice or a way of getting in the flow and turning down the volume of your conscious mind. It can be actual meditation, exercise, a self-care routine, cook, create, play music, paint, or anything that relaxes your mind.
- **Access your subconscious consciously.** Close your eyes a let your mind relax.
- Did you wake up to the answer to your significant question? If yes- then yay! If not – keep trying – every night is a chance to practice.

- Think about times you've made choices based on fear or excitement. How'd that work out?
- Think about times you just 'knew', no emotion, just felt it was the right option. How'd that one go?
- Using a deck of regular playing cards, using only ace through four, shuffle and flip over the cards 'predicting' which number will appear, ace through four. This exercise is tougher than the last. Record your score each time and see if you can push it over fifty percent accuracy.

See ya on the next page... logically.

Day 4: Logic

"The intellect has little to do on the road to discovery. There comes a leap in consciousness, call it intuition or what you will, the solution comes to you and you don't know how or why."
– Albert Einstein

WHAT IS INTUITION **NOT**?

At the opening of this course we defined intuition; however, I feel that it's important to identify not only what intuition is, but also what it isn't.

In previous chapters, we established that intuition is NOT an emotion therefore, blindly following your heart isn't a method of working with your intuition. Intuition doesn't have emotion … it just knows.

Intuition is NOT logic, therefore doesn't require thinking, rationalizing or any other type of thought process. Intuition doesn't require thinking… it just knows.

But it is through both desire (emotionally charged) and thinking things through that combine with intuition to be the best and most effective method for navigating your life path. I know it's confusing in the beginning, but once you can clearly differentiate between emotion and intuition, and logic and intuition, you will breeze along your ultimate journey.

Intuition doesn't feel and it doesn't think.

Remember back to multiple-choice tests in school. Anytime you went back and second-guessed an answer, it was usually your first choice that was correct. Intuition is most often the first 'hit'; logic jumps in second and over-thinks the answer and sometimes completely changes the outcome.

"Good intuition usually tells you what to do long before your head has figured it out." – Michael Burke

"Your intuition and your intellect should be working together… making love. That's how it works best." –Madeleine L'Engle

Mind chatter is a very interesting phenomenon. We can all talk ourselves into things and out of things by going through what seems like a logical thought process. All the while our intuition is just under the surface – probably rolling its eyes – and already has the answer you are trying to discern. How can you tell?

Get out of your head. Let your intuition slide the pieces of your intellectual puzzle around with out trying to control or reason.

Have you thought hard about making a purchase? Maybe you were in a changing room trying to decide whether a shirt was looking good, or in an electronics shop debating cost verses bells and whistles on a new gadget.

There you are… 'does this look good?', 'is it worth the money', 'I can afford it, but do I need it?'. Who are you talking to? Yourself. There you are talking to yourself. Abstractly, that makes two of you, the 'you' who's asking the questions, and the 'you' who is listening and quite possibly answering those questions. I know – confusing, but we all do it – yes?

Let your imagination take you back to a situation similar to the one above, where you are having a conversation with yourself. You can probably see it as a clear memory. While you were talking this through with yourself – which part of you was observing the whole thing? That third part of you that was just watching but already knew if it looked good, already knew if it was worth the money, already knew if you needed it. Your intuitive self was there all the time and while you went on with logic and emotion, it just sat there and waited for you to come to your senses. Do you remember the outcome? It's good to journal these things as they occur or even after the fact. Times like these help deepen your awareness.

> *"Your intuition knows what to do.*
> *The trick is getting your head to shut up so you can hear."*
> *– Louise Smith*

Let's get your 'spidey senses' fired up again.

- Find a comfortable place to sit straight – nice and aligned from the base of your tail-bone to the top of your head. Relax your shoulders and breathe easily.

- Close your eyes a let your mind focus on the number one goal on your list, and feel the emotion behind it. The excitement, fear or desire. Those are just feelings – they come and go as you think about your goals.
- Imagine what it will feel like when you achieve your number one goal. Let that emotion wash over you as you explore your heart. Ask questions, be willing and open and get into the possibility that this could unfold for you.
- Allow your mind to wander to the pieces of the puzzle that might make up the bigger picture. Ask 'what needs to come together to realize this potential?' 'What magic needs to happen to make this real?'
- Watch and listen – maybe nothing happens – maybe you feel you get an inkling, or maybe a full-on solution pops into your conscious mind. Your intuitive hits may take hours, days or weeks as your subconscious is working hard at fulfilling your desire.
- When you feel you have explored that number one item on your wish list, open your eyes and go about your day. Your subconscious is doing the work for you behind the scenes. You've given it instructions.
- Stay aware and watch for signs, solutions, and progress.
- If your #1 item has begun to manifest, go on to #2 … or maybe you've decided on something different by now.

"All great people are gifted with intuition. They know without reasoning or analysis, what they need to know."
– Alexis Carrel

"The intuitive mind is a sacred gift and the rational mind is a faithful servant. We have created a society that honours the servant and has forgotten the gift."
– Albert Einstein

INTUITIVE DEVELOPMENT EXERCISES

- Continue journaling your intuitive experiences.
- Continue a meditation practice or a way of getting in the flow and turning down the volume of your conscious mind. As mentioned earlier, it can be actual meditation or anything that relaxes your mind.

Access your subconscious consciously:

- Continue asking questions before bed every time you are seeking solutions to problems. Your dreams, or the few moments as you first awake hold loads of relevant information accessible only briefly. Write 'em down.
- Think about times you've made choices based on other's opinions or advice? How'd that work out?
- Think about times you just 'knew', but then second-guessed and changed course. How'd that one go?

See ya when you turn the page... I can feel it.

Day 5: Action

"There is a voice inside of you that whispers all day long,
'I feel this is right for me, I know that this is wrong.'
No teacher, preacher, parent, friend or wise man can decide
What's right for you--just listen to the voice that speaks inside."
– Shel Silverstein.

ACTING ON INTUITION

Sometimes I'm chicken to act on my intuition and other times it's a breeze. It's one thing to identify an intuitive hit, but quite another to take action on it. Courage and trust are the first obstacles, and another is risking our ego – we might feel a sense of shame or disappointment if we are wrong. Our inner-skeptic is not helpful, so put yours to the side and take the leap!

What we are doing here is crazy! Think about it... direct access to unconscious knowledge? Yes. We are talking about knowing of a situation without specific data or evidence; analytic reasoning is not part of the intuitive process, nor is an emotion or anything else except some weird sensation that is neutral, unemotional and most likely spot-on. Yup – it is nuts! It works like magic.

Pretty cool stuff.

Crazy or not... just as you can become more comfortable making decisions when you apply logic and reasoning, you can also become more adept at trusting your intuition when you use it more frequently over time and the results range from somewhat accurate (in the beginning) to very accurate (with practice).

You WILL be a rock-star with practice. Start with little things that come to you and 'test' yourself. Have fun with it and engaged in the spirit of play. This takes all the worry and seriousness out of the equation and builds confidence in preparation for life's bigger questions.

We haven't talked much about 'gut feelings', but working with your gut is a good place to practice acting on your 'spidey senses'. Your gut contains neurotransmitters that are subconsciously connected to your intuitive regulator, so if you get a gut feeling, pay attention.

You may feel your 'spidey senses' kick in when you vibe a person, place, situation, a decision to be made or a problem to be solved.

Vibes encouraging you to take a step *forward* may come in the form of:

Unemotional clarity, flutter, warmth, expansion, easy breath, relaxation, feels 'right', calming sensation, lightness, inspiration, a sense of resolution, goosebumps, tingles, a 'yes' or any other feeling of positivity that bubbles up.

"Trust yourself. You know more than you think you do."
– Benjamin Spock

Vibes encouraging you to take a step *backward* may come in the form of:

Unemotional clarity, heaviness, headache, tightness, coldness, retraction, restricted breath, anxiousness (high alert), feels 'wrong', uptight sensation, clenching, inspiration, a sense of unease, goosebumps, heebie-jeebies, a 'no' or any other feeling of negativity that bubbles up.

"This is mysterious. I cannot visually, with my physical eye, see the forces that act upon me from within and without, and yet I cannot deny their existence. If I try, I suffer. If I surrender, allowing them to act upon me, and if I work with them, I feel exhilarated; I become filled with the joy of life."
– Jonas Salk, inventor of the Polio Vaccine

As I mentioned earlier, at times I'm chicken to act on my intuition and other times it's a breeze. For me, it depends on the risk factors, the drama or substantial change that could occur, or if other's will be impacted by my actions. It's easy when I'm the only one who will be affected – harder when others will be part of the mix.

However, I don't want to live with regret – so now I act on my intuition regardless, and am very gentle when others are involved. You and I are doing this crazy thing called Intuitive Development because we have had these things happen – and are ready to move past these statements.

"I knew I should have/shouldn't have done that."

"I wish I had trusted my gut."

"I knew what was going on but I didn't say anything."

"I wanted it so badly but I still walked away."

"I felt that I might have something going on, I can't believe I didn't check it out earlier."

"I knew that person was good/bad for me."

"I probably could have made that career move in hindsight, I was so nervous at the time."

"If only I hadn't second-guessed myself."

"I knew it, but felt I was the odd duck, so went along with everyone else."

"I should have, could have, would have."

Your intuition is your internal GPS, always guiding you in the 'right' direction. It is your best friend; it has your back, has intimate knowledge of what you truly desire, will do anything to protect you and help you stay true to yourself along your life path. It's worth acting on.

"Intuition is the compass of the soul."
— Anonymous

READY TO TAKE ACTION

- Find a comfortable place to sit straight – nice and aligned from the base of your tail-bone to the top of your head. Relax your shoulders and breathe easily.

- Close your eyes a let your mind wander to a decision, relationship, situation, problem or anything that could benefit from your intuitive guidance.

- Connect with your breath and just breathe easily while your mind wanders and wonders.

- Let your mind be curious and explore the whole dynamic and allow as much information to sift through your consciousness. Albert Einstein believed that "Intuition does not come to an unprepared mind." This exercise gives your subconscious mind as many pieces to the puzzle as possible.

- Trust your gut feeling or any other vibes that bubble up. Initial feelings (not emotion) are relevant in the ultimate solution.
- Continue to breathe easily while your mind wanders and wonders, allowing for curiosity and expansion.
- If you get a nudge during this session, then great! But if you don't, it's okay, your subconscious is working on it for you in the background. Insight may just pop into your consciousness, or it may bubble up the next time you are silent and still.
- When you feel ready, disconnect and go about your day.
- Stay aware and watch for signs, solutions, and progress.

"When your intuition is roaring loud, follow it."
– Anonymous

"Deep down you already know the truth."
– Anonymous

INTUITIVE DEVELOPMENT EXERCISE
Take action on your intuitive hits:

- When you feel a vibe asking you to take a step forward or back away, act on it and journal the experience. Keep a record of your hits and misses. Remember the hockey player, Wayne Gretzky's wisdom, "You miss one-hundred percent of the shots you don't take". So you may as well start shooting now!

Next: safety and protection.

Day 6: Self Care

"Intuition is really a sudden immersion of the soul into the universal current of life." — Paulo Coelho

I love to feel alive! and that's what happens as you head down this intuitive path. You feel deeply. The more intuitive you become the more sensitive and self-aware you become. For this reason, it's good to look after yourself, to be kind to yourself, to protect and clear, and to avoid carrying everyone else's 'stuff' around.

SET BOUNDARIES

'No' is just as good a word as 'yes'. Overwhelm occurs when we say 'yes' too often when we actually meant 'no', or when we feel we need to please someone. It's freeing to both parties to say 'no' right out of the gate, no awkwardness or discomfort will loom on the horizon if you both know that it's not on your plate. Take on what you feel is good for you and leave the rest. Pacing yourself is delightful and allows for more intuition in your life.

PREPARE IN ADVANCE FOR OVERLOAD

Know what to do ahead of time when you do feel overwhelmed or depleted. Have an action plan for retreat. It could be a walk outside, meditation, time at your altar, a cleansing and protection ritual, crystal therapy, a massage, listening to music, reading a book, enjoying a relaxing bath … or even just taking a deep breath and counting to ten. Be prepared and have your own version of a time-out at the ready.

GET OUT IN NATURE

Nature is the ultimate source of intuition and feel-good energy. Signs and symbols, synchronicity and all the magic of the world will increase the more time you spend heart to heart with Mother Nature, the great nurturer.

MEDITATE IN SOME FORM OR ANOTHER

You've already got this.

JOURNAL

You've got this too… right?

CREATE A MANTRA

A mantra is a word or series of words used to infuse energy into your being. You can repeat the word or phrase during meditation, or use it anytime throughout your waking hours. It can be a simple word such as 'love' or 'joy', or a phrase such as 'I am safe, I am love, I am happy'. I used 'I am peace' for years until I no longer felt agitated or triggered in most situations. Mantras work incredibly well.

USE YOUR FAVOURITE TOOLS TO CLEANSE AND PROTECT

Are you a crystal rock hound? Do you love working with aromatherapy? Do you sage or smudge? Your favourite tools can be used during your intuitive development… and maybe you'll be guided to something new!

DEFINE YOUR COMMUNITY

Not everyone is good for you and believe it or not; you're not good for everybody. We all have triggers and can be either the sender or the receiver of those provocations. Find value and respect in your relationships, tuning in to those who bring out the best in you and those with whom you feel a healthy connection.

A good exercise is to sift through your social media friends and feel what it's like when you visit their page. Do you feel joy, happiness, empathy, sympathy, friendship and connection or do you feel jealousy, envy, distance and distrust? Clean up your tribe and you clean up your vibe!

PRACTICE SELF-AWARENESS

This can be both joyful and gosh-darn painful.

A moment ago I mentioned that not everyone is good for you and believe it or not, you're not good for everybody. Self-awareness helps you 'see' where you are adding to the human adventure and when you are making a little mess out of things. I remember Caroline Myss saying "Believe it or not, there is somebody in therapy because of you." Whoa! Brutal!

When we have insight and self-awareness we can see the results of our words and actions. Once we get past the discomfort of self-revelation and stop cringing at our past selves, we tend to develop greater empathy, act kindly, forgive easily, and life gets better. We become responsible for what we are 'putting out there', and it feels good. Actually… it feels great!

BE POSITIVE

Don't buy into the bulls#*&. There is 'fake' positive (loads of it out there!) and there is 'authentic' positive. Come from authenticity and be amazed at how the world treats you! Yes, you can fake it till you make it at work or after watching the evening news… but there is a better way. Be still and search inside for your 'good vibes' and identify a true-blue one-hundred percent-for-real positive thing going on in your world. Pull it out and cherish it for a few seconds … feel that? Nice!

"Trust your intuition and be guided by love."
— Charles Eisenstein

"Your intuition is the most honest friend
that you will ever have." - Doe Zantamata

PROTECTION VISUALIZATION

- Find a comfortable place to sit straight – nice and aligned from the base of your tail-bone to the top of your head. Relax your shoulders and breathe easily. Your feet on the floor.
- Close your eyes a let your mind focus on your breath. Feel the air moving in and out of your body.
- Imagine breathing white light, not just air, but white protective light.
- Imagine breathing this light in through the top of your head, filling your body, and exhaling out through the bottoms of your feet.
- Continue for a few minutes – just breathing white light.
- Imagine the following mantra in your mind, or say it out loud: "I am safe and protected, centred and grounded, and connected between heaven and earth."
- When you feel ready, open your eyes and relax for a second before going about your day.

"Pay attention to your gut feelings.
No matter how good something looks,
if it doesn't feel right – walk away." - Anonymous

INTUITIVE DEVELOPMENT EXERCISES

- Continue journaling your intuitive experiences.

- Continue a meditation practice or a way of getting in the flow and turning down the volume of your conscious mind.

- Journal self-care methods you use and note which modalities work best for you. Allow your intuition to guide you to the best possible means of self-care.

Oh oh ... next page is the last day... and there's a test.

Day 7: Final Takeaway

"At times you have to leave the city of your comfort and go into the wilderness of your intuition.
What you'll discover will be wonderful.
What you'll discover is yourself." – Alan Alda

WHAT TYPE OF AN INTUITIVE ARE YOU?

Read each of the following statements and rate the extent to which you would agree that the statement is true of you using the scale below. These items have no right or wrong answers; just respond based on what is true for you.

Circle the number that applies to your experience.

1=definitely false 2=mostly false 3=undecided 4=mostly true 5=definitely true

1. When tackling a new project, I concentrate on big
    ideas rather than the details.   1 2 3 4 5

2. I trust my intuition, especially in familiar situations.   1 2 3 4 5

3. I find it difficult not to care.   1 2 3 4 5

4. Familiar problems can often be solved intuitively.   1 2 3 4 5

5. There is a logical justification for most of my
    intuitive judgments.   1 2 3 4 5

6. My approach to problem-solving relies heavily on
    my past experience.   1 2 3 4 5

7. I don't do well in crowds.   1 2 3 4 5

8. I tend to use my heart as a guide for my actions.   1 2 3 4 5

9. My intuition comes to me very quickly.   1 2 3 4 5

10. I feel connected to nature.   1 2 3 4 5

11. My intuition is based on my experience.   1 2 3 4 5

12. I often make decisions based on my gut feelings, even
    when the decision is contrary to objective information.   1 2 3 4 5

13. People seem to seek me out for support or to tell me
    their problems.   1 2 3 4 5

14. When making decisions, I value my hunches just as much as I value facts.   1 2 3 4 5

15. When I have experience or knowledge about a problem, I trust my intuition.   1 2 3 4 5

16. I often feel emotionally overwhelmed.   1 2 3 4 5

17. I've had enough experience to know what to do most of the time without trying to figure it out from scratch every time.   1 2 3 4 5

18. I don't like conflict.   1 2 3 4 5

19. If I have to, I can usually give reasons for my intuitive hits.   1 2 3 4 5

20. I have a hard time setting boundaries.   1 2 3 4 5

21. I enjoy thinking in abstract terms.   1 2 3 4 5

22. I see things differently and often pick up on things that others miss.   1 2 3 4 5

23. I try to keep in mind the big picture when working on a complex problem.   1 2 3 4 5

24. When I make intuitive decisions, I can usually explain the logic behind my decision.   1 2 3 4 5

25. I believe I am a "big picture" person.   1 2 3 4 5

A. Total your score on questions 1,5,8,9,10,12,19,21,23,24,25   _____

B. Total your score on questions 2,7,10,13,16,17,18,20,21,22,25   _____

C. Total your score on questions 3,7,8,10,13,16,18,20,21,22,25   _____

The highest score reveals your strongest level of intuition. A, B or C

A = Intuitive Evaluation is your greatest strength. *Intuitive Evaluation happens when a decision is reached based on subjective feelings.* Your intuition comes from your ability to pick up on patterns, process information around you and come to conclusions effortlessly, although the reason why the decision was made may be difficult to articulate and is not fully conscious.

"It is by logic that we prove,
but by intuition that we discover." – Poincaré

B = Intuitive Insight is your greatest strength. *Intuitive Insight is a decision reached or a problem solved often triggering the "a-ha" moment.* Your intuition comes from your ability to process information non-consciously combining bits and pieces of knowledge with each other in new ways to come to conclusions effortlessly. The more experience you have in a particular area, the greater results you will have in that area. The more you know – the greater your insight.

"Trust your hunches. They're usually based on facts filed away just below the conscious level." – Joyce Brothers

C = Intuitive Empathy is your greatest strength. *Empathy is the ability to sense energy from other people.* You may even be able to absorb another's energy and feel the same intense emotions in your own body. Your intuition comes from your ability to sense other people and environments, process the information and come to conclusions effortlessly, although it may be difficult dealing with the information. Self-care is critical.

"Could a greater miracle take place than for us to look through each other's eyes for an instant?" - Henry David Thoreau

Now you can pursue your innate intuitive skills and soar! Maybe you have skills in all of these arenas, or two are predominant. Explore! Engage in your intuitive brilliance and enjoy a life of insight, clarity and flow.

I hope this section was insightful, helped you appreciate your own amazing talents, and revved up your 'spidey senses' to a whole new level.

mediumship

How to Follow the Clues
By Elizabeth Rasta

Serendipity: finding good things without looking for them.

The book was on the table. Sarah, my daughter, had left it there. It was the catalyst for my journey into mediumship. That day I picked up the book. It was about the magic of the moon, and I read it cover to cover.

I had read Tarot cards for over twenty years, had a full-time job, and was raising three daughters, a dog and two cats. At that time, Tarot was my joy. Sundays were the day I put aside time to enjoy my cards, learn, and study the metaphysical world. But that particular day when I randomly read that book left on the coffee table, I decided it was time to set intentions and start using moon magic to manifest. Opening the door for me to love myself again.

I was (and still am) grateful for all the opportunities in my life, but was having difficulty separating my illusions of fear from all those opportunities.

That summer Sarah travelled and worked in the interior of British Columbia (in Canada). Lo and behold, it was where the author of the moon book was offering psychic readings. Sarah went for a professional psychic reading and was so impressed. By the end of the read, both Sarah and the psychic felt that it would be beneficial for me to have a session as well.

So I went.

A few short minutes into the reading, the psychic told me I was a 'medium', and in the future we were going to work together, to bring healing and light to the planet. She also said I was to find a mentor or teacher, and it would all take place in a building with the name 'five corners'. This shift in my mindset would be a catalyst to transform my future.

A few months later, I was invited to a charity event that included psychic readings from apprentices. I brought my daughter, and off we went on another psychic adventure. As I was waiting, a magical and serendipitous shift occurred in me while observing the event organizer guiding the participants to sit with the readers. When she addressed me, I immediately

170

knew that she was to be my teacher and mentor. I knew I had attended the event just to meet her as my Solar Plexus chakra kicked into gear, and I urgently signed up for five consecutive classes called, 'Learning to Hear Yourself'.

The work in the class slowly cracked my outer shell open. I was hearing my inner voice clearer than I ever had heard myself before. I was trusting my gut again, it brought peace to the surface of my life. The connection to Spirit gave me hope, direction, the courage to move forward, and love. This love for myself that I had never felt before. Pure White Light Love.

I craved more.

And I gave myself more by reading extensively on the mastery of love. I made time for different classes with different teachers and continued higher learning from my mentor. My mentor made an offering of a one-year program for mediumship, in which I hastily enrolled. It meant studying, working, and driving thirty kilometres each way, but it was worth it. Plus, the location of the studio where my studies took place was called 'five corners' – just as the psychic had told me!

Serendipity indeed!

I soon realized the work and effort I put into my studies was self-healing. Forgiveness, compassion, and allowing love into my life were part of my destiny. As I healed my heart, the light was extended to all those around me. Spirit brought me to the Tarot and mediumship to usher in peace and freedom.

Each day I strive to invoke healing of my heart through the angels, I set intention that all of us on the planet may expand the love in our lives. It is the willingness to explore new avenues, to heal at a soul level, and to qualify ourselves worthy of success. By following Universal clues and my intuition an amazing synchronistic journey has brought me to where I am today. I am so grateful for the richness of all the experiences of serendipity.

"Loving everything about yourself – even the 'unacceptable' – is an act of personal power. It is the beginning of healing."
Christiane Northrup, MD.

How to Follow the Clues

"One discovers love through the practice of love."
– Paulo Coelho

Mediumship is a practice of purposely meditating on the communication between Spirits of the dead and living human beings. To become a medium, you are often guided or called into the spiritual world of healing others through the communication of speaking or hearing messages from those crossed over.

You may wish to find a facilitator or group to work with, and be formaly trained to use this gift; some church groups even study mediumship together. Or you may like to gently investigate the subject on your own.

As you build your mediumship practice, try bringing awareness of the serendipity in your life through these daily mantras:

- Every circumstance is a possibility to heal. I invite peace and harmony.
- I listen to my emotions, I am healing, I activate my inner power of love.
- I set healthy boundaries.
- I balance the scale of giving and receiving.
- When I chose to love myself, I raise the vibration of the collective conscience.

Things to know about Mediumship:

- Mediums work with the light of Spirit, how you perceive that is up to your individual beliefs and experience. It is always best to bring in Divine guidance and timing through the portal of loving light.
- A fundamental practice of Mediumship is to quiet your mind so that you can hear or visualize Spirit. Meditation is a useful tool for stillness.
- Spirit will bring only what the human spirit can handle on this earthly dimension; you can never force a connection.
- Empathy and sympathy, are relevant to the connections. They help with being non-judgemental.

- Generally, those drawn to mediumship have a strong desire to work with others in a healing capacity.
- Association practice brings a language with Spirit, for example, when I see daisies in my connections, I know I'm channelling messages of childhood.
- Mediumship takes practice to open channels to the spiritual world, but also needs closure and clearing after each session, with grace and authentic gratitude for every connection.
- As you become fluent in your language with Spirit, it will help your channels open with ease – such as hearing, visualization, smelling, and a true knowing.

To begin to be a medium, you will be working with Spirit and you will be provided with information through signs, symbols, and inspiration to enable you to be a more evidential medium. An evidential medium is one that provides evidence – proof that someone or someplace truly existed.

If Spirit has led you to be a medium, it will assist and build the knowledge you have acquired in your life, lessons, and experiences. These experiences will help validate and provide evidential messages in communication. To keep these messages up to date, it is important to add new information and experiences. Learn something new to add to your conscious learning and creativity each day.

Become aware of your surroundings and the people around you. I find it helpful to journal my impressions. The greater your conscious awareness, the more Spirit will have access to information, which will enhance your communication.

To be a medium is a calling that taps into your psychic channels. And to be aware that you are a being of light, through your Divinity and your higher consciousness working together, always working in the light. If you choose to answer the call to mediumship, you may learn and grow using the light, and allowing your gifts of transmission to connect ultimately with spirits past.

Tap into your psychic channels, and learn different avenues to connect:

You may choose to focus on one or more of the main methods of connections. There is Clairsentience, the ability to acquire psychic knowledge through feelings -- learning to honour your feelings. Clairaudience, hearing what is inaudible -- paying attention to what you hear in your mind -- as well as with your ears.

To enhance your Clairvoyant ability – the ability to see things visually in your mind's eye or even as a visual energy pattern -- you may consider meditating with Lapis Lazuli, a blue crystal that assists in enhancing psychic vision. As your Clairvoyance evolves, you will notice your ability to perceive in a different form, beyond the ordinary, in mental images, dreams, and auras.

To enhance your Claircognizance ability – the ability to simply know something in your mind -- you may consider meditating with Clear Quartz, a transparent crystal that assists in clearing your thoughts and concepts, promoting positive, loving, and helpful ideas and thought patterns.

You can also strengthen your connection to Spirit through learning about the Chakra System. Both psychic and medium emanations are received and transmitted through auric energy, which in turn can access the specific chakras that are associated with the 'claires'. Everything is made up of energy, which constantly moves and vibrates. Seven primary colours – red, orange, yellow, green, sky blue, indigo, and white are associated with our chakra system. The chakras and their corresponding colours help with symbolism, creativity, imagination, aura work and our chosen method of connection to Spirit energy. Colours around a Spirit, can help identify aspects of a personality.

Once you begin to recognize these different avenues of connection, practice with them. Sit and listen to yourself. Look closely at what is around you, notice small details, ordinary or not, practice seeing colours, lights, thoughts, and about how small details make you feel or react. Journal your new reactions, what was ordinary now becomes extraordinary.

THE IMPORTANCE OF PRAYER

Connecting with your higher Divinity, your source of light, is crucial with any psychic or medium work. Make it routine. It is vital for aiding in healing, for your mediumship to be in the highest good for all. Prayer confirms love and support in our practice and in our lives. Prayer brings communion when we open our hearts to a power greater than ours alone. Prayer is important in preparation, and it is powerful and proven to create a loving respectful link to Spirit.

Pray with gratitude, in time of need, but also for peace, or prayer to say hello and develop relations with Divinity. Pray to protect, but to also understand. Simply speak from your heart to the Divine source. Faith is the key, know you are heard and always loved. Creating Sacred Space is simply a way to hold the energy of Spirit with honour, love, and grace. Call in light to enhance your meditation as well as psychic abilities, and to bring you to a safe place for your mediumship practice. You can burn sage, light candles, play music, spray infused waters, use crystal bowls, or hold a crystal, all to bring in light through Spirit. Before you start working with Spirit, find your sacred routine, or elements that bring the light body to your work. Create a loving, inviting environment for spiritual connections and communication. Use flowers, spiritual icons, spiritual images, burn incense, again all to enhance your spiritual space.

Work regularly in the space you created, it will become infused with spiritual energy. The most important part of creating this space is to always bring loving intentions. Breathe in love and Spirit for a clear loving intention between you and the Spirit World. Always share thanks and gratitude to Spirit for hearing and honouring intentions.

Pay attention to what is around you – like the colours, how they make you feel, and what energy centre on your body they affect. For example, green reminds me of the outdoors, peace, Christmas, and the heart.

Practice seeing and breathing in colour, let the rich spectrum of colour fill your body with spirit. Mediums use their right side of their brain to achieve altered states. This is where communication takes place. Building a mediumship practice takes time. Find your soul community and work with them.

Share your love of Spirit. Each day, gracefully allowing Spirit to enter and fill you with light, love, and laughter. Have fun with learning, stay light-hearted, be open with yourself about your own truths and help those that are searching for their truths. Spirit only brings us what we can handle and grow from.

Blessed be your work,

Elizabeth

magic of love

Intuitive Games to Open Your Heart!

By Sharon McArthur

"Magic is believing in yourself,
if you can do that,
you can make anything happen!"
– J.W. Van Goethe

Do you believe in love and magic? Oh, the power of believing...

Magic is defined as the power to make impossible things happen by saying mystical words or doing special actions. It is a special, attractive, or exciting quality. Magic is a mysterious quality of enchantment a feeling of great pleasure, delight, captivated, to produce, alter or cause by or as if by magic. Magic and magical can also be used to say that something is wonderful and exciting.

Your magic resides in your heart and when it is in a state of loving resonance and aligned with your mind, your body and your Spirit, it is like medicine. You feel better, more relaxed, more joyful, and better able to handle stresses that come up with ease and mindfulness.

Modern science is coming to the same conclusions as our wise ancestors. That is, your heart holds the magical key to your happiness, your health, and your ability to create thriving relationships and meaningful work.

It is okay to live a life that others do not understand, and those who do not believe in Magic may never find it.

"Real Magic is not about gaining power over others:
It is about gaining power over yourself."
– Rosemary Guily

Eckhart Tolle teaches, *"No matter how long your journey appears to be, there is never more than this: one step, one breath, one moment – NOW!"*

I have been helped along my journey as I began accessing all kinds of Love healing and the many modalities. Love healing presented itself in a multitude of ways such as, bodywork, angel therapy, colour and light therapy, energy work and dance. I began to ask myself "What am I attracting here?" "Who's attracting Who? Or What is attracting What?" I felt as if I had been simply guided by energies that govern my Spirit and well being.

This time in my life opened me up to all kinds of new experiences, expansion and things I did not even believe in or had not known about before. I have gained a peaceful Spirit; I trust, surrender and remember I'm here for growth and love.

It left me with expanded awareness and a deep, deep knowing that my mother is with me in Spirit, hears me and loves me even more than ever!

One day, I chose to experience a psychic intuitive reading. I was blown away when my Mom came through in a session with information only I could know; beyond a shadow of a doubt. It was Magic! It completely resonated with me. What a blessing and an unexpected gift; it changed my life forever.

Having had such a profound experience left me with a deep, deep knowing that my Mom is with me in Spirit. She still hears me and loves me dearly. Thank you, Mom, for your light and love.

What we love, once enjoyed, we never lose. All that we deeply love become a part of Us.

And get this – since that day, my heart has grown back even bigger and better than before! Emotionally, spiritually and yes, …physically.

I had a heart murmur for over thirty-three years. As I was growing and healing with the pain and finally the joy of my mother's love, my daughter turned thirty-three and 'magically' I no longer have that hole in my heart. It has healed miraculously. I asked my Doctor "where did it go?" But she could not explain it? Crazy right? Woo hoo!

And THAT, my friend, is the MAGIC of LOVE.

WHAT IS LOVE?

Love is the highest energy vibration. Rumi wrote: *"We are born of Love. Love is our Mother."*

L.O.V.E.

L living
O one
V vibrational
E energy

"Love is the river of life in the world." – H.W. Beecher

WHAT IS MAGIC?

Seek magic every day! Embrace your beliefs and turn them into positive actions every day. Dion Fortune stated that *"Magic is the art of changing consciousness at Will."*

M.A.G.I.C.

M mastery
A attention
G gratitude
I intuition
C connection

"Magic is not a practice. It is a living, breathing web of energy that, with our permission, can encase our every action."
– Dorothy Morrison

FINDING MAGIC IN LOVE

I would like to share with you my personal story of love and magic.

My mother was truly my first love, and she loved me unconditionally. With her passing, her physical death at age eighty-six. I experienced the greatest loss of Love in my life.

My heart was broken. I cried an ocean and was at my lowest low. I just couldn't catch my breath. I had lost the sunshine. I remember asking my Mom to come down from heaven and kiss me when I was sleeping each night. It was a long and painful journey from deep sorrow and lost Love. As the Beatles song laments, *"It was a long and winding road."*

"Yes, science helps us to prove facts, yet Intuition guides us to discoveries." ~ Paulo Coelho

Thank-you! Mom, I will always be with you! For as many years as the grass grows, the sun shines and the rivers flow. I can feel you now and I can't wait to dance with you again. You are my sunshine; I love you forever and for always. Keep shining, sparkle, sparkle on.

Knowing that my Mom's love lives on in my heart, and learning so much about the unseen world, and being open wide to allowing the possibility of some pretty wild stuff, I have come to realize that gratitude and happiness go hand in hand, just like Magic and Love.

Thank you Universe, Mother, Father, Goddess, God!

magical games
For Spiritual Expansion

You and I already hold the power of magic within us, for we are made up of stardust, pieces of the Universe and limitless possibilities.

When your soul nature is balanced and harmonious with joy, you will be at peace and feel connected to all of life. Remember, what we think we create, what we feel we attract, what we imagine we become.

Is love a feeling or a choice?

Is magic a feeling or a choice?

Is gratitude a feeling or a choice?

Is kindness a feeling or a choice?

THE WONDER GAME 'AKA' THE FREE GAME

Can be played daily

STEP 1: Ask the Universe; "I wonder what I will get for free today?… wonder, wonder, magic, magic". Then let wonder and magic have a turn.

STEP 2: See what shows up. It might be cash, a coffee, or a gift. It may be something as lovely as a smile from someone, loving-kindness, a door held open, a feather or a flower. It's always a mystery as you watch to see what shows up.

STEP 3: No matter how big or small your 'free wonder' is, acknowledge it as 'profound'. Recognizing it helps set the stage for the next time you play!

STEP 4: Once received, give thanks, drop deeply into the attitude of gratitude.

'I AM THE QUEEN OF GRATITUDE' PROJECT

Oh, the POWER of gratitude. It's incredibly strong. This is a simple game with loads of benefits… so it's much more than a game; it's a way to improve your life.

End and start your day with what you are grateful for.

When you climb into bed and are ready for sleep, think about all the people, places, things, and situations that you are grateful for today. You can keep a journal, or mentally scroll through the events and faces of your day to FEEL the gratitude warm your heart.

In the morning, as you become wakeful, FEEL into the gratitude of a new day. Journal or mentally note your feelings of gratitude as you look forward to the infinite possibilities brought by a fresh start.

There is a multitude of proven benefits of gratitude. Not only can it improve your physical and psychological health, it makes you generally a happier person.

Gratitude is the acknowledgement of kindness with thanks, (from the Latin word gratus). Studies have shown, those who cultivate gratitude find tokens of appreciation every day, on their own.

Gratitude works like magic. It instantly changes from negative thinking to a positive mindset.

Gratitude makes you feel more gratitude; it expands and grows. Gratitude creates GOOD feelings and makes you more joyful.

Cultivating gratitude is a skill that takes mindful practice to produce a lifetime of happiness.

We have the choice to develop our attitude. Attitude means our nature, opinion, and perspective, towards things and people. Gratitude is an attitude of gratefulness, thankfulness, appreciation and acknowledgement.

Let's seek it and express it. Through this personal gratitude connection, you can aim to improve your circumstances and well being, and the well being of others by sending them positive energy and healing.

Benefits at a glance: The science of gratitude is correlated with vitality and energy, physical, emotional and mental well being.

1. **Health:** Increased energy, improved sleep.

2. **Emotional:** More relaxed, more good feelings, more resilient.

3. **Personality:** Optimistic outlook, increased self-esteem.

According to gratitude researcher Robert Emmon's, Gratitude is just happiness that we recognize after the fact, that may have been caused by the kindness of others. Gratitude does not make us happier, it is happiness in and of itself.

Happiness is a choice. Happiness is not something that you get in life. Happiness is something you bring to life. Cultivating your attitude of gratitude is a tool to create personal happiness. Enjoy!

"There is no path to happiness, happiness is the path.
The way is not in the sky, the way is in the heart."
– Buddha

THE 'I AM' AFFIRMATION GAME

The words we choose can have a profoundly empowering effect on our lives. Any words (good or bad) that come immediately after "I am" has a powerful impact beyond measure.

How to play the 'I am' game:

Say "I am", either out loud or in your mind. Then add a word that describes the things that are gloriously wonderful about yourself. This is great for improving your self-worth, self-image and self-confidence. Look for fun ideas about you that may be lost from childhood and bring them back for extra joy.

I am healthy. I am happy. I am loved. I am abundant. I am creative. I am grateful. I am going on and on. I AM THAT I AM. Healthy I am. Happy I am. Loved I am. Abundant I am. Creative I am. Grateful I am.

Get specific and descriptive with your personal qualities: I am good at 'this' or 'that'. I am a conscientious pet owner. I am a considerate son. I am lookin' good. I am a good shoulder to cry on. I am physically capable. I am learning life lessons with grace. I am getting good at this game.

I could go on all day.

THE SELF-LOVE GAME

This game can make me cry or laugh. Self-love was not something I was taught growing up. The source of love is within you. The key insight is that love begins from loving oneself.

Silently or out loud, begin by saying "I love my ___ and my___ loves me".

I always start with my heart and say. "I Love my heart and my heart loves me." Then I move on, "I love my eyes and my eyes love me". At times I break it down further, "I love my ears for all I can hear. I love my throat for allowing me to sing and speak. I love my legs that carry me when I walk".

You can do a scan throughout your entire body if you choose, or you can ask to be aligned with your highest potential and greatest source of happiness by starting a conscious conversation with your body via your chakras or the living energy you can feel in your physical self.

TRY doing this, in the mirror looking into your eyes and repeating the words. I love you! I really do!

RIDE THE LOVE WAVE GAME

Your beautiful and kind vibes can create a positive tsunami-sized impact. Set your vibe of the day into motion and gently create a ripple effect. It's fun to watch the effect you can have at work, in your home and amongst strangers during your daily rounds as others inadvertently ride your wave.

I often ask myself, "What energy am I spreading?" If it's true (and it seems that it is true) that everything is energy, and energy is everything, then can it be contagious? In this game, choose a type of positive energy you'd like to 'spread'. Maybe it's kindness, joy or peace. There is also huge power in kindness, generosity (the act of giving), being happy, soft and open, and of course, the expression of gratitude. LOVE is my go-to vibe, and I find great delight in watching it work its magic on others.

During your day, keep your eyes and ears tuned in for an opportunity to spread your vibe of the day. Be gentle in your energy, not pushy; it could be your smile, a kind word, or maybe you just send the vibe in your mind without saying a thing. Play with this game and find your own way to work the magic, even humming a tune can change the energy in a room. The Beatles had it right, "All You Need Is Love", is my happy song.

Responding kindly and gratefully to a situation helps you be more resilient, more flexible, happier and healthier. This has a ripple effect on the person who is giving, the person who is receiving, and remarkably, the people who are witnessing. You always have a choice with how you act in the present moment and everyone benefits from expressions of kindness, gratitude and good vibes.

I believe love is infinite and love is everywhere. My favourite Mantra is: I Give love, I Live Love, I Am Love.

"The greatest thing you'll ever learn is just to love and be loved in return."- Eden Ahbez

FIVE GOOD THINGS

A quick switch from feeling grumpy to good.

Not your day? Things are a bit off? Nothing seems to go right?

Try this quick and effective exercise: Write down five things you are happy about. Feel it. Recognize why they make you happy. Just remembering five good things, can change your outlook and help you feel a little lighter. Sometimes the magic is an energetic shift that might even help solve your current struggle!

LOVING KINDNESS or METTA MEDITATION

LOVING OURSELVES FIRST- Rejoicing in our own goodness fills us with joy and love for ourselves and a great deal of self-respect. By first practising Metta towards yourself you are building the essential foundation for being able to offer genuine love to others. Contemplating the goodness within yourself is a classical meditation, done to bring light, joy and rapture to the mind.

Joy has so much capacity to eliminate separation that the Buddha said, "Rapture is the gateway to Nirvana".

Imagine you are in the middle of a circle of light, a protective eggshell, or the safe and protected image of your choice, and begin with self-contemplation.

Reflect on the good things you have done such as recollecting a time when you have been generous or times you have been caring. Perhaps you can think of a time when it would have been easy to hurt somebody, or tell a lie, or to be dismissive, yet you made the effort not to do that. Perhaps you can think of a time when you overcame some fear, reached out to someone, or dared to change and give something up that freed you.

Once you feel appreciation for yourself repeat the Metta in your mind three times. Loving Kindness - Metta *"May I be at Peace"*.

IT'S A WRAP!

So I ask, "Is your future written in Stone or Pencil... What do you BELIEVE?"

Have fun exploring your beliefs (Belief = accept something as true). Can you accept being One with the earth, the sky, the cosmos, and All that Is living one vibrational energy? Perhaps this is what our wise ancestors knew.

Don't forget to also thank yourself for everything you do for yourself and others. Remember that the greatest magic and miracle is your life and the lives of your loved ones.

So YES I believe in Magic... MAGIC IS LOVE!!!

Spreading Love and sharing JOY!

J just

O one

Y you

Namaste, blessed be, Om Shanti Shanti Shanti,

Magical Sharon

PART TWO

Personal Growth & Holistic Healing

The Frequency of forgiveness

By Sadhana

"To forgive is to set a prisoner free and discover that the prisoner was you." – Lewis B. Smedes

FORGIVE AND FORGET, ARE YOU KIDDING ME?

The idea of releasing negative thoughts, emotions or experiences can be terrifying. The longer you have held onto these feelings, the greater likelihood that you not only identify with them, but you may also actually believe that they are you. Imagine forgiving a partner for betrayal, a close friend for deceit or a parent for sexual abuse. Similarly, what would it feel like to forgive yourself for being gullible, naïve, violent or anything less than honest? In this chapter, I will share with you my personal experience in letting go of a painful past and give you the tools to begin the process yourself.

The process of letting go has nothing to do with condoning the action or inaction of yourself or others. It is a process of releasing the power the memory has over you, so you can find freedom and ultimately, peace. I use the word action to refer to any emotional, mental, spiritual or physical action or inaction that created a negative memory or pattern in your life. These memories are usually so deeply etched in the core of our beings that frequently we don't know they are there until we are triggered.

I'm certain that you can think of a time when something happened that set you off swearing, yelling, crying or sweating. It could have been as innocuous as someone cutting you off in traffic, an old song playing on the radio or a child spilling a glass of juice. As the emotion made its way to the surface you may have paused and wondered why you reacted the way you did, or maybe you automatically reached for your favourite security blanket: denial, cookies, vodka, the gym, violence – anything to numb the pain. Chances are you weren't even aware of what was triggered, you were just aware that you needed your blanket.

I want to reassure you that the practices I offer in this chapter are not about dredging up the past – their intention is to help lessen the effects of the triggers and move forward freer, cleaner and lighter. If you are not aware of what is at the root of your reactions, practices of forgiveness will begin to gently nudge their way up against the stored memories and bring them closer to the surface where you may choose to access them or not. If you are aware of what sets you off, then you are one step closer to finding your freedom.

Forgiveness practices are one of many ways to release energy. It is never an easy journey, but if you have the courage to practice regularly, I promise that you will come out the other side transformed – and feeling much lighter! And to address the proverbial elephant in the room, WHY! Why in the world would I want to forgive? Can you still hear yourself shaking as you said, "I will never forgive you for this!" You want to forgive because the toxic energy of those words and every associated negative emotion lingers in both your energetic body as well as your physical body. Memories, whether they be negative or positive, conscious or subconscious, are stored in the body on a cellular level. Each memory resonates at a different frequency and is stored in a part of the body that matches the frequency of the emotion associated with the experience. For example, heartache is stored in the lungs, heart, and breasts. Lies and secrets are stored in the throat, thyroid, and parathyroid. Accordingly, there is potential for disease to manifest in these organs if the emotions are not released. However, these simplified examples are meant to encourage the desire to enter into forgiveness, not illustrate how emotional trauma manifests as disease.

As with anyone's patterns, mine are layered in story and remained subconscious for most of my life. Some of you may recognize them as your own patterns as our stories are universal. For me, the unwinding process began about 16 years ago in a marriage counseling session. As a mother of three young children at that time, I found it hard to justify both the time and the money spent endlessly talking, crying and making little progress. While I was able to identify issues quite early on, traditional counseling did not offer practical steps in moving forward. I needed to find a different approach if I were to find healing and grace. Perhaps subconsciously, knowing the methodology wasn't working for me, I abandoned psycho-therapy and jumped feet first into the waters of yoga, shamanism and every kind of mysticism I could get my hands on.

All the practices suggested in this chapter are about moving and releasing stored energy so that your physical, mental and emotional bodies can become clearer, cleaner and freer. My experience with "talk therapy" is that an inordinate amount of energy (words, thoughts, emotions) is repetitively put into the pain/experience/story and the process has the potential to amplify the perception of victimization and increase the degree of reactionary impulses, rather than release it.

Being in your pain and feeling what arises when you recall an experience is an important part of healing. There comes a point however, when you are ready to begin releasing and having a few tools in your belt can be of tremendous relief at that time. Understanding that you are not your pain and that you have the power to let it go is a huge realization. Perhaps, in talk-therapy, you can eventually arrive at the point of letting go, but for me, that was not the experience. I needed a different approach. There are many paths to realizing your wholeness, what I offer here are practices that worked for me and have worked for many clients. My prayer for you is that eventually, you learn to live in a place of greater equilibrium between pain and pleasure. Ultimately, that is where peace and freedom are found and that is the purpose of the practices offered in the second part of this chapter.

When I began to peel away the layers and see my stories from the perspective and wisdom of ancient teachings, I slowly began to understand what needed to be done. There were many actions that I needed to forgive myself and others. One transformative experience happened during a shamanic training course where we were asked to go back to the time of conception and explore some personal and difficult questions to better understand the root of current and on-going issues. We were asked to research the circumstances and emotions surrounding the time we were in the womb, our birth experience itself and the early weeks of life.

Over the years, through many visits, phone calls and courageous questions, I have pieced together parts or versions of the story of my conception and birth. After high school, my mother went to the Canadian Armed Forces basic training in Ontario where she met my biological father - a handsome young man whom she dated a few times. I was conceived on a weekend sojourn to Montreal on a cold, winter night. Shortly after, unable to finance further training and unaware of her condition, my mother returned home to her small, close-knit hometown in Saskatchewan.

My mother told me that it was her father who recognized the symptoms of pregnancy and began to make plans for what was then considered an illegitimate baby she was carrying. Even though an aunt and uncle had offered to raise me, so I could remain in the same town, my grandfather would have nothing to do with it. My mother was under the strict authority of a powerful patriarch. Her mother (my birth grandmother) was living in another town and perhaps, had there been communication with her, circumstances may have been different.

My mother was escorted to a home for unwed mothers in Vancouver, British Columbia where she lived for a few months until my birth. She kept mainly to herself at the maternity home except for mealtimes or when she was doing chores with other girls. She chose not to contact my biological father as she presumed that he would not have wanted a long-term relationship. I was living in a womb of loneliness, despair, confusion, pain, and guilt. Perhaps an even stronger ripple that was being created was one of lack of power or free will.

I was placed with my adoptive parents soon after my birth and grew up in a loving family. My parents were always open about the fact I was adopted. My younger brother was also adopted as were other neighbourhood children. I never questioned my adoptive parents love for me, nor did I consider the young mother who gave me up for adoption. It never occurred to me that there may be issues or unresolved emotion surrounding being an adopted child. Sadly, my adoptive father died when I was thirteen. His departure from our family left an indelible mark on the three of us. Upon his death, what was triggered in my brother and mother was so powerful that it shifted my course for the next several decades.

If a glimpse of abandonment rose to the surface, I did not see it. Instead, I focused on caring for the other two people in my life. A caretaker pattern burst forth that grew like jungle vines on steroids. If you have seen the first Harry Potter movie, you may remember the scene where Harry, Hermione, and Ron fall through a trap door and find themselves tangled in a vine called "devil's snare". Hermione soon realizes that if one relaxes and eases into the vines that one will be released. However, the more one struggles, the more one is entangled and potentially strangled. Looking back, I wish I had had the foresight to be in my own pain, to lean into it and accept it. Instead, I reacted and became entangled in my own vine of emotional drama. In short, my reaction to my brother and mother's inability to cope with my father's loss was to fix everything – or at least try to.

I took on the role of confidante, cook, housekeeper, counselor, mediator, and parent at thirteen years old. It was exhausting and suffocating. For years, I masked my pain in perfectionism, excelling at school, in sports and leadership roles. And in my sorrow and desperate need never to be abandoned again, I also made friends with kids who smoked and partied. At the time, however, I was not aware of why I made the choices I did, other than it kept me away from home. These patterns that developed early on, laid the groundwork for unhealthy relationships, excessive caretaking and a need to remain in control.

I had no idea when I began my journey with yoga about sixteen years ago that anything was wrong, nor that the unraveling process was going to be life-altering. I took to yoga like a dog to a bone. I devoured my classes. I listened intently to the cues for physical postures, ruminated on the sounds of chants and found breath practices took me to a home that I had never known. As my practice began to grow and I found ease in my body and Spirit, I began to notice shifts in my life. It was around this time that my clairvoyance skyrocketed, and my third child started having spiritual experiences.

Unraveling the Patterns

One of the emotions that surfaced in marriage counseling many years ago was that I just wanted to be looked after. I no longer wanted to be brave and strong. I wanted to be held, protected and cared for. I (thought that I) needed a husband who was present and attentive, whose arms I could curl up into at the end of the day. However, finding myself in a marriage where I was responsible for so many and so much had become overwhelming. I was so caught up in caretaking for my family, friends, and community that I was not able to see the trees for the forest. If fear of abandonment was lurking, it was deeply buried in my subconscious.

The divine has a way of continually presenting obstacles or putting us in situations until we finally realize that we are in a pattern and something has to change. Yoga was my saviour. I was fortunate to be introduced to teachings and practices from many traditions. I resonated deeply with the practices and it unexpectedly awakened unfamiliar, yet wonderful feelings.

The process of letting go was guided by marvelous teachers. They presented themselves as I was ready and each, in their own way, took me to new levels of understanding. I met shamans and lightworkers from many countries and disciplines. The more I studied and the more I practiced, the clearer and braver I became.

I saw my stories from a different perspective. I became a witness to my life. Suddenly life was happening for me, not to me. I revisited many relationships and events in my past and began to forgive myself and others. I remained deeply committed to healing practices for months at a time. If, however, I lost perspective and was sucked back into old patterns, the Universe manifested some pretty harsh and direct situations to get me back on track. One of those happened the day my grandmother died. (I mention here that it was my adoptive father's mother because there were still unresolved issues regarding my adoptive father's departure 30 years earlier.)

It was the day of an important figure skating competition for my eldest daughter. In utter disbelief that no other family member could deal with the situation at the nursing home and that my grandmother's room needed to be cleared out by the end of the day or everything would be disposed of, I left my daughter at the skating rink in the care of her coach and other skating parents . When I arrived at the nursing home, I was informed that the funeral home had not picked up my grandmother's body. The supervisor asked if I would be able to come back later. Not really comprehending why or what was going on after being summoned and delivered what seemed like an ultimatum, I explained that I needed to attend to the task at hand. I was confused, shaking and exhausted. With my newborn asleep in her pram, I entered my grandmother's room and spent some time sitting with her dead body.

I was surprised how little my grandmother seemed in the body bag. Even though she was just over five feet tall, her personality was larger than life. The room was icy cold. Every conversation I hadn't had with my grandmother flooded my mind and I saw each of them as a missed opportunity to understand who I was and how my story had unfolded the way it did. There was much to forgive. In the process of emptying drawers and clearing out her belongings, I felt an ethereal presence comforting and guiding me. At the same time, I was cognizant of her cold body lying behind me. I was bitter and angry. This was not the first grandparent or great-uncle whose care had consumed me.

That day I began to weed out my collection of self-imposed responsibilities and truly look at what a mess of busyness my life had become. I vowed to be more authentic in my relationships, to stop pleasing people and to simplify my life. I was not at a point where I truly understood my patterns, but I did recognize that the unraveling of "roles" would become part of my healing.

Each of the masters I studied with shared the same message: our stories are not who we are. Our stories are the accumulated human experiences in which we have chosen to participate to advance on a soul level. While that statement might not sit comfortably or be beyond the scope of this chapter, it is an important piece to start to digest. We are spiritual beings living a human experience – and a chosen one at that!

Let go of the Stories

Through the exercises and practices that follow, I hope that you will begin to see and feel the beauty of the frequency of forgiveness. It is magic medicine. All the stories and their associated memories and emotions, conscious or unconscious, are a part of you. You have a choice to hold onto them or to let them go. In letting them go, you will remove the power the memories have over you and you will begin to feel lighter and healthier. And – the beauty of these practices is that you don't have to understand "why" anything has happened. Know that it is the ego, not your soul who wants to know "why". Eventually, in this lifetime or another, on this plane or another, you may understand "why", but at this particular moment, it doesn't matter.

The frequency of forgiveness is one of the frequencies of healing. It is a gift from the divine much like prayer, sacred music or gratitude. It resonates at such a high frequency that it has the power to heal the human body, relationships, and community. Ancient teachings from many parts of the world acknowledge that healing work does not only affect the one doing the work, but also has the potential to heal many generations in all directions of time. Let us begin.

Practices of Forgiveness

Find a spiral bound notebook or one with pages that are easy to tear out – one with not too much ink on the paper so if and when you choose to burn pages, they burn cleanly. This is your Forgiveness Journal and is going to be your companion over the next few months and maybe even years as you work through the process of detaching yourself from your stories and begin to see the world and your life from a much wider perspective.

FINDING FORGIVENESS IN YOUR BREATH

As in every yoga class, meditation and reading I offer or receive, it begins with the breath. With your journal and pen close at hand, find a comfortable and quiet place to sit or lie down. Support your body with blankets and cushions and make sure that you are warm. If you like, set a timer for five minutes. Subsequent days you may try eight or ten minutes or longer. You may wish to record your voice reading the following passage pausing where it feels natural to create space through silence:.

Take a few moments to adjust your body so that you are completely comfortable. Feel your body begin to settle and close your eyes if you have not already done so. Become aware of your breath. Observe the next few inhales and exhales. Now take your attention to the breath in the chest. Become aware of your lungs, your heart, the whole ribcage. Breathe in and out of the front ribs, the back ribs, the right side, the left side. Be aware of the whole ribcage and notice any parts that move more easily than others. Just follow your breath in and out.

Become aware of the exhale breath. Follow the exhale all the way to the end. Surrender into each exhalation. Lean into its softness, knowing that with each exhalation is an opportunity to let go, to release, to surrender. If it feels right, find a word, an emotion, a name or even an object and repeat it softly or silently with your exhale breath. Exhale what no longer serves you. Create space by letting go. Simply follow the breath or your word. Be aware of eleven more conscious breath cycles.

Release your word. Release the awareness of the exhalation and return to your natural breath. Gently move your fingers and toes and slowly transition to wakefulness. Take as much time as you need.

JOURNAL PROMPTS:

- How did the breath feel in your chest?
- Was it as easy to move the front ribs as the back? Left side? Right side?
- Was any part of the rib cage not moving at all?
- Did keeping awareness in the chest area stir anything up?
- What words, thoughts or emotions arose?
- How did it feel to exhale that word?
- If you feel compelled, make a list of all the 'words' you would like to exhale.

Energetically, focusing on the exhale breath will help to release negative e-motions (energy in motion) creating a sense of spaciousness in your mind, heart, and life. Repeat this practice often for maximum benefit.

FORGIVENESS IN THE PHYSICAL BODY

The next practice is a guided meditation around the body. As you move your awareness from body part to body part, you may feel sensations of warmth, coolness, a shudder or twinge. Know that these are energetic releases. You may also experience the need to cough, sneeze, pass gas or yawn. These also are the body's way to release what it no longer needs. Emotion is stored in the physical body, so it follows that if we focus our mind on a body part that is fatigued, sore or injured, emotion or memory may arise. My experience working with many students is that this practice works at a subconscious level and it is not common to be aware of what is being released. You may be aware of the physical manifestation of the release, but not the emotion or pattern attached to it.

The beauty of this practice is that you just follow the guided meditation around the body and let the mystery unfold. Whether you are aware of any injuries or ailments, it doesn't matter, the energy will work its magic as it is needed and as you are ready. This practice feels wonderful and you may even fall asleep the first ten times you try it. That is okay. Eventually, you will stay awake and begin to explore the practice on a deeper level being aware of sensations and energy moving through your body.

Like the previous practice, you may wish to record the following script in your own voice and then follow along with the recording. You may need to record it a couple of times to get the pauses and pace just right. When you get to the body parts, keep the pace steady. Are you ready to let go? Lie down on the floor, grass or a sofa (a bed is not recommended as you will likely fall asleep). You may need a cushion under your knees to provide comfort for your low back. It is also a good idea to cover up with a blanket as your body temperature will likely drop during the guided meditation. Begin:

As your body begins to settle, take time to make any adjustments necessary so that you can remain still and comfortable throughout the recording. Press into the back of your arms and tuck your shoulder blades under a little. If your low back is bothering you, raise your hips off the floor and shift your pelvis forward. This will lengthen your lower back. Then settle back down to the earth . Bring awareness to your breath and take a few deep inhales and exhales. Be aware of what is beneath you, what is over you. Close your eyes if you have not already done so. Give yourself permission to let go and soften into the earth below your body.

Be aware of the air, the temperature of the air on any exposed skin, the warmth of your clothing or blanket. Breathe in and breath out. Say to yourself, "I will stay awake and aware." Become aware of sounds – sounds all around you. Scan from sound to sound not remaining on any one sound for too long. Find the furthest sound you can hear. Bring your awareness closer and listen to sounds near you. Come even closer and listen to the sound of your own breath or other sounds of the body.

Know that every instruction is an invitation. Allow your heart to be your guide. Silently repeat the following intention three times: I am releasing stored emotion from my body. I invite healing and freedom into my life.

Beginning the rotation of consciousness around the body: As each body part is named, take your attention there. Either internally repeat its name, picture it in your mind or just touch it with your awareness. The body remains still throughout. Take your attention to the right hand. Right hand thumb, index finger, middle finger, ring finger, little finger, palm, back of the hand, wrist, lower arm, elbow, upper arm, shoulder, underarm, right side of the torso, hip, upper leg, knee, lower leg, ankle, top of the foot, instep, bottom of the foot, right big toe, second toe, third, fourth and fifth.

Move to the left hand. Left-hand thumb, index finger, middle finger, ring finger, little finger, palm, back of the hand, wrist, lower arm, elbow, upper arm, shoulder, underarm, left side of the torso, hip, upper leg, knee, lower leg, ankle, top of the foot, instep, bottom of the foot, left big toe, second toe, third, fourth and fifth.

Stay with the practice and move to the top of the head. Forehead, right temple, left temple, right ear left ear, right eyebrow, left eyebrow, eyebrow centre, right eye, left eye, bridge of the nose, tip of the nose, right nostril, left nostril, right cheek, left cheek, upper lip, lower lip, teeth, tongue, jaw, right collar bone, left collar bone, the hollow between, right side of the chest, left side of the chest, heart centre, upper abdomen, navel centre, lower abdomen, pelvis.

Move to the back. Right buttock, left buttock, small of the back, middle of the back, right shoulder blade, left shoulder blade, upper back, spine. Feel the spine from the tailbone to the back of the neck. Back of the head, top of the head.

Be aware of the right leg, left leg, right arm, left arm, both legs, both arms, the whole front, the whole back, the whole body, the whole body, the whole body.

Once again you are invited to repeat the following intention 3x: I am releasing stored emotion from my body. I invite healing and freedom into my life.

Feel your body connected to the earth below. Become aware of your surroundings. Remember the room, the details of the room. Become aware of sounds. Take a few deep breaths. Begin to move your fingers and toes. When you are ready take a full body stretch and slowly transition back to your seat. Move slowly. When you are ready… open your eyes.

JOURNAL PROMPTS:

- Were you able to remain awake and aware?
- Do you recall where you drifted off?
- Did you feel any unexpected sensations?
- How would you describe them?
- How did the intention feel in your body? Describe it.

This practice is part of a more comprehensive yogic practice that can be customized to work toward healing specific physical, emotional, mental or spiritual issues or concerns. It is a simple, yet powerful practice that can be done anywhere. With a little practice, you will be able to guide yourself into deep, peaceful relaxation and explore the subtleties of the body/mind connection.

"The weak can never forgive.
Forgiveness is the attribute of the strong." - Mahatma Gandhi

Forgiveness and the Full Moon

When the sun illuminates the moon to its fullest shape, deep and dark emotions can creep their way to the surface. This mysterious monthly phenomenon can be used to its advantage by entering into a practice of forgiveness. Often what is illuminated has been lurking in the shadows for some time and can be challenging to face. During this time, the ocean's tides are amplified, and this too is mirrored in our physical bodies giving rise to unpredictable emotion.

The practice is to work with moon energy – to use it advantageously to clear patterns of long-held resentment, regret and pain. On a fresh page in your journal (one that you can remove), write your name at the top. On subsequent pages, write the name of others who come to mind. Then begin to write. Write without thinking, without editing. Just write and write and let it all come spilling out. On the page with your name, write what you forgive yourself for.

I forgive myself for saying: I forgive myself for never saying: I forgive myself for all the times I . . . I forgive myself for all the times I never . . .

I forgive myself for thinking: I forgive myself for wishing: I forgive myself for feeling: I forgive myself for being:

On the pages with the names of others, write what you forgive each of them for.

In the few days leading up to the full moon, you will begin to feel the pull of her energy. Work with her energy as you write. There is no limit to what might pour out of you if you can give yourself permission to release. Once you are complete for this month, on the night of the full moon or the day after, remove your pages from your journal. Bring some matches or a lighter and head to the beach, a clearing in the forest, your backyard or kitchen sink. Be as elaborate or simple as you like with your fire ceremony. Under the luminosity of the full moon, burn your pages. Offer the emotions to the divine, back to the Universe so that you no longer carry these burdens. Gift yourself this freedom and enjoy the spaciousness it creates.

This is a practice that you can do every month. If you are not aware of the moon cycles, one of the easiest ways to follow the moon is to download a moon app on your phone. Each month you may choose to focus on a theme or different aspect of your life, or you may need to repeat the same names and words a few months in a row.

A variation on this practice is to create a FORGIVENESS JAR. Cut up strips of paper and place them in a jar. Each time you are reminded of something you need to forgive yourself or another for, write it on a strip of paper. You can have this jar available as an on-going project. Perhaps have different jars for different people. Each month burn your strips of paper in a little ceremony under the full moon.

Ho'oponopono

The ancient Hawaiian practice of forgiveness called ho'oponopono consists of a few simple words that have the potential to create major shifts in every aspect of your well-being. Traditionally, this was done as a family or community ceremony to improve the energy of everyone affected by another's wrongdoing. In your effort to unwind painful memories, never forget that you are only one soul affected by the action. If shouting was involved, there were likely passersby who considered getting involved and will remember the experience. If the incident happened publicly, there may have been many witnesses affected or triggered by the action. The ego wants to make the stories and painful memories personal. Perhaps, you remember a time when you witnessed, heard or saw something that deeply affected you, though you were not directly involved. The web of life, the interconnectedness of each and every soul on this planet is real. This is one practice, that may move you closer to feeling its presence.

Ho'oponopono can be practiced by yourself facing a mirror, with a few strangers or acquaintances at a meeting, or with large groups of people. The reason for forgiveness does not need to be shared or spoken. Simply look into your own or another's eyes and repeat the words. You may feel the energy move. If tears arise, allow them to flow.

Please forgive me. I am sorry. I love you. Thank you.

You may wish to bring a past incident to mind and take a few breaths to consider all the people involved and how forgiveness could benefit others. Always remember, the work you do will touch others in ways you never expected. If it is possible to hold hands with another, as you gaze into each other's eyes, the energy and effects of the practice will be amplified. If that is not possible, you may wish to hold a photograph or a physical object symbolic of that memory. Then, wholeheartedly, slowly repeat the words: *Please forgive me. I am sorry. I love you. Thank you.*

Final Thoughts

The practices suggested in this chapter have been part of my life for many years. I once asked a teacher if it was possible to clear a karmic pattern in one lifetime. She paused, not wanting to disillusion me I suppose, and said that she didn't think so, but that great progress could be made. These patterns that we perpetuate throughout our lives have likely been repeated in different variations over lifetimes. Just keep doing the work and expanding your awareness and all will be well.

I also want to encourage you to be creative and adapt any of these practices to better suit your lifestyle. The most important thing is that you are doing them regularly. It is better to practice ten minutes every day or every other day than to practice for one hour for 30 days in a row and not again for another six months. Integrate these practices in a way that is manageable so that it is easy for you to do one or more of them.

These are subtle practices that will, over time, break down the scars from old wounds. They will physically, emotionally, mentally and spiritually lighten your sense of being. You will experience a shift in perspective. It will become easier to let things go and allow grace into your life.

The frequency of forgiveness is peace.

Working with Chakra

power

Excerpt from Oracle Workshop Curriculum

The seven major chakras relate directly to our physical (material) state, and our higher consciousness (spiritual). The subject of chakras is incredibly rich and complex. This section is an abridged version to pique your interest and give a basic understanding of this energetic network that can help improve your precious amazing life.

Chakra means 'wheel' in Sanskrit, so named because they appear spinning on a two-dimensional plane when viewed from the front. However, they are vortices of energy, more like tornados, located in the etheric body, whose function is to transmute energy into matter according to our desires, beliefs, and programming. Like the meridians in Chinese Medicine and acupuncture, chakras can't be seen with the naked eye. If someone has surgery, neither meridians nor chakras can be found; they are energetic channels and portals. Just as the earth has ley lines (paths of energy), the human body has a similar system (nadis), where energy flows throughout the body. The entry point being the chakras, and within each chakra lies the seat of our consciousness, psychic awareness, intuition and spiritual development. Each chakra is a doorway allowing energy to affect particular areas of our bodies, emotions, thoughts.

The seven major chakras are spaced from the base of spine to the crown of the head with their openings, like vortexes, towards the front of the body pulling energy from the opening and concentrating it along the spine. Here, energy (prana) is moved vertically by the nadis (Sanskrit for tube or pipe).

There are three primary nadis which run from the base of the spine to the head, connecting through the chakras. The Ida (feminie, receptive, creative) on the left, the Pingala (masculine, active, analytical) on the right and the Sushumna (grace, benevolence), in the centre. Hindu philosophy professes that clearing the flow of prana (energy) along the nadis and in the chakras lead to purity and liberation.

Simply put:

- The 1st or Root Chakra vibrates to red and is connected to survival, security, vitality, energy and passion.
- The 2nd or Sacral Chakra vibrates to orange, and is connected to creativity including procreation, also pleasure, the gratification of desire, the desire to connect.
- The 3rd or Solar Plexus Chakra vibrates to yellow, deals with will and willpower, interpersonal emotion, intrapersonal emotion, self-esteem.
- The 4th or Heart Chakra vibrates to green and is associated with love, compassion, altruism, and abundance. The heart centre.
- The 5th or Throat Chakra vibrates to light blue and deals with truth, communication, self-expression, choice, and the directing of one's will.
- The 6th or Third Eye Chakra vibrates to indigo, works with understanding, wisdom, intuition, perception of meaning, and spiritual perception.
- The 7th or Crown Chakra vibrates to violet and white, connects us to the divinity in each of us; the doorway to higher consciousness.

Thoughts, feelings and sensations we currently experience, and all memories from the past, are recorded and stored within our subtle body energy system. The chakras reflect the general state of our well-being physically and spiritually. They react to internal and external stimuli, fluctuating from day to day and from event to event, as we deal with each experience. The chakras activate and transform our emotional responses, the nadis, channel and transport, while the aura acts as a reservoir.

When one chakra is under-functioning (lack of energy) or over-functioning (excessive energy), the state of this chakra may affect the state of other chakras. This also holds true when one chakra is open, flowing and functioning well, it positively influences other chakras. Chakra balancing can remedy problems and balance the flow of energy. The ability to deal with any situation depends on the condition of each chakra. A balanced chakra, open and flowing freely presents the ability to react effectively, while a blocked or off-balance chakra impairs this ability because our perspective is restricted by the condition of the chakra.

The chakras represent seven primary stages of metaphysical development. Each chakra operates independently and as a part of the whole.

1st or Base Chakra	material world experiences	I AM
2nd or Spleen Chakra	emotional world experiences	I FEEL
3rd or Solar Plexus	personal will experiences	I CAN
4th or Heart Chakra	unconditional love experiences	I LOVE
5th or Throat Chakra	expression of truth experiences	I CHOOSE
6th or Third Eye	perception & vision experiences	I SEE
7th or Crown Chakra	divine will experiences	I CONNECT

CHAKRA SYSTEM: THE POWER TO BE FREE

Emotional, mental and spiritual forces flow into physical expression through the chakra system. The energy created by our thoughts and emotions runs through the chakra system and is distributed into our cells, tissues and organs. Understanding this process gives insight into how we can, and do, affect the state of our body, mind, and circumstances in our lives. We have the power to create your own shift.

The main purpose of working with the chakra system is to create wholeness within oneself. Moksha is the Sanskrit word for liberation or release. It is the ultimate freedom and the goal of chakra clearing. The idea is to transmute anything heavy, negative or hurtful into free flowing prana.

How good would that feel?

Amazing!

When you become aware of the energy around and within you, you can recognize aspects of consciousness from the physical and the spiritual, and actively bring them into balance and harmony. If things aren't feeling right, with chakra clearing, you have the power to do something about it using simple tools such as meditation, conscious awareness, mantras and the ideas expressed on the following pages.

Freedom is yours to create; help yourself.

1st Chakra / Root Chakra

Sanskrit name: Muladhara (moold-ha-ra) meaning 'root' or 'support'

Sound: LAM

Location: Base of the spine

Colour: Resonates to red

Element: Earth

Petals: Four

- **Associated Consciousness:** Survival issues, physical relationships and concepts, patterns, materialism and our primordial flight or fight responses. It also deals with the archetypal collective of people (tribe), and regulates the flow of life force energies, universal and earth energy, for physical sustenance and vitality.
- **Associated Physical Body:** Limbs and organs including legs and feet, large intestines, spinal column, rectum, bones and the immune system.
- **Associated Crystals:** Garnet, Bloodstone, Red Jasper.
- **Signs of Balance:** Feeling safe, secure, and stable.
- **Signs of Imbalance:** Anxiety, fear, worry, nightmares, feeling of being disconnected, disassociated or left out. In the body: lower leg issues, pain or weight gain.

How to Balance the Root Chakra

Active grounding will balance the 1st Chakra. Take a walk in nature, touch a stone or a tree, let yourself feel solid and stable. Place one of the associated crystals on the Root Chakra, or hold the crystal in your hand and express the sound 'LAM' either out loud or in your mind.

Each chakra associates with an affirmation. The affirmation for the Root Chakra is "I am". You may choose to repeat the affirmation "I am" as a grounding tool for solidifying the 1st Chakra and regaining your sense of self, safety and security.

2nd Chakra / Sacral Chakra

Sanskrit name: Svadhisthana (swad-hiss-tuh-na) means 'where your being is established'

Sound: VAM

Location: One inch below the navel

Colour: Resonates to orange

Element Water

Petals: Six

- **Associated Consciousness:** Symbolism, dualism, and polarities. How we relate to and interact with others and how we form and maintain relationships, expression of emotions, pleasure, movement, sensation and our ability to nurture. Affects our personal visions and relationships stimulating our need for growth and change. Associated with sexuality, repressed emotions and trauma.

- **Associated Physical Body:** Sexual organs, pelvis, lower back, urinary elimination and reproductive system, colon, small intestines, and immune system.

- **Associated Crystals:** Carnelian, Orange Calcite, Stilbite.

- **Signs of Balance:** Feeling in the creative flow of life. Playful, sensual, sexual and non-sexual pleasure.

- **Signs of Imbalance:** Addictive or compulsive behaviour, sexual dysfunction, fear of change, emotional instability. In the body: infertility, impotence, or menstrual issues, lower back, kidney, or stomach disorders.

How to Balance the Sacral Chakra

Water is associated with the 2nd Chakra - bathing, swimming or floating will help balance the energy of this chakra. Recognize that feelings are part of the human existence and can be appreciated as a reflection of one's reaction to circumstances as they shift from joy to gloom and back to joy. Journal your feelings or find a healthy way to express your emotions to discover your personal peace and calm. Place one of the associated crystals on your Sacral Chakra, or hold the crystal in your hand and express the sound "VAM" either out loud or in your mind. The affirmation "I feel" is a tool to embrace your emotions, enhance sexual comfort, regain your sense of self-worth, and keep you in the flow of life.

3rd Chakra / Solar Plexus

Sanskrit name: Manipura (mon-ee-poor-a) means 'city of jewels' or 'lustrous gem'

Sound: RAM

Location: Solar Plexus, above the adrenal glands, below the sternum

Colour: Resonates to yellow

Element: Fire

Petals: Ten

- **Associated Consciousness:** Personal empowerment, how one feels about their personal power and the ability to control the direction of one's life.
- **Associated Physical Body:** Metabolic system (regulation and distribution of metabolic energy through the body), the muscles, adrenal glands, liver, spleen, gall bladder, lumbar vertebrae, and pancreas.
- **Associated Crystals:** Citrine, Amber, Yellow Tiger's Eye.
- **Signs of balance:** Feeling confident, motivated, purposeful, reliable and able with a sense of responsibility.
- **Signs of imbalance:** Feeling uptight, aggressive, nit-picky, low self-esteem, feeling stuck. In the body: fatigue or weight gain.

How to Balance the Solar Plexus Chakra

Moving your body will balance the 3rd Chakra; the Solar Plexus or 'place of the sun'. Get active in nature, especially on a sunny day. Place one of the associated crystals on your Solar Plexus Chakra, or hold the crystal in your hand and express the sound "RAM" either out loud or in your mind. The affirmation "I can" is an empowering tool to open the 3rd Chakra and regain your sense of purpose, personal power and self-worth.

4th Chakra / Heart Centre

Sanskrit name: Anahata (an-a-hat-a) means 'sound made without two things striking', 'unhurt' or 'unstruck'

Sound: YAM

Location: Heart area

Colour: Resonates to green (sometimes pink)

Element Air

Petals: Twelve

- **Associated Consciousness:** Reflects our ability to express love - both self-love and love of other people. Compassion, care towards others less fortunate than oneself, a loving relationship between family members, or an intimate relationship. Capacity to move beyond self-love into unconditional love.
  The Heart Chakra is the most critical of all the chakras because of the interplay between emotions and perceptions. It unites the energies above (spiritual) and the energies below (physical). It integrates the mind and body. Love energy that combines the need of the soul with the challenge of the physical world to experience.

- **Associated Physical Body:** Heart and thymus gland, and influences the immune endocrine and circulatory systems.

- **Associated Crystals:** Emerald, Green Aventurine, Rose Quartz, Rhodonite.

- **Signs of Balance:** Empathy, compassion, unconditional love, and the ability to love and forgive yourself and others. Healthy relationships. In the body: heart or circulatory problems.

- **Signs of Imbalance:** Hatred, selfishness, jealousy, fear of betrayal, and self-disdain. Unhealthy relationships.

How to Balance the Heart Chakra

The practice of loving-kindness will balance the 4th Chakra. Pass out compliments, smile at others and offer forgiveness where appropriate. Find a way to help others; volunteer or be a confidential listener. Place one of the associated crystals on your Heart Chakra, or hold the crystal in your hand and express the sound "YAM" either out loud or in your mind. The affirmation "I love" is an empowering tool to open the 4th Chakra and regain your kind and loving nature.

Fifth Chakra / Throat Centre

Sanskrit name: Vishuddha (vish-oo-dha) means 'essentially pure'

Sound: HAM

Location: Throat

Colour: Resonates to sky blue

Element Ether and sound

Petals: Sixteen

- **Associated Consciousness:** Communication and higher creativity, how we express ourselves and our desires and how we connect with other people.
- **Associated Physical Body:** Throat, vocal cords, and neck area, and is associated with the thyroid and parathyroid glands and all forms of self-expression.
- **Associated Crystals:** Blue Lace Agate, Turquoise, Larimar.
- **Signs of Balance:** Healthy discernment, confident choices, truthful communication as authentic expression comes easily and naturally.
- **Signs of Imbalance:** Difficulty making decisions, tuning into one's authentic self, or expressing true needs. Afraid or unable to share opinions and desires, gossip, and difficulty listening to others. In the body: neck or shoulder pain, thyroid imbalance.

How to Balance the Throat Chakra

The practice of authentic speech will balance the 5th Chakra. If you feel speaking up for yourself is too painful or difficult, start with writing your feelings and personal needs and wishes in a journal. Get your vocal cords going and sing or chant. Place one of the associated crystals on your Throat Chakra, or hold the crystal in your hand and express the sound "HAM" either out loud or in your mind. The affirmation "I choose" is an expressive tool to open the 5th Chakra and regain your momentum in the world.

Sixth Chakra / Third Eye

Sanskrit name:	Ajna (uh-juh-na) means 'to perceive' or 'to understand'
Sound:	AUM
Location:	Between the eyebrows
Colour:	Resonates to indigo
Element:	Light (and Akasha)
Petals:	Two

- **Associated Consciousness:** Ability to see the world around us and to perceive without prejudice how things really are. A bridge from the physical plane to the spiritual planes, opening to other realities and potentialities of a multi-dimensional universe. The Third Eye is light, colour, seeing, visualization, clairvoyance, holographic realities, also our greatest teacher of fear and love.
- **Associated Physical Body:** Pineal gland.
- **Associated Crystals:** Lapis Lazuli, Sodalite, Amethyst.
- **Signs of Balance:** Strong intuition, inner wisdom, ability to envision outcomes and the release of the ego.
- **Signs of Imbalance:** Overly attached to external circumstances, cynical, or unwilling to embrace others' points of view. In the body: headaches, eye, or vision problems.

How to Balance the Third Eye Chakra

The practice of meditation is the best tool to balance the 6th Chakra. Sit quietly with your eyes open or closed and allow your thoughts to swim through your mind without 'thinking' about them as they float by. Visualization meditations are also incredibly useful for stimulating and opening the Third Eye. Place one of the associated crystals on your Third Eye Chakra, or hold the crystal in your hand and express the sound "AUM" either out loud or in your mind. The affirmation "I see" is an expressive tool to open the 6th Chakra to gain clarity and focus.

Seventh Chakra / Crown Centre

Sanskrit name:	Sahasrara (sa-huss-ra-ra) means 'thousandfold'
Sound:	Silence. Just Listen.
Location:	Top of the head
Colour:	Resonates to violet (sometimes white)
Element	Fohat (One Universal Energy)
Petals:	One Thousand

- **Associated Consciousness:** Spirituality or understanding of the relationship we have as spiritual beings in the physical experience - the gateway to higher realms of consciousness At a physical level the Sahasrara deals with the mind and the brain, represents our conscious and unconscious thought and our ability to tap into the collective consciousness.
- **Associated Physical Body:** Cerebral cortex, central nervous system, associated with the pituitary gland.
- **Associated Crystals:** Clear Quartz, Lepidolite, Howlite.
- **Signs of Balance:** Strong Spiritual connection, enlightenment, connection to one's Higher Self, contentment and peace.
- **Signs of Imbalance:** Feeling lost and lacking in purpose, existential depression, materialism. In the body; headaches, fatigue, and mental health issues.

How to Balance the Crown Chakra

The practice of silent meditation is the best tool to balance the 7th Chakra. Sit silently with your eyes open or closed, allow your thoughts to swim through your mind without 'thinking' about them as they float by. Place one of the associated crystals on your Crown Chakra, or hold the crystal in your hand and be open to thoughts, ideas and impressions that come to your mind as you sit in silence. The affirmation "I know" or "I connect" are expressive tools to open the 7th Chakra to connect with Spirit, infinite possibilities, and a blissful state of Spiritual union.

Meditation to Balance 7 Chakras

Sit comfortably, yet straight, visually aligning your Chakras Root to Crown.

Feel the breath flowing through your body, filling your lungs and sending sweet oxygen to your bloodstream, then exhaling the carbon dioxide and feeding the trees in your environment with nourishment and transmuting your exhale back to oxygen.

Now feel your breath flowing through your body, and imagine filling your lungs with love, sending sweet love to your bloodstream, then exhaling anything that isn't love to be transmuted for the highest good and back to love. Continue breathing like this until your feel completely full of loving-kindness.

Bring your attention to your Root Chakra and visualize a bright red ball of light glowing and spinning. Affirm 'I AM' and gather a feeling of safety and security and self-worth. Know who are. Seek to brighten any dullness in the red light at the Root Chakra. Breathe love.

When you feel solid, bring your attention up to the Sacral Chakra and envision a bright orange ball of light glowing and spinning. Affirm 'I FEEL' and gather a feeling of equanimity. Feel who you are. Seek to brighten any dullness in the orange light at the Sacral Chakra. Breathe love.

When you feel peace, bring your attention up to the Solar Plexus Chakra and envision a bright yellow ball of light glowing and spinning. Affirm 'I CAN' and gather a feeling of empowerment. Honour your can accomplishments and acknowledge what you are able to do. Seek to brighten any dullness in the yellow light at the Solar Plexus Chakra.

When you feel empowered, bring your attention up to the Heart Chakra and envision a bright green ball of light glowing and spinning. Affirm 'I LOVE' and gather a feeling of loving-kindness for yourself and other sentient beings. Acknowledge the power of your love. Seek to brighten any dullness in the green light at the Heart Chakra. Breathe love, lots and lots of love.

When you feel a deep and loving-kindness in your heart, bring your attention up to the Throat Chakra and envision a bright sky-blue ball of light glowing and spinning. Affirm 'I CHOOSE' and gather a feeling of truthfulness and honesty for yourself and other sentient beings. Know your own truth and respect the truth of others. Seek to brighten any dullness in the sky-blue light at the Throat Chakra. Breathe love.

When you recognize your truth, bring your attention up to the Third Eye Chakra and envision a rich indigo ball of light glowing and spinning. Affirm 'I SEE' and gather a feeling of intuition, vision and wisdom with the humility to continue learning and to be open-minded. You can see things from many points of view and can see what lies before you. Seek to brighten any dullness in the indigo light at the Third Eye Chakra. Breathe love.

When you feel ideas, intuition and insight open before you, bring your attention up to the Crown Chakra and envision a clear, loving, bright ball of light glowing and spinning. Affirm 'I CONNECT' and gather a feeling of unity with Spirit, whatever you believe that to be. You can feel the connectedness between the spiritual and material realms. Seek to brighten any dullness in the Spiritual light at the Crown Chakra. Breathe love.

When you feel the strength of your connection to the realm of Spirit, bring your attention back to your loving breath. Imagine breathing into your chakras as well as your lungs. You may breath into each individually, or run the loving breath energy up and down your body through each chakra.

When you feel done - renewed, refreshed, and complete. Give yourself a big, beautiful, meaningful, loving hug, and carry on with your wonderfully balanced day in greater flow and with a boost of energy.

Understanding & Utilizing Dreams

Excerpt from Oracle Workshop Curriculum

Sleep is meant to be restorative and healing. We are alive and well – just in a different state of consciousness than when we are awake. Although it may feel as if 'nothing' is happening when you sleep, there is a great deal going on. One of the most fascinating is dreaming.

Dreams offer two important resources to our lives. Firstly, dreaming is incredibly therapeutic. Recent research (Mark Blagrove, Swansea University, Wales 2019), has shown that intense dreaming activity occurs when our brains are working hard to process recent, emotionally powerful experiences, basically providing self-induced therapy. Dreams give us an outlet to process our emotions. There is nothing more to 'do' with this knowledge other than ensuring you have a good, healthy night's sleep. Theta brainwaves are naturally produced in this wonderful stress-release dream state and seem to amplify when you are processing a high emotional experience, helping you process difficulties organically. Dreaming helps you feel better, develops peace of mind, and helps calm emotional upset.

Secondly, dream interpretation can help us identify areas in our lives that could benefit from some conscious attention. They send unfiltered messages from your subconscious mind to help deal with life issues. Some dreams are easy to figure out while others are incredibly complex, but it is worth the time it takes to explore your dreams because they often have answers to conscious and unconscious questions. There are no filters to hold back what a dream is trying to tell you, no denial, no justification, and no opinion; they tell it like it is… if you can decipher the code.

Dreams can expose our worries, diagnose our ailments, reveal thoughts and emotions we have tried to ignore, enhance creative ideas, and suggest improvements in lifestyle, family dynamics, career paths, and relationships. With such a plethora of information available to us as we lie horizontal – it seems crazy not to make good use of this useful tool to enrich your waking hours.

Then again, our dreams seem surreal, abstract and nonsensical. How does the mishmash of images and strange impressions make any sense? They are so fantastically bizarre at the time, can they really be delivering helpful information? The answer is yes.

When we remember our dreams, (not everyone does, nor do we remember every dream we have), the memory of the often disjointed images can invoke feelings. We may feel sad, fearful, joyous, inspired or downright terrified. However; dreams can be used to help us resolve issues, connect with others, or gain perspective. They offer useful information that may not otherwise have 'come to mind'.

Our subconscious has access to every bit of information and every situation we've experienced, and when we are dreaming, we have direct access to our subconscious. The symbols of our dreams are the language of our soul; they assist, enlighten, and heal.

Dreamtime is during REM (rapid eye movement) when Theta brainwaves are strong. Theta brainwaves have high amplitude and a low-frequency range; normally between 5 and 8 cycles a second. When awake, daydreaming or driving without being able to recall the last five miles are examples of being in a theta state. When you are sleeping, your dreams kick into full-blown technicolour.

THE SLEEP CYCLE:

Stage 1: Approximately four to five percent of the average sleep time. Light sleep, slow eye movement, and reduced muscle activity.

Stage 2: Approximately half of the average sleep time. Eye movement stops and brain waves become slower, with occasional bursts of rapid waves called sleep spindles.

Stage 3: Approximately four to six percent of sleep time. Extremely slow brain waves called delta waves begin to appear, interspersed with smaller, faster waves.

Stage 4: Approximately twelve to fifteen percent of sleep time. Delta brainwaves dominate this stage of "Deep Sleep". There is no eye movement or muscle activity.

Stage 5: Rapid eye movement (REM) accounts for approximately one-quarter of sleep time. Dreams occur during this phase. Physically, breathing becomes more rapid, eye movement is detected and sleep paralysis occurs. In most cases, the dreamer has no control over the images and feelings that occur during REM dreamtime.

Most people cycle through these stages three to six times per night.

Everybody dreams (unless they miss the REM sleep cycle), but not everyone remembers their dreams, or forget them quickly as they begin to wake up. Beta brain waves are a constant in the conscious waking hours and they overwhelm the quieter sleeping states. If you can stay quiet and do not 'chase' the dream, but allow it to bridge from your subconscious to your conscious mind, you can better remember the events and emotions of the dream. Journaling can help with dream retention, but repeat it to yourself before writing it down, because even the act of reaching for your pen and journal will cause the dream to fade. You may discover that your subconscious allows the dream to bubble up during the daytime when you are relaxed and not 'thinking'.

On average, dreams occur between three and six times per night although ninety-five percent of dreams are forgotten upon waking. Part of the reason for forgetting your dreams is because the Theta brainwaves fade and Beta brainwaves take over as you wake, cancelling out the subtle and delicate subconscious awareness. Thoughts and consciousness rise and dreams and subconscious fade. The more you move and think, the faster the dream slips away. If you struggle with remembering your dreams, lay quietly and let the dream solidify in your consciousness, have a pen and journal at your bedside so you can write the dream down.

WHY IS DREAM INTERPRETATION USEFUL?

- There is no denial in the dreamtime; therefore you will know the truth of any situation in your life which helps you deal with your current waking reality.
- Dreams give solutions to difficulties and problems in your life.
- Precognitive dreams give the gift of insight into future events.
- Dream interpretation accelerates your personal and spiritual growth and peace of mind.
- Dreams come in the service of health and wholeness.
- There is no such thing as a dream without meaning.
- Dreams often reflect inborn creativity and the ability to face and solve life's problems by processing information gathered during the daytime.
- Dreams can aid in finding solutions that would be challenging for the awake ego to face.

- All dreams reflect the dreamer's relationship to their lives and environment and may represent unconscious desires and wishes.
- Dreams can relate present experiences to the forgotten past in preparation for the future.
- Working with dreams regularly improves relationships with friends, lovers, parents, children... even pets.
- All dreams aim to improve quality of life, offer clarity, and aid discernment.

Types of Dreams

1. Housekeeping Dreams: Suggest ways to deal with issues in your life.
- Often based on current events.
- Occur to help you 'get your house in order', a mental clearing up of events or emotions.

2. Archetypal Dreams: Teach you something important about yourself.
- Relate to a universal energy system - the collective.
- Usually occur at significant times or transitional periods in your life and may invoke a sense of awe, or that you have learned something crucial or significant.

3. Precognitive /Superconscious Dreams (Psychic)
- Often there is no clue the dream is pre-cognitive until after the event has occurred.
- You may feel shocked or surprised upon awakening with an urge to call someone to verify.
- Superconscious dreams may bring images from other realities.
- The dream may be unusually vivid, with an obvious reference.
- Loved ones crossed-over or light-beings may be present.
- The dream may be inspiring and meaningful with a relevant mode of application.
- The dream may not be precognitive at all, but only coincidence, a false memory, or the dreamer unconsciously connecting known information.

Dream Interpretation

What goes through our minds just before we fall asleep likely affects the content of our dreams. Events and situations from our day show up in our dreams. Memories, including suppressed memories, may steer our dreams and can be used to heal past trauma.

With the exception of prophetic dreams, you put everything in the dream. If you dream about your brother – you subconsciously put him there. If you dream about a car, you determined the colour, make, style and era of the vehicle. Everything in your dream is created by the dreamer. Unless it is a precognitive dream, the images are all bits and pieces, reflections and concepts offered up from your own experiences; an invitation to yourself to do some personal or spiritual growth, to take action, or gain insight into something you'd prefer not to face in the daylight hours. Very, very useful information indeed.

Interpreting the dream leads us to discover that all the nouns of our dream are actually parts of ourselves. We are everyone and everything in our dreams. The dog in your dream is an aspect of you, so is the road, the flower, your sister, and how they behave or what they represent is an aspect of the dreamer.

The dreamer's 'aha!' of recognition is a function of a previously unconscious memory and is a reliable touchstone of dreamwork.

DREAM SYMBOLS
- Personal symbols (something important only to you)
- Archetypes (the bully, the heroine, the traveller)
- Cultural/universal symbols (i.e.: elderly people may represent wisdom, water may mean emotion or life force)

Can you make yourself dream about particular issues? The jury is still out, but Edgar Casey suggests we ask questions while awake, be sincere, and then 'sleep on it'. You may find solutions to problems, answers to questions, guidance or desires revealed by morning time.

Is there a 'good' dream and a 'bad' dream? They can feel good or bad, but all dreams help you get back into your life. They help you reconnect with your natural style of being and living.

Dreams can reveal moods and their sources; they can cause you to think about something you may not have thought of, they can show possibilities, and help you to see things in a different light. They can also bring challenging issues together that might be difficult to face during a waking state.

Nightmares cause upsetting emotions and may represent challenges to us, forcing us to the edge of our tolerance. They may be caused by stress, fear, trauma, emotional difficulties, illness or the use of certain medications or drugs.

Lucid dreams occur when the dreamer realizes they are dreaming, often in the middle of a regular dream. At that point, the dreamer may have some control over their dream.

DREAM THEMES

Some dream themes appear to change over time, they shift based on personal and external circumstances reflecting what is going on in your life and what is happening in the world in general.

Common dream themes include falling, flying, being chased, unable to move, sex, no home – or altered home, school-related, family-related, being attacked, being nude, eating, being imprisoned, insects or snakes, being killed, taking an exam, being smothered, being paralyzed, losing teeth, arriving late, a living person being dead, a person now dead being alive, being dead, killing someone, finding money, wearing the wrong clothes, trying to do something and struggling, weather or storm-related, fire, flood, violence, romance, plane crash, sensing someone, being a child, encountering God, an angel or some Spiritual essence.

How to Interpret a

1. Simplify the dream to its basic theme. (As a story or TV show)
2. Who are the characters in the dream and how do you feel about them?
3. What is happening and how does it feel?
4. What symbols appear? What do they mean to your intuition? What do they mean in an unabridged dictionary?
5. What associations and dynamics occur in the dream?
6. Are there memories that have bubbled up? Solutions to problems?
7. What action is being called for by the dream?

A SAMPLE DREAM

I dreamed that I was swimming in a beautiful azure tropical ocean.

Two colourful fish swam ahead of me as if they were leading me to a special place.

I seemed to be able to breathe underwater.

I couldn't see anything but blue, then a sandy ocean floor and finally a small tropical island.

It felt like someone special was there – but I couldn't see who.

I woke up.

The feelings were peaceful, excitement, anticipation, happiness and love. To me, the archetypes were the ocean (emotions) an island (haven, solid world) and two fish (relationship).

I was swimming in a beautiful azure tropical ocean. INTERPRETATION: I was deep in my 'good vibe' emotions.

Two colourful fish swam ahead of me as if they were leading me to a special place. INTERPRETATION: I (the fish) led myself (me) to somewhere special (also me).

I seemed to be able to breathe underwater. INTERPRETATION: I was comfortable and at ease and able to do what I needed to in the situation.

I couldn't see anything but blue, then a sandy ocean floor and finally a small tropical island. INTERPRETATION: Things were slowly revealed to me. I could see my emotions becoming grounded and stable. The island part of me was there to balance the emotional part of me.

It felt like someone special was there – but I couldn't see who. INTERPRETATION: I felt that a part of myself was ready to have a better relationship with myself or possibly I was seeing myself ready to have a balanced relationship with someone else.

I woke up.

A SAMPLE NIGHTMARE

I dreamed that I was having a picnic on a hillside with my family.

I walked towards a woman standing away from everyone.

Three or four prohibition gangsters in 1920s roadsters with automatic weapons drove between me and the woman and killed her.

I tried to get help but no one could hear me.

I ran to help the woman, but she was obviously very dead and was lower on the hill.

I chased after the gangsters in the cars but they were getting away, driving down the hill. All of a sudden one car backed up towards me and I could see the license plate.

I woke up.

The feelings in the dream were fear, panic, helplessness, heroism, and frustration. The archetypes were bad guys, death, victim, attempted hero and family.

I was having a picnic on a hillside with my family. INTERPRETATION: Life is good, family is important, I am in a high (top of the hill) place.

I walked away towards a woman standing away from everyone. INTERPRETATION: I walked away from myself to see what this other version of myself was doing. She was (I was) at the same height on the hill (the hill is also me).

Three or four prohibition gangsters in 1920's roadsters with automatic weapons drove between me and the woman and killed her.

INTERPRETATION: I drove up and killed a version of myself. My subconscious put the cars, guns and 'bad guys' in the dream. They all represent an aspect of me.

I tried to get help but no one could hear me. INTERPRETATION: I tried to save myself but was struggling.

I ran to help the woman, but she was obviously very dead. INTERPRETATION: I couldn't save myself.

I chased after the gangsters in the cars but they were getting away driving down the hill – all of a sudden one car backed up towards me and I could see the license plate. INTERPRETATION: Things are going downhill. I tried to stop myself from killing myself, but when I almost couldn't, I backed up and showed myself how I could save myself.

I woke up.

At this point in my life, I had recovered from heart disease and was not taking as good care of myself as I should. Coffee was back on the menu and my diet had gone back to 'anything goes'. The dream came to show me the important things in my life and how my situation could go downhill if I wasn't looking after my health.

Dream Practice

EXERCISE: Pretending Offers Useful Information

Picture someone you have an 'issue' with. It can be anyone from a family member to a cartoon character. Don't try - just let it come. Don't 'do' anything - just let your imagination show you the person. What are they doing? How do they appear? Is there an emotion?

Continue to watch without thinking or doing anything. Comment on what happened.

Note that everything that the character you 'pretended' did or said behaves the way you orchestrated knowingly or not. Did you provide yourself with any useful information by imaging?

EXERCISE: Working with Your Dreams

1. Using a journal, write down your dreams as soon as they come to your conscious mind.

2. Ask: How does the story/symbols relate the dream to your life? Is there a relationship? What do you recognize? What is foreign?
3. What parts of your dream are reflections or projections of yourself?
4. What action can you take on your dream? How can you apply your dream? Is there any action or communication required?
5. Evaluate each dream. Practice, practice, practice! Do the dance with your dreams, and get comfortable with them.

"Follow your dreams, they know the way."

The Colour yellow

Excerpt from 'Finding Yes: The First Step'
By Kendall Anne Dixon

I didn't come to my first Energy Awareness class twenty years ago willingly.

Not really.

I had already been meditating on my own for many years, not to mention I had lived with my father and stepmother during high school; they were professional psychics and held weekly healing groups that included meditation at our house, which I attended. Having been a shiatsu therapist for over ten years, giving energy healings and massage, I really thought I 'knew this kind of stuff.' I was only there because I was desperate. I had developed an autoimmune disease (ulcerative colitis) and hadn't worked in almost a year. Unable to tolerate solid foods, I had lost thirty pounds, and according to my doctor I had recently been a single digit away from needing a blood transfusion. I look back on that time with confusion; how could someone so ill and desperate for help be so unwilling to receive it? Simple – no learning space. Without knowing it, I was a closed door. I had no idea that I didn't have a learning space. I was there, wasn't I? I had paid for the class and shown up. Yet the inner state-of-being that helps create learning space is so much more than just showing up physically, and I didn't have it.

The most important aspect of learning space is willingness, and I had at least the smallest amount needed to come to the class. I was a sincere student if nothing else. So one day I arrived early, took one of the chairs that were arranged in a semicircle in the teacher's living room, and prepared for class, practising the new centering and grounding tools I had recently learned. Even though on some level I thought I already knew this stuff, I was there and at least in the smallest way willing to learn. The other students filtered in, and after a brief touch-in, our teacher had us close our eyes for a short review meditation, but instead of following along with the others, I found myself going deep into an old memory. I was very young, maybe three years old, and standing beside my sister. A woman was in front of us, but the sun was in my eyes, and so I couldn't see her face. She's asking my sister what her favourite colour is, and she says, 'Green.' I feel like I want my sister to like me, I seem to know that she doesn't, and that she doesn't want me there, so when the woman asks me what my favourite colour is, even though I want to say yellow, I say green. I'm hoping that when my sister sees that I'm the same as her, she will like me better. Instead she is furious.

'It is not! You're just saying that because I said it!'

Now I'm angry. 'It is too!' I shout back.

The lady says, 'Now, now, girls, you can both like the same colour.'

The meditation ends, and I open my eyes feeling totally confused. The other participants are sharing their experience, but for a change I'm quiet. It was clear to me that something had just happened; without a doubt that was a real memory, but other than that I hadn't a clue as to why I'd spontaneously remembered what seemed like a totally inconsequential thing. I can't stop thinking about it though. Yellow, yes of course it's my favourite colour. I seem to know this as truth, yet in this moment I'm suddenly aware that I've been saying green my whole life. Every green shirt, skirt, and dress my mother ever bought because I'd insisted it was my favourite colour comes to mind, and I feel nauseous. I know that yellow is my favourite colour, but I'm also aware that if you had asked me even moments before this meditation, before this strange memory, I would have said green. Is it possible I've been living a lie? And who cares anyway? Do adults even have favourite colours? I can't understand why this seems to matter, yet clearly it does because a sense of anxiety and confusion slowly creeps in throughout the rest of the class. It's just that so much of my life was up in the air, my not being able to work due to being ill, that this one thing I felt certain about, that at least I know about myself, was suddenly very important.

I begin to panic, thinking, what else don't I know about myself? I notice it's time to leave, people are getting up, taking their bags, putting on jackets, and heading toward the door. I stand up and wait while my teacher finishes talking to another student. She's aware of me and also, I suspect, that I'm feeling very confused.

She looks at me as the student finishes with her, and I realize I don't know where to begin, what to say. She has a calm yet straightforward demeanour and is wholly herself in a way I'm not comfortable with, and I find myself fidgeting. I'm not even sure what the problem is. I feel like it's totally wrong that I've lived my whole life until now thinking green was my favourite colour, when all along it is yellow. At the same time I feel completely silly; I mean, who cares what one's favourite colour is? Still, there is something I don't understand, and that makes me very nervous; I like to understand things. No, I need to understand things.

I don't remember what I said to my teacher, but I do remember hearing her final words to me repeating as I walked home that night.

'All I know is, you can never really lose yourself.'

This isn't very comforting. I'm feeling like I don't even know who I am anymore. I've just discovered something fundamental about myself, and that seems totally wrong; it feels like this is something I should already know. What else don't I know about myself? What other lies am I living? Without thinking it consciously, I'm questioning this meditation practice. Do I really want to find out? What else will emerge? There are a lot of things in my past that I remember as being really terrible, especially from my childhood. I'm not sure at this point I really want to go down this path because who knows where it will lead?

I remember that walk home. It had rained while we were in class, and all the cherry trees that line the street to my apartment were in bloom. Every time a breeze came up some of the water would fall out of the blossoms and drop down my neck, making me look up. At that moment it occurs to me that this is a choice point. I feel certain that continuing to take this class will mean change. This lost and confused feeling is uncomfortable, and maybe I don't want to know these things. Who cares if I wanted my sister to love me enough that I would lie? Telling a lie and living it as truth is bigger than just fibbing as a child, and somehow I know this is the real issue.

As I approach the entrance of my building, something occurs to me: haven't I always had this problem in all my relationships? I tend to go with what the other person wants, trying to get them to like me, giving up opinions, preferences for movie choices, and even where I want to live, until finally I gave up on relationships instead. I have come to believe that the only way I can be me is to be alone. It occurs to me that this issue might be connected to those energetic boundaries my teacher had alluded to when I first met her.

As I key open the door of the building and swing it wide, I'm feeling a stone in my throat. I don't like this one bit. I went to meditation class to feel better, less stress, not worse. This is the last thing I need, I think, as I enter the elevator.

When I get to my door, I open it and step inside and turn on the light. For one brief moment I stand perfectly still, holding my purse and umbrella. I'm in awe, and can't believe what I'm seeing, and I hear my teacher's words pass through my head – 'You really can't lose yourself' – as I see my apartment as if for the first time.

It is entirely in yellow.

The paint is yellow.

My desk is yellow.

The bedspread on my bed is yellow.

I've always loved yellow, I've always known it, and I feel my heart swell. I've just never let myself have it, admit it, live it.

I sit down on the couch, jacket still on, and take in the newness of seeing yellow all around me, something I've clearly always known on some level, even if I haven't lived it consciously. I'm not lost, just not remembered.

After some time I let myself question my meditation practice and it occurs to me that it might be fun to find out more about myself. Maybe these classes will help me find some things out that I want to know.

With the tiniest bit of willingness that I brought to the class, the exact experience that I needed to open me to learning came. It was as if my entire identity was like a house of cards, and an invisible hand had seamlessly snuck in and removed the one card that would take the others down. That identity was keeping me from knowing myself as *essence*, from experiencing the inner truth of who I really am. But I would never have been open to that if I hadn't had that memory because I was too busy believing that I already knew who I was. The next class I arrived a very different student. I came not only willing but curious; what else don't I know about myself?

Six years later I sat in my new, freshly painted office where I was opening Awaken Wellness, my first Meditation and Massage Studio in 2006. I had graduated from my teacher's training course two years prior, and it was time for me to have my own place. I sat on a padded folding chair in front of the seven chairs in a semicircle awaiting the arrival of my preregistered students. I took in the room, from the light-yellow paint on the walls that beautifully offset the dark-green carpet (my favourite colours) to the subtle art on the walls. I spent a little time meditating, preparing myself, and setting the energy for the class, as well as opening my own learning space for teaching.

The students arrived, and after they introduced themselves I told them a little bit about my experience with these tools and how much they have helped me.

'I ask that you give yourself a learning space; that means creating the space to learn something new. If you want a plant to grow bigger, you put it in a bigger pot. As adults we only grow by learning, so give yourself a big space to learn in. This also means making it a safe space. Not comparing to others if they are having an experience you aren't, not criticizing or judging yourself. It also means having a possibility space. You don't know if there is something here for you, and neither do I, but you won't know unless you give yourself the opportunity to try. Try it first before deciding. Finally, you can't learn anything new if you think you already know. You might have practised various types of meditation and energy work before this, but for the moment set them aside, and be open to having a new experience with what is being offered here. Learning space is more than just showing up for the class; it's a state-of-being.'

They were sitting in front of me wide-eyed and alert. Open, receptive, ready.

To know ourselves as energy, as love, we must be willing to embrace the unknown, and to do that, we must be willing to learn something new. This story is the lesson... to become open to learning who you really are... the signs are everywhere.

Journey of self

By Kathleen Willis

Challenges can evoke a journey to the Spiritual side.

During my twenties, thirties, and early forties, I was struggling in a difficult marriage. Over twenty-three years the reationship gradually became more and more uncomfortable for me, and when I finally found the courage to physically remove myself, I was an addict, an alcoholic.

After leaving my marriage, I almost immediately started up a new relationship with someone younger than me, who was also an alcoholic. Like attracts like. Less than three years later, August 2009, I was black and blue unable to move for several days, having been badly beaten up.

What a wake-up call!

Shortly after recovering from this more recent abusive relationship, I started meditating. Every night at six in the evening I would lie on the floor and listen to Osho guide me in *Body Mind Balancing*. Each time I would fall fast asleep. It took a year before I was able to stay awake through the entire meditation.

In late 2011, I was guided to meet a group receiving heart conscious channelled messages about how things work in the higher realms. Since that time, I have been studying the information which came through. The messages channelled were: Divine Blessings, Virtues and Qualities, Universal Laws, and the growth patterns of twelve dimensions connected to a thirteen chakra system, from root to crown.

My journey of awakening is distilled there. From experiencing what does and doesn't work, to learning how to create balance with peace, love and joy both within and without (or in the world around me), following the philosophy, 'as within so without'.

In 2012, I began to study the channeled information from the higher realms, and in 2015, I was encouraged by my Guides to start looking at the patterns of angst I had created in my life.

Every morning — same chair, same time — I drew cards from the Thoth Tarot deck and from an animal totems deck called, Medicine Cards, to receive messages and look at the situations of disarray from my past. Every day I sat learning not to judge what I saw.

Sitting in pain, in order to heal through the pain was very difficult. There were days when I dashed the cards to the ground, in great distress, my ego reacting in extreme ways.

At the same time I was studying the teachings of the higher realms - the Divine Universal Laws, Blessings, Virtues, Qualities, and Dimensional Growth Patterns - and was taught to consistently drop out of my mind and 'sit' in my heart.

In my heart I was shown we have a colourful tri-flame of blue, pink, and gold, full of warmth and wisdom. I found each of these flames have attributes, Divine Qualities.

The blue flame was infused with understanding, forgiveness, the Divine Mother's Essence, and the knowledge that She forgives everything, and that 'God' is not punishing.

The pink flame offered compassion, humility, and grace. It came with the ability to observe without judgement, and hold the highest vision for one's self and others and to understand the balance of self-love and self-worth.

As I contemplated the golden canary yellow flame I realized it carried the Essence of the Divine Father, a sign of gratitude for what I had learned from all my experiences. The good, bad and ugly, had all been experienced for my sacred purpose, and even greater balance including love from within.

The blue flame was probably the most profound as I found myself going back in time, in this life and past lives; observing and forgiving, forgiving myself, others, and offering and asking for apologies, some in person, some etherically.

I was able to forgive myself for not expressing and experiencing myself and others as Divine.

As I did this work, my external reality began to change, to shift. With fortitude, that willingness to be in the heart, to listen and know we are naturally kind, interconnected beings, I found myself surrendering deeper and deeper into the love of self and love of All.

My ego — reassured — relaxed, and all anxiety was eliminated. Calming the spikes of emotional turmoil by using Divine Qualities, such as forgiveness, compassion, and the deep gratitude for all my experiences, rejuvenated me.

I began to reach out to help in the addiction recovery community with deep understanding, empathy and compassion. It was through the pain of my own experience that I discovered the ability to be anywhere with non-judgement, with love, to hold the highest vision, especially for our most disenfranchised. From our sorrow can come our joy, gratitude for life purpose.

My volunteer work has become my joy and my passion - especially working with women in recovery. The more I forgive myself, and develop compassion and gratitude for myself, the more I reach out to help others.

From my aforementioned channelling from the higher realms, I learned sacred purpose is what we are most passionate about. It is what we can't wait to wake up in the morning to do, and it's something to discover on an ongoing basis. I find the deeper I journey into my heart, and the wisdom of the tri-flame, the more my purpose unfolds before me. It is the call to help create a balanced planet in all ways, to lift up our most disenfranchised into a place of equality, to create societies that work for everyone,. We each have a unique purpose that can be found when we are ready and willing to listen to benevolent guidance with one's heart.

We have Guides who are with us 24/7. I am in great gratitude for my mine. Their loving counsel and direction, and especially the first nudge to practise meditation that began my journey of awakening. That nudge has lead me to today, and has gifted me with the consistent daily practice of sitting still in my heart.

Everyday I like to sit in meditation, dropping from mind to heart like a pebble into a pond — same time, same chair — with a notebook for my insights from 'heart listening'. Coming to a place of balance is an ongoing practice.

When I'm triggered by an internal emotion, usually from an external event, the question I am guided to ask myself is: "How is this _____ (situation, relationship) connected to the past?"

- I close my eyes, see images from the past that come to mind, and jot them down.
- As I do this work I see repeated patterns, or the negative self-talk that created similar situations — with different people over the years — comparable scenarios of angst, again and again.
- When I see the repeated patterns, I am guided to sit in the pain, really feel the pain, rather than run away from it. Feel it to heal it and then surrender to love.

Then, from there, to use 'I Am' statements:

- I Am Forgiveness of self/others, therefore I Am Peace
- I Am Compassion for self/others, therefore I Am Love
- I Am deep Gratitude for self/others, therefore I Am Joy

These affirmations help us to feel the Divine Mother and Father's Love, awakening our heart consciousness to balance our masculine and feminine energies within. Divine Qualities can be extended to oneself and everyone else and especially to our early caregivers - in my case my Mum and Dad - flowing that love equally through both feminine and masculine energy helps create a solid foundation.

QUESTIONS FOR CREATION OF BALANCE WITHIN

Because we tend to create similar situations over and over, without realizing what we are doing, here are questions I have been guided to ask myself. Sitting still with these questions may help you too:

- Have I forgiven myself, others, and the entire situation?

- Am I compassionate, able to observe without judgement, can I hold the highest vision of Love for self, others, situations?
- Can I find the gratitude, somehow, for this experience? Finding that gratitude for the most difficult of circumstances, eliminates anxiety, lack and physical pain, then helps create more situations we can truly be grateful for. Like attracts like.

Tenderly understanding our experiences and being in a place of forgiveness, compassion, and gratitude truly creates peace, love, and joy!

"Owning our story and loving ourselves through that process is the bravest thing that we'll ever do."
~ Brené Brown

The Imagination

manifesto

By Michelle Rose

Never has there been a more exhilarating time to use the wildly pleasurable advances of your imagination. To walk through your day, spinning on this perfect planet brimming with well-being, while observing and participating in the plethora of all that is going on around you and at the same time, using the power of your ability to focus in your imagination. A valuable skill to cultivate. The ability to choose to *deliberately* to conjure images - to mould and handpick your inner world for the singular purpose of pleasing and satisfying yourself in the moment creating a beneficial domino effect. It can be done at any time, in any place, during anything that is going on within or around you. That my friends, is what this section of this book will teach you how to easily do.

Many of us, have been externally responding to the very 'real' life events that have taken place thus far. We have knee-jerk reactions to conversations with our parents, husbands and wives, to our children, employers, jobs and whomever and whatever enters our life experience. Most of us have allowed our reactions to become automatic functions. However, we have come to understand that what we focus on is creative and with our focus, or deliberate intention, we can change everything. This is not a chapter on how to manifest your desires, there is plenty of material about that all over the world. The purpose and function of this chapter is to magnify and shine the spotlight on the absolute power of your focus and wake up the passion and life force of your imagination. To focus into your virtual reality. To use your imagination to improve your personal world. In the very real here and now – you will see it, taste it, touch it, and wonder at the ways the abundance of synchronistic circumstances and events magically unfold around you. Of course, words do not teach. But if you are willing to give this a try, in the next thirty days, you could be a walking, talking example of what happens when you regularly and on purpose step into your virtual reality. Your life as you know it to be, the one you are in as you are reading these words now, will be very different, very new, and full of things that please you.

It is insightful to know that we are made up of energy, vibration, and that our wonderful brains are transmitters and receivers of vibration and energy. You may have heard the saying that 'where our attention goes, energy flows'. Some people are triggered by that sentence because if things aren't going that well, it may definitely feel like you're not thinking these thoughts – not creating your own difficulty. It sometimes feels like these thoughts are thinking you and that you have to protect yourself by justifying why everything is the way that it is. But this is not the case and it is easy to change. It is just a change of perspective away. Boosting our creative mind power is not only a wildly important skill to cultivate, but we have never been given a better arena, or better resources all over the world to pick and choose what we like, what we prefer, what we enjoy, what stimulates us or revs our engines and therefore what we want to have in our virtual reality landscapes.

What is a virtual reality?
It is anything you want it to be.
You are the architect. You are the creator.

This life has just about all of our attention does it not? We live in a digitally diverse, socially inhibiting time and the way information is plucked and carefully distributed to individuals through every digital platform has served us greatly in many ways. For the most part – life is great, but we sure are an insatiable bunch, aren't we? It could be so much more.

Maybe you have had an 'off' day or an 'off' month or an 'off' thirty years. The first thing would be to stop beating up on yourself about it. Let your frustration be the means to have your 'aha' moment gently turn you around and launch you into your virtual reality. Start enjoying the fun of your imagination. It is always there, will never go away, forever present, and all yours, and no one other than you can tap into it.

Spiritual teachers may suggest that you enjoy the fun of giving your attention to what pleases you, trying to show us all where we could be going because where you could be going can be infinitely more pleasurable than where you are. And that my friends, is why virtual reality is so much fun. Yes, your 'now' may be limited. If you were to only pay attention to where you are right now, it is a tiny piece of your life overall, is it not? It is very brief in comparison to all of your past and the future before you. If we give our attention to only our present and past - whether that past was what happened two minutes ago or two thousand years ago - we do not use the power of the Now as effectively or efficiently as we could. And yes, it is a lovely thing to look into your past, present, virtual reality or future, as long as what we are looking at is causing some good feelings to bubble up inside of you. Are they ringing your bells, are they turning you on, are you feeling uplifted by them, are you feeling inspired? Are you feeling hopeful? Are you sated before you fall asleep? Can you feel a certain level of satisfaction even when you're doing things you wish you would rather not have to do but doing it anyway thanks to societal norms of today? Because if our attention is on what went wrong, or what annoyed us that day, or in that moment (and the moment is gone) if our attention right now is on what irked us in the past, you hold yourself in all that and keep very much alive in you what went wrong in the past. Spiritual teachers have said that your Now doesn't know if what you are thinking about is the past, present or imagination. You're beaming that signal regardless, and if it is true that we have all this power, and all of our power is right now, then it is kind of a foregone conclusion that what we are obsessing over is what we will get more of? It doesn't have to be that way, and maybe you don't do that, but looking at the way the world is today, I think it is safe to say that some of us tend to do just that. But the past is serving us enormously well. Take your past into your arms, lavish it with kisses and thank it meaningfully because it has helped you define so clearly what you prefer, what pleases you, what you find deeply interesting, what nourishes you, what you want and what feels pleasurable to you.

"Your imagination is not necessarily a departure from reality"

Try it for thirty days. When your timers go off, step into your virtual reality. The purpose of this chapter is to help inspire you to dive into virtual reality many times a day, to give you some tips and tricks to help you boost your imaginative abilities, and to help influence your landscapes/dreamscapes when you're in there. But the real purpose of this piece is to help you see clearly things that aren't there and move all the immovable things. To make your mind as clear as a movie screen and paint the sky any colour you want it to be, blue with clouds in it, purple, or completely covered in stars. Your virtual reality is yours - all yours - to do with as you please moment to moment. Make it a place of respite, make it a place to find solutions and invent ways to live out parts of your favourite books or experiences you've had before. Move your body in exactly the way you want it to move, dance, run, jump. You can do anything that you want, you are the architect. You can run your fingers through your child's hair if you can't be with them right now. You can converse with that special person about that thing that you want to talk to them about. Kiss that stranger. Be as bold and as beautiful and flexible and nimble and playful, responsive and light. Go in there to see your favourite rock star or idol, or your dead loved one, or favourite athlete or idol and converse with them, give them the mood you want them to have, speak to them, get tips from them and adore them and praise them and be praised and laugh and go on adventures and do everyday things with them. Visit with animals at a level of perfect oneness, swim in the ocean, swim in the sky. Fly. Go in for the fun and the freedom of it, the aliveness and friskiness and playfulness of it, for the sounds and the smells and the materials. For the music, the instruments, for the passion, for the artists and construction, the pure creativeness of it. Feel how sensual and sexual it can be. Feel the textures and smells and the tangible realness of it, the unlimitedness of it.

Create anything. Make everything exactly as it suits you to any moment. You are the creator and you can make it any way it pleases you, feel how it wants to please you. Make it fun, make it playful. Make it everything you have ever wanted to experience.

Never has there been a better time to enjoy
the fun of your imagination.

Not having to leave your house to experience the speed and exhilaration of skiing downhill in the Swiss Alps, or flying at 50,000 feet in a Lockheed Martin F-22 Raptor stealth fighter jet that can do tricks like fly upside down. But does everything need to be bouncing off the wall enthusiasm? Is there not power in ease or satisfaction? Maybe you want to sink a golf ball in a hole in one, or hear the sound of waves crashing on a pebbly beach. Or recreate the moment your pet or child did something new and you just want to watch it over and over it. Or kicking a soccer ball around with friends, or singing and playing your heart out like Lady Gaga and Bradley Cooper on a stage somewhere with the blinding lights and screams of thousands of people. I know for me, the vision of two impeccably dressed people, completely in their own world, dancing the waltz on the street corner with lace and chiffon and the twirls and the flutters of her dress and his expert handling always makes me smile. Then stepping into her metaphorical shoes and feeling his warm kind but firm hand on my waist while skilfully guiding me through the dance while seeing through his eyes the elegant column of her throat as she leans back, dips and relaxes her neck over his support. I find this a truly wonderful way to be in traffic.

A 30-Day Self-Experiment

Here is what you are going to do to build your own real-time virtual reality. We are going to be shaping the clay of your mind deliberately. 'Deliberately' is the name of the game. For some, imagining things that aren't there is a skill that needs to be built on, and like any skill, practice makes perfect. Practice on purpose is where the power is. It can and will get stronger and clearer the more it is used. Here's how it works: Pick up your cell phone and set thirteen timers. Set the first one for fifteen minutes after you wake up and the last one for fifteen minutes before you go to sleep, after or during your bedtime routine. Then space it out throughout your day. Make sure to apply them to all of the days of the week. You don't have to use an abrasive loud ringer (unless you want to), it can simply be put on vibrate. Because for many of us our cell phones are usually an arms reach away for most of the day, it is an easy way to stay on track. If for whatever reason you miss your timer that's okay. When you get to your phone and see the icon stating your missed alarm, proceed to your exercises then. A sample timer schedule could look like this.

8am, 8:30am, 9:30am, 11am, 12pm, 2pm, 3pm, 4:30pm, 5:45pm, 6pm, 7pm, 9:30pm, 10pm.

When your timer goes off, you are going to do the Lightbody Exercise. For those that do not have a cell phone, try to do this exercise every hour (or every time you check the time).

First, imagine in the trunk of your body a small white light that grows bigger and bigger until it encompasses your entire body and the space around it. The light could grow slowly, or it could engulf you in between the space of a single heartbeat. You could, if you so please, imagine that that light blasts out of you and in a wide thick stream encircling the planet on which you stand. Then widen the stream of light until its swallows the earth whole in pure light. This does not need to take more than five seconds. Sometimes it helps to look at it from a different perspective, maybe you shrink yourself down a bit or look at yourself from a different angle encased in pure blinding light. Maybe you picture the Earth the size of a beach ball or marble and illuminated with light.

It takes will and it takes focus.

Next, you will play a little game of self-imposed virtual reality. To do this, simply imagine a scene that makes you feel good. It does not matter what the scene is, and it helps if it isn't something that is a pressing, strong desire within you. Just imagine yourself having fun. Use as many details as possible, and through the detail and fun atmosphere of your imagined landscape, the possibilities are truly limitless. You can spend anywhere from five to twenty seconds or more playing this game.

You will do this every time your timer goes off and after a couple of days, you may find yourself doing it in between the timer as well. Don't fight the feeling, instead milk it with all the detail you can muster.

Be easy about this, and be playful about it. It takes focus and it takes will. But not only are you completely capable of using your attention in a different playful way, it also becomes easier and easier after each passing day. By day 30 it will come as easy to you as seeing what's physically there. By making a decision to do this and knowing your power to focus is not only your universal given power, it is the *only* thing you have 100% control over. You have the free will and the power to focus. Your power to focus your attention is the most powerful tool you have.

Maybe you will go underwater and laugh because it feels as warm as bath water, and then dive under exploring the colours and sea life, and instead of the muffled sound of hearing underwater you'll hear with perfect clarity the song of a Humpback whale. Maybe you'll reach out your hand and stroke the side of its gargantuan body as it gracefully moves through the water, and its rough but soft rubbery skin is so soothing maybe you press your body closer and rest your cheek on it and hold on while it glides effortlessly through the water, and maybe it breaches the water, its spout blowing water that sprays out and over you. Maybe it is dark and the sky is full of trillions of stars, maybe one of those stars is shooting through the sky in a graceful arc. Maybe there is an iceberg nearby and the ocean is glowing with phosphorescence all around you.

Maybe you would be interested in careening down trails on your mountain bike going forty miles per hour, dodging trees and boulders, feeling your handlebars trembling and pushing your bike to the limit while being in complete control.

Maybe you want the pure exhilaration of jumping off the highest diving cliff. Maybe you turn on your heels and smile in knowing before you lean back and tip over the edge completely - feeling the drop in your stomach - the acceleration and momentum picking up speed until you feel the ice-cold water envelop you as you submerge.

Maybe you are still and standing knee-deep in a large flowing river waiting quietly and spotting a large fish swimming by and you thrust your hands into the water catching the fish with your bare hands.

Perhaps you pick up a kitten and feel its tiny warm body settle into your hands while it looks up at you with a sleepy but focused look. Feeling your feet in your favourite pair of comfortable shoes. Can you fly out to see the Earth just outside of our stratosphere? The blue glow? Just sit there for a second and feel the quiet and the glow of blue and feel its calm. Its surety.

What about sitting on a rowboat on a still lake? Trees and open spaces along the shoreline. Birds calling and fish jumping. Put your paddles in the water and hear it as you make the motion with your arms to let your paddle stir the water gliding you forward.

Maybe you could use some chill time so you go to Kansas and stand in the thousands of acres of golden wheat under the marigold sun.

Or maybe you're at the office and maybe you simply make the screen you are working at larger, or add a few screens and turn it into a supercomputer. Maybe you'll imagine the spicy burrito you have in your office fridge for lunch and pick up a clean spoon from the drawer to scoop out a dollop of thick organic sour cream. Maybe you'll swipe your finger through the cool cream and lick it slowly off your finger, savouring its deliciousness .

Maybe as you are driving there are lights up and down every tree, trillions of them, lining both sides of the road. Or maybe while you walk you will play with architecture Inception-style and effortlessly erect buildings and change floor plans or create blueprints from the ground up, or bend the sidewalk upwards, walk up, and appreciate the view from there. Or maybe you hear the bees buzzing around your bright rhododendrons, and smell the fresh air of your garden in spring.

Maybe you're on a basketball court and with every shot at the basket the swish is audible and it is like you're so on your game and you and your teammates are of the same mind and someone is right there exactly where you need them to be and setting you up exactly right and it is fun and you're laughing and everyone's timing is perfect and you just dominate the game.

Maybe you can conjure up the smell of Lily of the Valley, or the smell of your grandfather's cigar. Or freshly brewed coffee. Or lemon cake. Or lavender flowers.

Maybe you will run as fast as you can through the forest barefoot in a flowy white dress, or shirtless with loose pants, feeling the spongy forest floor with sunlight streaming through the trees just right and revealing elaborate golden spiderwebs. Maybe you swing from tree to tree like Tarzan, or jump to the top of the tallest tree and sit there looking out as far as the eye can see, or maybe you look down and spot fellow hikers and playfully ponder jumping down to give them a fright.

Maybe you go around the environment you're in and you playfully change objects into other things. This cup is now a goblet and this chair a lazy-boy or throne lined with diamonds and rubies. Maybe this doorway could be wider and taller and painted burnt orange, and this door with glorious detail is now emerald green. This hallway will be longer and let's put a door here and here and some stairs over here leading to the top floor. Let's make the ceilings see through and three times as high and make these windows wrap around the whole structure flooding the room in natural light.

Look to your left or your right and find an object, desk, chair, toy, couch, lamp, book and lift it into the air. Turn it around, open the pages flip through it and put it back down. Lift the couch and turn it to look at the back of it, or flip it upside down and look at the bottom, then right it and put it on the other side of the room. Sit on it or stand on it in its new place.

Maybe you just transport yourself into a gazebo and listen to the rain falling all around you. Smell the earth and the gardens in bloom and how it is magnified in the wet of the rain.

Maybe it's a successful first attempt at high jump, soaring way past the bar and landing in a fluid elegant crouch. Maybe you run up the side of a building and do backflips parkour style.

When your timer goes off, where are you? Are you at home or work?

Are you out on your boat or your patio? Are you with friends or fighting with a loved one? What do you want right now? Not so much physically, but what emotion would you like to have right now? Ease? Relief? Happiness? Peace? Not so much monetary or a new item like a car or house, but what would really please you right now that's easy to see. Is your child laughing? Walking up to your spouse and holding them tight? Feeling appreciated or encouraged? Step into your virtual reality and lightly and breezily play out what is wanted at the forefront. If it incurs negative emotion it will spit you out, so then you have to come at it in a more general way -- off the topic -- but feel it out because it just might work perfectly for you. Maybe you're in traffic and you can push with your mind all of the vehicles on the road to the side and create a wide-open path for you to drive through. Or maybe you push a button to initiate the flying sequence of the vehicle and you lift into the air and fly over all the cars. Maybe you put someone you really want to hang around with next to you. How are they sitting? Look at that smile and the way they laugh. Feel the easiness of being with them as you expertly and easily handle your flying car.

Or maybe you pick up your water bottle and with your mind make it effervescent and watch it through the glass, the thousands of tiny bubbles all floating upwards, listening to them gently bubbling. Then make it go the other direction and watch them all float downward. Swirl them around like a snow globe.

Do things you want to experience, maybe you want to stand on the edge of the tallest cliff edge and look down before you run and leap off the edge and feel yourself free fall.

Make it playful, make it fun, and let your imagination go. Do this for thirty days in a row.

I conducted a focus group of open-minded individuals that were willing to play my little game and some of the things they told me blew my socks off.

"Within the first three or four days, life just seemed to be reacting differently to me. Like the world really was my oyster."

"I just feel great. Like consistently great. Good things just keep happening to me."

"It feels to me like I have access to thoughts and ideas I've never had before."

"I've built my dream house from the ground up! I know the layout, where all the windows are…I've actually looked out of all of those windows and know each view, I have felt the carpet under my bare feet and have baked a pie from scratch

in my dream kitchen, using my dream oven and hearing my dream oven timer go off. It was unreal. No, it was super real!"

"Since I started this (I'm on day eleven) the TV has been off a lot more. I'm just finding I can entertain myself so much better than what's on other programs and even with social media I'm finding I'm just enjoying my own company way more and I really don't need those other things to entertain me."

"I swim in the ocean and can feel the salt dry on my skin as I walk up my stairs topless with the warm sun shining down on me. I can make it so real and it is genuinely so pleasurable."

"Even if I'm in the middle of something that has my full attention, when the timer goes off I can change the colours of something around me and even just the slight manipulation is amusing to see. And it's that feeling of being slightly amused that interests me. It doesn't always have to be building muscle cars (my go-to) or sitting in a hockey arena watching my favourite team kill it."

"I love butterflies, and so I put them in my virtual reality often. And it is so funny because it is like everywhere I look in real life, I see butterflies! In books, on clothing, on a bumper sticker, all over my garden. It makes me smile every time. One actually flew into the house the other day!"

"I was definitely the weirdo sitting on the train with a massive grin, deep in my virtual reality."

One participant, after a lifetime of having a very fuzzy not very colourful imagination found herself in what she described was similar to standing in the middle of the movie Avatar with all the humming vibrant plant life and the visceral life force connection, she could literally just think it up in the middle of her day no matter what she was doing.

Another said that she looked forward to when her timers went off, being able to use whatever setting she was in and being able to manipulate it to her choosing was so much fun, she felt like a wizard and how it genuinely changed her emotional set point regularly throughout her day. And how the things she wanted out of life just gravitated toward her. Never has she been more successful or happy. And never has she felt more in love with her mind.

Another in the group said that it has been over two months since she was in my focus group and emailed me to say that she's kept her timers on and consistently still plays 'virtual reality' every single day because of what it does for her life.

It is powerful knowing that your mind has no limit and with that non-limit the creative control we have of being able to not only see things that aren't there, but make them so pleasurable and so detailed, so real that it can very much be like its transporting you to a different time/space.

It's a matter of focus. It's a matter of will. It's a matter of wanting to switch things up in your life. It is a decision. Does meditation help? Of course it does. It helps every aspect of your life. Does meditation mean a bunch of different things to as many different people? Of course. For this exercise, the type of meditation that this is about is this one . Wear loose comfortable clothing and sit or lay down in a comfortable place of your choosing. Turn on a bathroom fan or listen for a sound that is uninteresting to you but consistent. (Air conditioner, heavy rainfall etc.) Now relax your body, breathe normally, and turn your attention to the sound. If your mind wanders bring your attention to the sound and gently put your whole attention back to the sound. Relax into the sound and quietly listen. After a minute or two of focused attention you will feel some light tingles or floating in the head and or body. That is your energy on the move, energy in motion. This is a sign of a very successful meditation. To supercharge it, keep redirecting from the sensations to the sound. Don't work hard at this, if its feels like work you are trying too hard. There are no mantras. This is not the time to ask questions and receive answers; its just for a gentle break of the mind and a conscious realization of your connection to Self. This is easy. It is easy to listen to a sound. It is easy to give yourself permission to do nothing but this impeccably important work of chilling out and giving your mind some quiet. It is easy to blend you with You. Fifteen minutes a day is all you need, and -- what's that saying? -- if you're too busy to carve out fifteen minutes of your day then you need to sit for an hour. This Zen proverb is not only right, it is really onto something. The idea that we as a society measure that the more you do the more you are worth is the most flawed premise of our world today. As a human Being, in this time and space reality never has there been a more glorious time to practice the pure knowing of our goodness, our rightness, our pure knowing that shouts at us from a cellular level that "the better you feel the more good things you allow". That feeling of feeling good is the 'gas in our cars' that propel us forward to everything that we ever wanted. Doesn't that just feel better knowing that? Doesn't that just feel better knowing that you are worthy of good feelings just for being focused here into these physical bodies? Don't you like knowing that you are good, no matter what you have lived, no matter what is around you and no matter where you are standing right here and now, and that you deserve good? Doesn't it feel great knowing that from this place of feeling good, all these astonishing very real inspiration and synchronistic events are being hand plucked and perfectly orchestrated and executed just for you in ways we couldn't have thought up if we tried? And you coming into and realizing your power just skyrockets and don't you feel good knowing that feeling good is at the basis of who we really are? Give yourself the imaginings. Treat yourself to the pure pleasures that seeing with your mind brings, things that just ring your bells, if for no other reason than its fun and it feels good. Do it because you are meant to feel good. Do it because it is your natural state of being. Do it for your love of yourself. Do it for the confidence, do it for the joy. Do it for all that came before you who are here with you cheering you on. Do it because you deserve to see the power of your focus, of your deliberate focus.

For those of you that say, "what if I don't know what I want to visualize?", start with movement. You could start with sitting on a swing on a sturdy swing set and go back and forth building your momentum. Feel the wind pick up and the dip in your stomach as you lean backwards feeling it swing you back and forth, back and forth, legs going up and down increasing your speed and smile and breathe and lean back and be suspended. There are no problems here. Only solutions. Only peace. Only pure love flowing to you, only pure, positive energy focused at you. Loving you. Guiding you. Appreciating you. Helping you. Loving you. Leading you. Finding you. Knowing you. Watching over you. Holding you. Guiding you. Inspiring you. Loving you. Get into an endless loop of that and see what happens in your real life as soon as today.

There is only love here for you. Love and the pinching-off of love. But love is all there is. Being shown consistent real life here and now - evidence of truly seen you are, how completely taken care of and how blessed you are, now that is one heck of a way to live!

good grief

Navigating Loss with Love

By Karen Armstrong

My first memory of grief was witnessing my mom on the phone with the shocking news that her dad had unexpectedly died. The phone dropped to the floor as she screamed, and the shivers of her shrill pierced through my body as I felt her panic. As a highly sensitive empath, I immediately gasped for breath as though my own heart had stopped in the wake of her pain. Her reaction was dramatically appropriate in the essence that she felt it. This is how we feel as Human Beings. As Spirit has shown me, "You feel the intensity of Love, whether feeling it as pain or bliss; it is the same energy." So any news of a perceived loss is perfectly felt and expressed in that exact moment. The wisdom, however, remains in the choice of how to respond, how to release the emotional energy and how to integrate the whole grief experience.'

When my brother died, we were both in our early 20s, fifteen months apart in age. His truck went off a dead-end cliff and plunged into the frigid water below. The panic (as I previously witnessed with my mom) didn't hit me until a few months later, and although it looked different than my mom's, it was the familiar, piercing shock of despair that aired a resemblance. I finally crashed into the reality that my brother was really gone - where everything seemed to shatter in one sudden, blurry flash. My dazed eyes hid behind shaded lenses and life would never look the same again. This was a significant blow to my seemingly simple life, so with these new shades of perception, I welcomed the label of 'her brother died'. This permitted me to continue feeling miserable, depressed and isolated. It allowed me to focus on how awful it was that he had died and how he died. It also perpetuated the significance that his questionable death left so many empty holes in the existence of so many lives. The police investigation eventually determined that it was black ice that caused his fate that day. Yet there was widespread confusion that gnawed at the ultimate question around his death; was it an accident or was it suicide? So while the jaws of despair continued to chew on my perception of reality, I grasped onto the strange comfort I found in the familiarity of the grief. Desolation had become my new normal and I had mastered ignoring my needs to keep fuelling this new existence. Labels, when we succumb to them, carry a tremendous energy load. I was 'that' person now, whom everyone expected to be grieving…and therefore I was.

After some time of going through the 'stages of grief', I was driving along an open highway on a beautiful sunny day and the song "I Can See Clearly Now" came on the radio. The warmth of the sun's rays wrapped me in a much-desired embrace and my body finally felt safe to relax as I melted into nature's gift of sun and song.

I can see clearly now the rain is gone
I can see all obstacles in my way
Gone are the dark clouds that had me blind
It's gonna be a bright (bright)
Bright (bright) sunshiny day
It's gonna be a bright (bright)
Bright (bright) sunshiny day
Oh, yes I can make it now the pain is gone
All of the bad feelings have disappeared
Here is that rainbow I've been praying for
It's gonna be a bright (bright)
Bright (bright) sunshiny day
Look all around, there's nothing but blue skies
Look straight ahead, there's nothing but blue skies
I can see clearly now the rain is gone
I can see all obstacles in my way
Here is that rainbow I've been praying for
It's gonna be a bright (bright)
Bright (bright) sunshiny day
It's gonna be a bright (bright)
Bright (bright) sunshiny day

~"I Can See Clearly Now" by Johnny Nash

The words vibrated through the speakers and saturated my cells with the profundity of Divine Messaging. Everything was okay. I was okay. Pleasantly surprised, I found myself singing along and felt something I hadn't felt in a very long time. It was Joy. I felt a glimmer of hope at that moment, through the magical power of music. The relief was more than welcome as the silent tears of joy cleansed my tired cheeks in the realization that I could feel this way again. And then, to my dismay, it was unwillingly and abruptly shut down. The grief default setting prevailed. "You can't feel happy. Your brother died. You're not allowed to smile. You have to be sad. If you're happy, then you don't care that he's gone." The nature of these thoughts continued to pour through me until they diluted the relief from grief and I found myself in a depressed driving mode once again. What just happened? Was I a product of societal grief conditioning or still in a stage of grieving? Or a combination of both?

GOOD GRIEF!

Good Grief: A slang expression or perhaps something more meaningful?

"Good Grief" is an exclamation to express surprise, alarm, shock, dismay, or some other, usually undesired emotion. It feels like a sarcastic expression of frustration, in a slow-motion slump, to accompany the words. The lineage of this expression, though, is linked back to God. "Good God" or "Good Lord" and while it can still embody a more derogatory expression, is it possible that it holds a hidden key to unlock a higher perspective that has the power to transform one of humanity's most prevalent suppressors that keep us at a lower vibration? Could it possibly lead us to a place of Surrender? Well, whether I liked it, desired to change it, embraced it, or not; this was the whole point to discover, on my journey with grief.

Grief defined according to Wikipedia: a multifaceted response to loss, particularly to the loss of someone or some living thing that has died, to which a bond or affection was formed. Although conventionally focused on the emotional response to loss, it also has physical, cognitive, behavioural, social, cultural, spiritual and philosophical dimensions. Grief is a natural response to loss. It is the emotional suffering one feels when something or someone the individual loves is taken away or is no longer available. The grief associated with death is familiar to most people, but individuals grieve in connection with a variety of losses throughout their lives, such as unemployment, ill-health or the end of a relationship. Loss can be categorized as either physical or abstract, the physical loss being related to something that the individual can touch or measure, such as losing a spouse through death, while other types of loss are abstract, and relate to aspects of a person's social interactions.

As life is constantly moving and changing, and experiences and connections come and go, we continue to evolve as deemed appropriate by our evolutionary needs. Yet based on the definition of grief, any attachment is ultimately going to lead to a form of grieving once that attachment is gone. Would that not lead us along a path where we are always in a state of grief, for one reason or another? My experience has revealed that all gains and losses are orchestrated as part of our evolution…and that the choice remains in how to respond to the experience. A choice of vibrational response; which doesn't create a gain or loss, but alters how we perceive it, respond to it and therefore, experience it. I've been taught, through moving the proverbial mountains, that it is not our vibration that determines whether we experience loss in any particular form. There is a powerful Universe that knows exactly what we need to help us evolve so that whatever we do lose, we will also gain on a much deeper level and the real freedom, again, lies in the choices we make about it.

We are all infinite spiritual beings, part of a whole, from one source of energy. That Universal source of energy is Love.

This has been instilled into me, not only by Spirit but also through exposure to many teachings from around the world. Although I do not adhere to any specific course or doctrine, I appreciate that, fundamentally, it always comes back to Love.

In A Course in Miracles, it says:
"Nothing real can be threatened. Nothing unreal exists.
Therein lies the peace of God".

If the energetic source of everything is Love, anything other than Love is only in our perception and therefore not real? Hmm...

Initially, I found this concept disturbingly frustrating. Grief had always felt very raw and real to me and I simply could not comprehend that it wasn't. Seriously!? How can someone say that the trauma is not true? How can they say my broken heart and the intense pain that I'm feeling, is not real? The complexities of grief and how each of us experiences it makes it impossible to pinpoint the preciseness of how to respond. Yet, while suffering amid culminated personal losses, I eventually learned the deeper meaning of what this meant - the meaning of choosing differently. Choosing to perceive via a different lens; that of Truth, instead of accepting the same lens of conditioned complacency. And that Truth…is Love.

Now, the last thing I ever wanted to hear, while drowning in my personal pool of tumultuous emotions, was that I needed to love myself more. While all my energy was being sucked down the drain just to survive, where was the extra energy to love myself more supposed to come from?

"Stop flailing." This is something my Spirit Guides have conveyed often.

"Huh?" The blunt delivery of those words has always shocked my ego into immediate and begrudged submission. The wisdom of "stop flailing" reverberates through all justifications of my ego's coping mechanisms, as I anchor the message yet again- becoming highly reactive and flailing creates the turbulent waves that I am desperately trying to survive. Gaaah. So I take a deep breath and feel my phantom flails subside.

What happens when we stop, breathe and relax? We float. Still in the emotional pool, and still nervous about sinking to the bottom, yet also having a more evolved/higher experience of it. When we float instead of flail, we experience surrender. We are in a position to receive and to allow our energy to be channelled in another direction…streamlined into our own healing heart.

This is how I learned; and not just a "yeah yeah, love heals all" notch in the spiritual ego tool belt; but really learned how self-love is the foundation for healing the world.

The Universe dances to the tune of our infinite perfection - with notes that we are made of love, no matter what is going on around us. Only in reflection, did I realize that grieving, in any capacity, does not change that. It is an experience of responding to an external influence and it has the profound power to permanently shift our perspective. If everything is Love, then anything other than Love is in the perception of what is being experienced. That perception is false when it is seen through the glasses that were worn during a previous experience and has a default setting in our nervous system. So while the experience was real, that doesn't make what was thought about it real. It is not wrong - it is just lacking love and therefore not Truth.

With different lenses, the opportunity to see, perceive and respond differently, is then presented, as the relationship with whomever or whatever, isn't taken away. When the lenses change, it's no longer a loss…it's a liberating shift that activates a more evolved perspective and therefore, adventure with life.

Surrender.

If you lose your job, you're not unemployable - you have been liberated to change jobs. If you lose your home, you're not homeless, you have been liberated to change where you live. If you lose your health, you're not permanently ill - you have been liberated to make changes affecting your body - to either remain in it or leave it and change form. If you lose a partner in a relationship, you're not alone - you have been liberated to have new experiences with others. If you lose a loved one to death, they haven't left you behind- they have been liberated from their physical body, with the ability and desire to foster a different connection with you.

Yes, choosing to perceive through the lens of Truth can feel almost impossible at times! These liberating experiences can cause a great deal of stress and distress... and requires the inner Light Warrior to look fear directly in the eye - with courage, resilience and faith- to rise and thrive beyond the challenges that only fear can present.

I have often questioned, "In a world where there is so much beauty created from Love, why is there also so much pain? If there is so much Love, how is it possible that there is so much chaos?"

"You feel as deeply in pain as you do in love," my Spirit Guides reminded me again. "It is all the same energy. Feel the contrast in your perception. You can rise above it - to see beyond fear and feel the Truth."

We are all awakening to the Truth of Love, which entails navigating through a complicated maze of Truths to be revealed, and as a process of releasing, will feel the grief as old patterns, beliefs, lineage lines and attachments are cleared from our life and our energy bodies. This process takes us from the old paradigm; our three-dimensional world, to the new paradigm, referred to as many things, including awakened consciousness and multiple higher dimensions.

There are many studies, theories and variables available to consider when a person is grieving from a third-dimensional perspective. Without weaving through the tapestries of a grieving process and/or an ascension process, we can more simply help ourselves and one another- no matter what we're struggling with- by choosing differently.

CONDITIONED RESPONSES

As we are all aware, feeling grief as a human being sucks terribly. At times, I felt the excruciating stabs in places I didn't know I could feel pain.

These daggers seemingly have the potential to pulverize our very existence and leave us feeling totally defeated, isolated and sometimes unsure of how we're going to continue. While the process of grieving is necessary -- the energy wants to leave our bodies -- it can feel debilitating to the point of total depletion. What is that? Why do we feel so out of control? How do we allow that to happen?

I started pining for answers as more questions bubbled to the surface.

Is it possible that we're conditioned to be attached to the grieving itself?

Is it a way for us to justify what we don't understand and a way of feeling alive amidst the chaos and clutter of societal structured expectations, only because we don't know how to break free of what we are exhausted from feeling?

When I was willing to acknowledge the fear-based security blanket of conditioning, clarity was revealed - like a weeping child bundled up in a fuzzy blanket- the reassuring comfort in feeling grief was found. There is comfort in feeling the pain. There is comfort in staying wrapped up in the energy that helps us feel closer to the departed, with whomever or whatever form that takes. It hurts horribly and it creates entanglements of self-sabotage; however, it also connects us to what is familiar and is therefore strangely soothing.

When something is being experienced as any of our previously sanctioned bereavement responses, whether it rides a vast spectrum of melancholy, anguish, heartbreak, or devastation, is it possible that we are conditioned to perpetuate those feelings to justify this lack of understanding? We are spiritual beings that have the capacity for a truly magical evolution while on this playground planet and having a very human experience. So when someone or something we care about has been unexpectedly or unwillingly eliminated from our conscious existence, our automatic response is to perceive it as a dreadful burden, with the capacity for unfathomable layers of radical awfulness. Even so, as I learned, diminished discernment is simply an experience that's lacking love. It's not wrong...it is just the perception we have when we are going through healing a wound of our ego while wearing old lenses, and it is all part of our individual awakening.

So much of what we are taught early on is to be afraid of what doesn't feel good. This is where I came to question whether grief is, at least mostly, a conditioned response. I had collected an exhaustive array of shaded lenses to choose from. They weren't based on the truth of Love, but they appeared to serve me well and with that, there was a twisted satisfaction that protected the survival toolkit of grief responses.

Watching my mom was very much a learned response. ' Bad news equals; Scream — check. Panic — check. Confusion — check. Shut down the emotional release — check. Say everything is okay when it clearly is not — check. Watching my mom was one of my first memories of grief conditioning. It wasn't a choice she was making as a mother to teach this. She was also taught, through her own traumatic childhood experiences, how to respond and what to do or not do…and her coping mechanisms were also on auto-pilot.

But what if she was able to celebrate her dad departing? What if she had gotten off the phone and immediately sat us down and explained that his soul left his body and that he was now free? What if, even though there was shock and sadness, she expressed how she was feeling? What if she explained that we won't be able to see him in his physical body anymore however we can have a new relationship with him in spirit? What if we were told that it's okay to be happy for him, that he is in a peaceful, loving place? And what if we were taught that when we're sad, miss him or feel confused, we can talk about it and cry and let the energy out, without feeling judged or that something is wrong with us?

To avoid the pain of loss with distractions and yet avoid happiness to prove we are in pain about the loss…sends us spiralling down a rabbit hole. What if we choose to grieve outside of the conditioning? If our conditioned response to grief is learned, then we can unlearn it and cultivate a different experience with loss in any form.

"GOOD" GRIEF

My awakening around grief revealed this other way of living it. And as I've shared, it's been integrated into my awareness as a form of reflective perception, linking the experience of grief in all-encompassing elements, back to that single source of all energy. Love.

It is in times of sorrow and grief, that we are challenged to dig deep and find the strength, courage and wisdom to help us move forward. Ultimately, what can be found during such times is the flicker of light within, where the embers of a distressed pilot light become ignited to shine brighter- and gives us a morsel of hope. Then, from a gradually higher perspective, we can see grief as a beautiful expression of the human experience. Whether the lens of perception remains a loss or evolves to liberation, it still becomes more about integrating the energy of loving and caring so deeply, that we feel the contrast.

Our Divine nature is to love, play and be in optimal health, vitality and happiness...and our Divine cellular foundation has a default setting to take us back to that space. Remaining lost in a loss causes repetitious ailments of grief to overwhelm our nervous system; while the embodiment of 'good' grief is there to shift the focus from the 'negative conditioning' to fuel that tiniest morsel of hope within. The Truth is Love. The fuel is Self-Love. Through cosmic alchemy, it grows and expands into a transformative shining force that ripples out and liberates not only the grieving one but everyone.

"You are still there for a reason. That reason is to LIVE. You can choose to live in love or live in fear, and you are free in that choice" as Spirit has consistently established. When I was willing to remove the shaded lenses, the Truth appeared- choosing to honour Love is the only real state of being and fear is the limitation of perception. And through repeated instructions from Spirit, I've learned that the very experiences that leave us feeling grief, are here to help us clear the denser energies out of our energy fields. The choice is to either fear what we are feeling and push the energy back down or love ourselves as we allow Surrender to fully heal our body, mind, heart and soul.

To me, it felt like the concept of releasing all the sadness meant that I had been completely emptied out and left to wallow as a hollow shell. And the thought of feeling nothing, having nothing or being nothing, was somehow worse than feeling constantly distraught with grief. Who was I, if I wasn't succumbing to the circumstances around me? Can I be powerful enough to feel such emptiness and still enjoy my life amidst the chaos? When plummeting into the spiral of chaotic perception, I had to choose; continue to feel victimized and out of control or STOP the spiral with the intervention of a different, clear, set of lenses - with no one to blame, no victimhood, no waiting for someone else to make it better for me. I had to choose differently and give myself the love I was waiting to receive.

Sometimes on our journey with grief, we see the proverbial 'light at the end of the tunnel', where we feel relief relatively fast. Sometimes it takes longer, while stunted by the effects of expectations. When we find ourselves in a repeated pattern of grief, are we still in the grieving process? Or is it the conditioned response that keeps us looping around a cycle of perpetual pain?

Good Grief is felt in the energy of pure self-love so that no matter what we're experiencing, we still know that we are okay. To go against the conditioning is to choose another way, that would allow us to experience the grieving process with more ease, more compassion and more love.

For me, the wisdom of choosing to honour love means taking care of the physical body. It means allowing all releases from the emotional body. It means honouring the memories of whatever is now gone by giving the Self more love than ever before. It means having the willingness to choose another way. With nothing to prove, nothing to hide, and nothing to fear, there is a miraculous reservoir of energy that's made available for extra self-care when feeling drained in disheartenment.

Grief transforms us. It's not something we move through or get over. It's something that we integrate and it changes us. Allowing good grief to change us, is how we continue our journey with the newfound wisdom that liberates us to shine brighter as we celebrate the very grief that brought us to this new place in life.

So in the wake of accumulated loss, I learned that there is another way; to grieve unconditionally, through Self Love.

I asked myself, "If I make the effort to feel better instead of worse, what is the worst that can happen? Can I truly feel good while riding the tsunami of grief, and then possibly experience grief as something good?"

CONDITIONED EXPERIENCE OR "GOOD" GRIEF?

Despite the vicious curve balls that I've witnessed retched into my reality, I have always maintained a level of gratitude in the awareness that my 'situation' was not as grave as others in the world. With that awareness, I am not here to justify any reasoning or degree of grief. When personal loss knocks at the door of your heart, the pain and confusion can be intensely overwhelming, regardless of who you are or what the perceived loss is. Those curve balls don't make an appointment in your schedule or wait for you to be more prepared to catch them. Like the game of 'Hide and Seek' that we learn when we are young, the conditioned grief responses are counting down "Ready or not, here I come." And like the twisted nature of that game, we're taught to find the best hiding spot, so not to be found - to somehow elude the haunting nature of being hunted and harmed with shock when grief bangs on our door. We are taught to live in fear and hide in the dark - where the dark acts as a false protector - while hiding from the darkness of grief as if it is the ultimate energy to fear.

When we are (knowingly or not) ready to evolve, the healing experience of grief makes no exceptions when showing up, and yet we do have the choice of how to experience it. The point of awareness and preparation is to accept personal accountability as the only one who can choose for oneself; continue to hide in, and from, the dark OR stand tall in your powerful light, igniting profound healing for yourself and the world, through awareness and self-love.

During a short time, I experienced the 'losses' that I always feared as the 'big ones'…ALL of them. First, I lost my physical strength and capacity of wellness through an accident, and then literally, one after another, in only a few short years, I experienced losing all of my financial security, my health, my home, all of my belongings, and four of the most influential humans in my life (all loved ones), all died within three years. With an overstimulated nervous system and a deeply conditioned response to grief, how was I going to survive these losses piling on top of one another like this? With each additional loss, the accumulating weight was driving me deeper into the rabbit hole of despair.

My first conscious moment of choosing 'Good' Grief over the conditioned response, was presented to me while I laid on the living room floor, utterly depleted from illness. It felt like I was being sucked into a vortex in the floor as the motion of tortuous despondency drained my life force energy. I can still hear the thunderclap as Spirit smacked the air directly in front of my face and my declining spin was abruptly interrupted.

"RIGHT NOW…choose a path; Love or Fear." My Guides were unfaltering in this urgent deliverance.

And what they meant, was that I had to choose whether to see the circumstances in the higher truth of Love - and that everything was been happening to help me evolve - or choose to see it through the limited lens of a lower perception.

"Is this an exit portal?" I asked.

"Yes," Spirit replied.

"Good, then I'd like to come Home. This is too much."

"This portal is closed for you, Dear. You are staying to continue your journey there."

Disgruntled and sarcastically I answered, "Well if I have to stay, then obviously I choose Love."

Unbeknownst to me during that conversation with Spirit, choosing Love meant losing my apartment, all of my furnishings and belongings, and scrambling around without a home for fifteen months. All of this was happening during a time that began while I was in poor health. This journey was gravely uncomfortable and stressful and I tried fighting it every step of the way. Yet I was continually given the opportunity to learn a degree of Trust that I had not imagined possible.

Trust in the Universe to lead me to the next safe place.

Trust in the people who showed up.

Trust that Kinja (my beloved cat) and I would both have food in our tummies.

Trust in me that I could handle it all. That I could somehow find those morsels of hope within me.

While sitting on the bed at one location early in my journey, I was sinking into the desolate tears of my reality. The allotted temporary stay was over and I had nowhere to go. This was it. I was actually going to be sleeping in the car with my cat (I was not parting with her — that was non-negotiable!). As I succumbed to the impairment of my self-inflicted blinders, the tormented cycle of negativity fuelled my shaking fists in an attempt to demand help from the Universe. And then Spirit spoke, with a sense of loving sarcasm, as if entertained by my current display of anguish. "If you stop flailing, we can show you."

I felt their Divine humour, however, did not share their enlightened view. I took a few deep breaths and tried to compose myself. Snuffling, I asked, "Okay, now what?"

"Be patient," my Guides said, and I could feel their collective grin.

Less than a minute later my phone buzzed. It was a text from someone with whom I wasn't close to at the time, but was aware of my situation. The text read, "Hey, if you and Kinja need a place to stay, you are welcome to sleep on my couch for a bit."

Completely stunned and beyond relieved, I cried new tears, this time of pure gratitude.

I got the message again. "You have a choice to see with Love. Love puts you into a place of both seeing and receiving the miracles. Take care of yourself so you feel good no matter what's going on around you. Allow Life to unravel and help you, by clearing all dense energies out of your body, while you honour who you are and give yourself loving care."

Throughout the range of places and people that I stayed with, the default conditioning would eventually cycle back and I would resort to struggling, resulting in a state of perpetuated worry. By this time, I was dizzy in disparities from fighting the volatility of the vortex. When will this end? What about my health? Where will my new home be? How will I possibly get back on my feet again? Will. This. Ever. End? In my endless quest for answers, Spirit continued to give the same message over and over and over, throughout those fifteen months...

"Do whatever you need to do to create peace within yourself. Trust. Enjoy this adventure. Everything is taken care of. Take care of yourself so that you feel good. BE LOVE so you experience the vibration where you can see the miracles that are already occurring."

With a desperate sigh, I agreed. What did I have to lose by heeding their instructions? First, I did whatever I could to make my external spaces more comforting and put energy into being positive and grateful. As I nurtured my healing heart, I was able to feel glimpses of hope as my Trust continued to grow. So there I was, in the midst of personal chaos, putting my focus and energy into feeling good, and gratefully allowing my patience to wear thin as I waited for things to shift. Then something did start to happen. One by one, albeit with supportive intentions, people kept asking me, "How are you even standing right now?", "Oh man, if it was me, I'd be drinking by now.", "How is it possible that you're smiling?" There were also those, who were unable to fathom what I was experiencing, who either projected very harsh opinions of what I needed to do or not do, and those who simply turned away and wanted nothing to do with me and my current reality. So I became aware, once again, of the expectations and conditions we have around grief. With what little energy I had left to maintain my positive outlook, I internalized everyone's opinions with my feelings of despair that had been tucked away and went back to focusing on how awful it felt to be in such a state of loss because I didn't know what else to do. It seemingly took less energy to be in the space of grief, where at least I felt supported, even if it was encouraging a mediocre existence, struggling in chaos.

Again, was I a product of grief conditioning, in a stage of grieving, or a combination of it all?

When we are chaotically spinning in our perpetual private black hole, regardless of what the grief is about, the last thing on our mind is how we're going to feel better or what we are going to do about it, as all our energy is put into surviving the darkness. Grief can feel like a clenching vortex that keeps us spinning through the cycle until, if not by choice, it spits us out to stagger back to the remains of our pre-grief life. Yet this is a self-fulfilled pile of shit - grief changes us, so it is impossible to return to the way we were before the grief experience. We will keep looping in the stench of this spiral until we choose to see it and experience it, differently. Juggling the willingness to change, with making, what feels like an impossible choice, can present as the most agonizing decision until it's finally made.

For the entire fifteen months and beyond, every single 'next place' was just as miraculous. Regardless of how I perceived the insufferable stress, it was perfect alignment every time, as each solution was presented to me within a day, if not hours of necessity. After being jolted from one moment to the next, for those fifteen months, I finally landed in my own private place. It was only through reflection that I was able to recognize that absolutely no amount of self-doubt, sabotaging self-care or fear, changed the fact that there was always a perfectly aligned place to go to and there really was a Divine Flow to everything that had happened. I felt a tremendous amount of grief through that time, with the perception that I had lost SO much. Yet, during the entire journey, I still had the choice, as Spirit kept teaching me, to give myself Love to feel better and take better care of myself. It was only in retrospect, that I was also able to embrace the bigger Miracles occurring: the wonderful people who had welcomed me into their homes and the experiences of true support and friendship that we mutually shared. Therein lies the true path of choosing Love.

During that same fifteen-month period, the passing of two loved ones, only three months apart, added an insurmountable amount of grief onto an already overloaded system. And yet the message from Spirit continued to remain the same. "Do what you need to feel a bit better now. Do something to honour the departed souls, to help you feel more peaceful. This is for you, not them." Since my resources were extremely limited, and they were in another province, I honoured their life journey by colouring each of them a designated picture that reflected an element of their life here. It was such a simple gesture and yet it helped me relax so that I was able to put a lot of unexpressed energy into something just for them. I also took out the back seats and converted the back of my car into a private cozy nook where I could go to be alone and feel the overwhelming emotions, as I gave myself the privacy to dive into the depth of pain with those losses.

Within three months of finally settling into my own place, the car that I miraculously managed to keep from being repossessed while I was without a home; the car that served as my only form of emotional respite, was gone as well. When Spirit told me, "the lease is up and you are to let it go", I snapped back, "No way! I almost lost this car every other month for the past year and a half, and I'm not letting it go now." Needless to say, sometimes we don't know what's best for us or what the Universe is aligning on our behalf. When I finally succumbed to the insistent pressure from Spirit that the higher path was to let the car go, I said, "okay, but how am I to live in my new home, in a rural location that has no public transit?"

Literally, within an hour, I was given a vehicle. It was a beat-up, old van that needed work and a massive cleaning overhaul! So with Divine Humour in tow, I tossed the grungy back seat, scrubbed everything, put new carpet in and jazzed it up with colourful pillows, mini lights and a prayer flag, and named it Goldilocks to honour the ramshackle gold tone of her coat. It was a shabby replacement, but with various, ongoing mechanical upgrades, it worked (most of the time), and it provided wonderful relief from the financial strain of payments while I was getting back on my feet. I was incredibly grateful.

I continued to make every effort to do what I could to feel better, make positive changes and focus on feeling gratitude for all the alignments that gifted me with the wisdom I had acquired. By this point on my journey, paying attention to signs, honouring my intuition, and listening to my Spirit Guides, had become my way of living.

The most profound nugget of wisdom - I had learned to fully Trust. As I settled into a stable home again, I embraced the numerous spiritual awakenings that enabled the necessary surrender to allow Spirit to work through me as a conduit in sharing the gifts I had been given. I was living a more conscious life. I was aware of choosing to perceive through the lens of Love, enjoying Shifters (a tool that Spirit had taught me over a decade earlier; a self-created list of things that help to shift my energy into a higher vibration), doing Ceremonies to honour experiences, feeling whatever was coming to the surface and asking for Guidance.

Yaaah!! I finally felt able to get excited and also relax into fully enjoying my life! The confidence anchored that I was done with the horrendous experiences of loss and I was ready to embrace all the awesomeness of standing on my own feet again! The Universe, however, had another plan for me, to practice all that I had learned. Two months into my peaceful life, another loved one passed away. Two months after that...well, despite all the acquired wisdom I was embodying, I did not feel ready for what came next.

Even though Spirit had tried to prepare me for over a year with messages that this time was coming, I would immediately reject the Guidance and go straight into deep denial. The simple fact, whether I wanted to admit it or not, was that whenever her health was anything but optimal, I immediately digressed, as all of my energy was spent helping her and taking care of myself was tossed aside. This was the big one for me and I knew it was imperative to practice all I had learned about the importance of self-love.

My guides' gentle response was crystal clear every single time and I couldn't get away from it. "She is mirroring to you when you need to focus on YOU. She is ready and preparing to come Home to Spirit but is demonstrating to you that you need to focus on your own self-care, while you prepare to let her go."

For the past sixteen years, this beloved sweet soul had been the one dependable constant in my life. Kinja was my fur baby, my friend, my confidante and my companion, that had been with me through everything. There was a lot of unprocessed emotion tied up in the relationship with this precious little being and I was not ready for her to leave the planet. We had made it this far and it was time to enjoy life! Right?

For those of you who have been the guardian to a furry friend, there is no explanation needed. Respectfully, for those who perhaps don't quite understand the impact of losing a fur baby, I ask that you try to honour, that for a fur parent, the pain and grief of that loss, can cause a ragged hole as deep and painful as any other tragic loss. When we feel the huge, burning hole within us that we identify as grief, the species, age, circumstance or any other detail, doesn't matter.

So the twisted knots in my gut set off the alarms as I was about to battle through the most dreadful deadlock. As I forcefully swallowed the cluster of courage lodged in my throat, the panic button was re-set.

Even after everything I had just been through, and with all the gathered nuggets of wisdom about grief, this still felt like the biggest loss of all and the trauma that I experienced while she was in rapidly declining health, was unbearably going to cause my own deathly demise. Anguished by my struggle to give myself loving care, all of my energy was being poured into caring for the soul who had been my consistent family for the past sixteen years. Partially because it was compounding the deeper, unreleased emotions from all the previously passed loved ones; and partially because she represented all that I felt was lost.

I had rescued her in memory of my brother, with the money he had in his wallet when he died. KIN (family) + JA (my brother's initials) = KINJA.

She had made the journey with me through everything and had become my 'everything' because I had 'lost' all else. So I really struggled to find any good grief in losing her now.

Yet when Spirit spoke, it was with the same wisdom that had become so familiar to me. "The bottom line is that you still have purpose down there and are not ready to come Home yet. Everything is divinely orchestrated for the bigger picture and right now it's time for you to be completely liberated. Allow the feelings of sadness and uncertainty to come out while taking care of yourself. The more you take care of yourself, the more she will reflect that state of being back to you."

That sounded like such great wisdom and yet even the concept of this impending loss felt so overwhelming, that the grief continued to intensify. The more she reflected my lack of care, the more I crumbled deeper into personal neglect, and all of my energy went into caring for her. The mirror was perpetuated and my terrifying pit of despair became darker and much deeper. Finally, in a panicked, desperate attempt to help her, I reluctantly did what I was being told - I shifted the laser focus from worrying about her to taking care of ME. And I was shocked at the result.

When I made the effort to feel better by taking care of my own needs, so did she.

When I made the effort to give myself love, so did she.

When I made the effort to eat, so did she.

When I made the effort to be social, so did she.

It was truly mind-blowing to me. This precious soul was perfectly mirroring how I was treating myself. Every time I let go of trying to control her outcome and instead, put energy into myself, she would mimic that effort. Even now, there are no words to adequately express how profound this was.

Ultimately, there was nothing I could do to change that it was her time to go. So for me, it stood to reason that there was nothing that I could do to feel better about it either. Yet, there she was, showing me that the more I took care of myself, the more she would also be at ease. It was like I was being forced into caring for myself, if only to make the transition experience easier for her, and as I had previously learned, this was the key to choosing differently.

While giving myself more loving care didn't extinguish the burning devastation of what was occurring, it enabled me to be more functional as a human. This then equipped me with the tiny morsels of light, which enabled me to listen and follow more Guidance from Spirit. This was welcomed with such soothing waves of relief, as I was supported through meditative experiences and communication with Spirit, especially when I unexpectedly needed it most. In one such experience, I prayed while coiled up on the floor beside her and surprisingly dropped into a deep meditation. In drastic contrast to my own body ball of tension, I was shown the peaceful loving ease of her transition once she was out of her body and my brother was at a rainbow bridge to greet her. At the time, I didn't quite comprehend the connection between the two of them and just chose to accept what I didn't know…all that mattered was he was there to greet her and it all felt SO blissful. The deep contentment followed me into consciousness, and I opened my eyes to find her asleep. My body had relaxed and she was resting peacefully. I was overwhelmed with gratitude, as we were both at ease and I was able to join her in the much-needed respite of temporary slumber.

Aside from those brief moments of spiritual clarity about her transition, it felt like I was being asked to high dive off a cliff, with full awareness of a hungry abyss below, seemingly anticipating my free-fall into a feeding frenzy of trauma. It felt like I was looking in the mirror of my mortality: if I dive into the unknown, will these winds of change whisk me away to a new place of liberation? Can I possibly float- or even fly- over the darkness of the unknown? Or will I be swept away by the gale-force winds of despair and be sucked into the abyss and lost forever? As drastic as my perception was and how it fuelled my fears, nothing changed the fact that I was standing at the edge of this cliff and I had no choice but to leap.

So here it was again; I had to Trust. Trust that she was about to feel more love, peace and joy, by being back in Spirit than we can possibly imagine down here. Trust that the timing of her death was being perfectly orchestrated. Trust that I was going to be okay and could handle everything that happens. I had previously had my own out of body experiences that gifted me with first-hand awareness of how amazing it feels, and yet it felt like my heart was being violently ripped apart, as I was grasping and pleading for her to stay, while also begging for her Soul to be free and letting her go. I had to leap.

As always, Spirit kept the guidance flowing into me, as I tried to balance giving her as much energy as I could while taking care of myself, and they were persistent to ensure that I made the effort to follow their instructions. "Create a plan to alleviate the fears of when she leaves her body. Allow the emotions, in all the rawness, to surface, and feel them as deeply as you can as you let them out. Focus on self-care, high vibes and shine as brightly as you feel able to, to create a positive environment for yourself, and therefore, also for her. Souls celebrate going Home every day and leave those left behind feeling totally lost. See from the higher perspective, as you float above the abyss, and allow it all to unfold with ease as you take care of yourself through the grieving (and celebrating) process."

During the painstaking last twenty-four hours of her life, two specific Angels hovered above her, ready to assist her out of her body, while my Spirit Guides gathered in the same room and continued to guide and support me as I lay on the floor beside her. I wouldn't leave her side, and when she reached out her fragile paw and placed it on my hand, I felt a damaging surge of doubt, guilt, blame and punishment, annihilate my heart. How could I help her? What was I doing wrong or not doing enough of, to make this better for her? Why can't I find the answers? Does she know how much I have tried to help her? Even though the veterinarian and I agreed on the course of her journey, there was an ongoing self-sabotaging spiral of self-judgement and I pleaded, begged and even tried demanding that Spirit help her! She was at peace, however, I knew that, in every attempt to leave her body, she was trying to stay because I was distraught. I wished only for her to feel peace and love but I also did not know how to live without her. I found myself at the bottom of the proverbial pit, gasping for breath, like it was my last one, in a desperate attempt to make a difference; except I had nothing left to give and was depleted of everything I thought I knew.

With anguished tears pouring out of me, I sat up and looked above to the Angels in the room and screamed: "THERE IS NO NEED FOR SUFFERING!"

There came an immediate and stern response from them. "Repeat Karen."

"THERE IS NO NEED FOR SUFFERING!" I did not understand why these Angels, who clearly knew what was going on, needed me to repeat it.

Again, "Repeat Karen."

Back and forth numerous times, They kept demanding that I repeat it. Why weren't the Angels doing anything to help?

As the tears poured with more compassion and an approaching profound awareness, I repeated yet again, "THERE IS NO NEED FOR SUFFERING."

The tender voice of an Angel was accompanied by a gentle embrace this time. "Repeat again Karen. And feel it."

As I fully collapsed to the floor, the words wept out of me. "There's no need for suffering."

BAAAM!! The truth of those words jolted a shockwave, as a vibrational escalade, through my entire body and then Kinja's body - and then blasted out in an all-encompassing ripple through the planet and back into the Universe! Seriously stunned, I couldn't move. Whaaaaat just happened?

Imagine racing on a highway - hastily, erratic, and barely in control because you are wearing glasses that are too dark - you simply cannot see clearly. Up ahead is a translucent screen and you have no idea that you're about to smash directly through it. The impact causes an energetic blackout, as the dark lenses of perception are dislodged from the tattered grooves around your eyes. The tension of prolonged perceptual hostility vanishes.

Your authentic vision is restored and you're now on the other side of the invisible veil. You see that you are still driving the same vehicle and it appears to be the same highway…yet it's somehow very different.

So there I was. The circumstances were the same, still on the floor, Kinja still dying in my arms, and it all still felt absolutely unbearable. Another layer of shaded lenses, however, was gone. It took me a minute to adjust to this significant shift in my human perception, but then it sank in.

This wasn't about her! She was peaceful and her exit portal was present for her to gracefully leave her body. Nothing could minimize the grief I was feeling, however, even in that darkest moment of the most anguished sorrow and uncertainty, it was still a choice that I choose Love or suffer in fear. There it was again. Only this time I felt it plunge expansively through the depths of my conscious awareness. There is no need for suffering.

I vowed right then- in an emotionally mangled mess on the floor- to love my Self more than ever before and to make it a priority no matter what. I had now been liberated into the sacred sanction of my own heart. And with her earthly role fulfilled, my cherished Kinja, her beloved soul, left her body shortly after, at 4:44 pm.

"Saying goodbye to her physical body is just that. It was her temporary vessel and she is now with you, back in Spirit form. Do a ceremony to free yourself from the attachment to her physical body." This felt like an impossibly harsh gesture while I was feeling such deep desolation, however, as specifically Guided, I held ceremony above her body, where I stood on trembling limbs and blubbered a list of all that she taught me and everything I was grateful for with our connection. It is noteworthy to mention that this list was something I was strongly Guided to create while she was still alive - and I was beyond grateful to have it prepared and ready to read aloud. My shaking words revealed a tribute to her quirky life and how she so lovingly and positively impacted mine. I blessed her Soul as it was now free. Even though I was choking in tears for the irreplaceable loss, when it was complete, I felt an actual detachment from her Earth-bound body, as a stronger connection was anchored to her in Spirit. I was gratefully astonished that I could, at that moment, feel any resemblance of 'Good' grief - yet there it was if I chose to embrace it.

The next few months were extremely difficult while navigating a constant negotiation in the declared battle between my conscious self and my ego. I vowed to honour Love for myself while riding the emotional waves, while my ego felt more comfortable in the conditioned response of grief. As I observed all of this from the higher perspective, I saw the interesting game of the ego - trying to keep me crawling in the comfort zone of anguish and fear, and even attempting to trap me there, by feeling guilty that I didn't do enough, that I am not enough, and that to prove my love, I need to show the world how my light has been dimmed or darkened completely, from all of the grief. It felt like the assurance of surviving the emotional waves was twisted into maintaining the turbulent waves. By this point, I could see how this conditioned game was designed - for a sole purpose - to keep me flailing in the chaos of conditioned grief.

The pain that is felt during the inevitable grieving period is indeed, invariably diverse; yet Spirit kept it simple. "That energy just wants to be expressed as it leaves your body, so let it out." I cried. I wailed and wept. I screamed. And I sobbed. The ferociousness of the emotional releases frightened me at times. I felt such intense pain in my head, that I thought something could burst. I felt such stabbing pains in my body that I thought something could rupture. I felt like I could actually die from the pain of this grief that was tearing through me.

The energy that erupted was a profound combination of grief that went back to my brother and the arduous childhood we shared. For me, this was now the mothership of grief that had landed and the powerful winds of this change blew open all caskets for deep clearing. Like a buried treasure, a lifetime of hidden, fragmented grief nuggets, from so many different losses, were now surging to the surface for release. As I pleaded to Spirit for help when the pain felt truly unbearable, I would instantly feel the warmth of an Angel embracing me and I'd find respite in a deep breath. The Angel would then, ever so gently, remind me after a deep emotional release, "Now go drink some water and make something healthy to eat."

Profound releasing occurs when we are ready to allow it fully, as our nervous system is innately equipped to handle it all - and when in a state of homeostasis, our bodies will integrate and heal whatever comes into our experience. With my personal declaration of choosing to honour love, I spoke gently with the vicious calls of grief within me; and with patience and compassion, I welcomed all of it to leave my body. Befriending these inner gremlins and inviting them to be free was exactly what they were waiting for. The more I welcomed the freedom from this energy, the deeper it went for clearing - and pervaded through lifetimes, grieving the darkness of vast tunnels of conditioned responses. A beautiful, new, cycle was being anchored in my nervous system - the more grieving energy that surfaced, the more I welcomed it…and the more it also wished to leave my body! This was only possible because I had chosen to do it differently this time. I chose to feel the cesspool of emotions that go with grieving, but I was choosing to do it with Love, which meant taking care of myself unconditionally. This allowed me to surrender, my body to be more at ease, and my nervous system to do exactly what it is equipped to do: balance and heal.

I was willing to allow this emptying out process to clear the depths of my being, of whatever burrowed anguish, sorrow, and heartbreak was ready to be freed. I was the patient and the nurse simultaneously. While I didn't know what it was going to look or feel like exactly, I welcomed the change that this depth of releasing embodied.

This is a choice that we make every day.

So every morning when I opened my eyes and my ego beckoned to take the lower road of conditioning, I visualized the crossroad and chose at that moment. I declared out loud, "I choose to be in a higher vibration today. I choose to honour Love."

What did that mean?

It meant taking care of my physical body; eating healthy food, drinking enough water, exercising (moving my body), breathing fresh air, resting when needed, and providing ample opportunity to sleep at night.

It meant doing things that I enjoyed. Allowing Joy and Freedom in my daily practice of living while benefiting from the simplicity of such immediate efforts.

I got out my Shifters List; the list of everything that helps to shift my energy. I revised it and made the daily effort to ensure that I was fuelling myself with it. As an example, I found a few new songs that resonated and gave me sparks of inspiration that made me want to dance.

I made plans to go out, even though I just wanted to stay home, where I was reminded of Kinja and all that she represented. When I was out and returned home, I welcomed whatever varying degree of release was necessary, over and over and over, until there came the day when I could return home and just walk in without a full-scale emotional melt-down.

I nurtured myself through the sorrow, while I allowed it to be fully expressed in an appropriately safe space.

Spirit had prepared me with the instructions to, "Take one step every day that is moving forward in the new life as you now know it. Clear out the old energy in every way. To honour your sacred space is to honour that some things no longer serve a purpose here."

While crawling in the aftermath of a catastrophic storm, we are confronted with a nagging choice; perpetuate the exhausted perspective while scrummaging amidst the scattered debris or start cleaning it up and create a new sacred space to appreciate the journey of contrast. Our choices determine how we experience.

For me, this action included removing items and re-arranging the apartment so that it didn't revolve around Kinja and her rapidly declining health. At the hand of urgency, created by my Guides, I started it the morning after she passed and did only one thing per day, while still honouring what felt right to keep a couple of special items as keepsakes. This was heart-wrenching to do however I am retrospectively so deeply grateful that I was so adamantly encouraged to do it this way.

Spirit's Guidance reminded me, "Further ceremony is unnecessary, however for YOU, it is a gesture of acknowledging, accepting, embracing, and honouring whoever has left. Do a simple ceremony to give Gratitude and create momentum. This is for you, not Kinja or anyone else. Everyone passed is at peace. Do this for YOU. It is simple, so keep it simple. Just give Gratitude. Then continue to give that same loving energy to yourself and watch it expand from within you. Choose Love and let the wisdom of the experiences anchor you, Kinja and everyone else…into Freedom."

Kinja's final transition back to Spirit was symbolic of the full liberation that I had also experienced. By choosing self-love and utilizing all such acquired tools, I had been relieved of the inhibiting grief energy that was congested within me, and throughout lifetimes of conditioning, the threads of time had been cleared to activate the full expression of my authentic self.

So in honouring her precious life here and to celebrate my newly enriched perspective about choosing to honour Love, I decided to spread her ashes in all three Provinces that we had lived in together. I went to several meaningful locations, said a simple prayer of gratitude to her for helping to liberate me of so much buried energy, and left a piece of rose quartz. With that, there are now several rose crystals back in the Earth that span from the Atlantic Ocean to the Pacific Ocean.

While departing the location of a ceremony in another Province, I pleaded for a sign from Spirit. I specifically asked for three balloons to appear together; one purple, one green and one blue, to represent three of the loved ones that had passed away and to signify that I was on track with how I was dealing with this grief. I asked for the balloons to be shown to me by the time I arrived at the airport, which was in two days.

Spirit responded, "Why not ask for a rainbow of balloons to represent all loved ones in Spirit and to signify all that you've learned about grief?" To which I replied, "I really need this sign from you and I wish to make it simple and more likely to occur."

I could sense a warm chuckle from all the Angels around me.

When I set the GPS for the two-and-a-half-hour drive to the airport, my intuition compelled me to go a different route…that was over three hours long! I was apprehensive, as it left no extra time for any delays along the way. Nevertheless, I listened. I had learned to Trust when receiving messages from Spirit and figured that I was being gifted with avoiding a prolonged traffic jam or possibly even something more stressful. I had never taken this route to the airport before, so I chose to enjoy the drive, wherever it was taking me. Well, unbeknownst to me, a monumental moment of revelation was about to occur.

While on the last stretch to the airport, on an unfamiliar, industrial road, I caught a glimpse of beautiful confetti pops of colour dancing in the distance. While I was intensively focused on calculating the allocation of time to return the rental car, check-in and get to the gate on time, I had completely forgotten about my original request for a sign.

As I drove past this seemingly random place, on an unplanned route, fireworks of joyful tears glistened in the shimmering rainbow light from the Universe, passing by a parking lot FULL of every colour of balloon imaginable! There I was, driving towards the same city where I recalled succumbing to the self-imposed expectations while grieving about my brother. He marked the beginning of me grieving by condition, and here I was, being showered in a rainbow affirmation, confirming that there is always a choice - we can choose differently. We can choose good grief.

When a journey has completed, it is a common condition to perceive it as a form of trauma or loss...whether it is the passing away of a loved one, the end of a relationship, losing a job, declining health or change in the physical body, a shift of possessions, or even a variety of ego deaths. But we are on this planet to Love & Play and as we go through the process to release the culmination of conditioned griefs, we not only have every right to feel the spectrum of emotions, we also deserve to rejoice in full celebration of each one.

To honour Love is to live authentically - to be honest with yourself about what you are truly feeling in your life. As an infinite spiritual being in a human experience, if you're being authentic, you allow yourself to feel it all, take care of yourself while doing so, and celebrate along the way! When you honour love as it is all there is, you are honouring who you really are. Then, you are in a position to truly make a difference, as you can only help another as much as you have helped yourself, and you can only love another as much as you love yourself. These words of wisdom from Spirit continue to remind me of the wonderful nature of our full potential...and is beautifully expressed via the poem, as written by Marianne Williamson:

"Our deepest fear is not that we are inadequate. Our deepest fear is that we are powerful beyond measure. It is our light, not our darkness that most frightens us. We ask ourselves, Who am I to be brilliant, gorgeous, talented, fabulous? Actually, who are you not to be? You are a child of God. Your playing small does not serve the world. There is nothing enlightened about shrinking so that other people won't feel insecure around you. We are all meant to shine, as children do. We were born to make manifest the glory of God that is within us. It's not just in some of us; it is in everyone. And as we let our own light shine, we unconsciously give other people permission to do the same. As we are liberated from our own fear, our presence automatically liberates others."

Life is a constant maze of learning, growing, evolving, and waking up to the choices we have through it all - and living consciously doesn't mean without experiences that cause grief, trial or tribulation. It means honouring the authentic expression of who we are. To think that we are ever done learning is just the plea bargain the ego tries to make at every triggering crossroad. The contrast of perception is acclimated into wisdom when we honour that where we are is because of where we have been.

It was the three-year death-anniversary of Kinja, and it struck an intense cord of recall, triggering my ability to allow other Beings to be on their own journey and not take on the self-righteous task of being in control of their life…or death. The delicacy of life was demonstrated again, as a dead sparrow revealed its last breath on my balcony. A familiar panic zipped through my body. In repetitious disbelief, I fell to my knees on the floor, holding my head as anguished tears soaked my face, while intermittently checking back to the balcony. Is it really dead? It is really still there? Why is it there? What did I do? Is there anything I could have done to prevent this from happening? Maybe it's just stunned? Can I make it not dead? If it's not my fault, why did it choose my balcony to die?!

Grief has claws. Claws that emerge to grip and strangle, or shake out any remnants of old perspectives. It is always a choice and it was mine to make - remain in panic and puncture the scars of an old response, or choose differently. Gratefully, I had learned to choose wisely. I permitted myself to feel the freak-out and then got up and prepared to honour the life that had changed form in my presence. While doing a ceremony over this precious creature, with its tiny wings and squinted eyes, I celebrated with tears, for a life that I knew nothing about, and prayed for the Soul to be free. My final acceptance in the moment of this soul's departure, remarkably also brought me to a deeper acceptance of all the loved ones whose time had ended here. The curiosity of this tiny sparrow's life brought forth the culmination of all the loved one's deaths and somehow anchored an even deeper appreciation of what a miraculous journey it is to be on this planet.

Yes, being human can feel impossibly draining, complicated and confusing. It is also awesome, full of miracles and a beautiful messy exploration! How we choose to experience it, is up to us. To remember that the Universe knows what we need to help us evolve is to allow the flow of Divine Timing and Orchestration. I am constantly being given the opportunity to practice this.

Just as I was floating in my own pool of serenity in life, basking in the comfort of stability and allowing a state of full surrender, my landlord innocently capsized me with the news of selling my home. The perceived container of stability instantly collapsed around me and I was swept into a stormy sea of emotions, where it felt like I was drowning in a tsunami of panic. O.M.G. I had to find a new home during a time of massive collective chaos and a skyrocketing rental market. Life has a way of pitching those sudden curve balls that have the potential to knock us over. I went from peaceful surrender to total panic with only two words: "sell condo".

Without thinking, I started pacing back and forth with such conviction, as though I was purposefully digging my own grave in this familiar pit of despair. This was an old response to a very real experience of 'losing' my home and all of my belongings once before. So while my heart palpitated, gasping for breath and trying to keep up with the racing thoughts of how to handle being 'homeless' again, I chose to do what had, by this point, been ingrained into me. I chose another way of looking at this perceived crisis. As I trembled in the potentiality of not having a home again, the words "I'm so f"ing scared." stumbled from my lips. Shocked, I heard a compassionate and yet firm whisper in response, "Are you really?" Only this time, it wasn't my Guides speaking; it was me. My human perception shifted at the moment, to choose differently and I simply asked myself "Are you really? Are you actually scared?"

Stunned by my own intervention, I paused the automatic panic play button to feel what was real and laughed out loud, "No, actually I'm not scared!" I was thinking scared, not feeling scared. The fog of old conditioning quickly dissipated and revealed the clarity of Truth that had become my trusted friend; at this moment there is no need for panic. I am full of Love. Everything is Love. I choose the lens of Truth so no matter what is happening, I am okay.

Interestingly, my mind attempted to lure me into 'squirrel moments' of finding a solid reason to panic. But even the ego eventually gets tired and with my determined resolution to choose differently, the Divine intervention would immediately yield "Bring it back to the moment". This faithful mantra echoed - like the tune of a favourite song - as my mind found peace in the persistent permission to find relief in surrender.

With that shifted perspective, I made myself available to see, and therefore experience, the miraculous alignments of my next home. When I chose to be real with myself, and remember the choice of response, the reality of losing my home became an exciting liberation of a changed address. And as I write this now, surrounded by packed bins for moving, I am filled with immense gratitude and excitement for this next adventure.

So be honest with yourself. Are you truly distraught? Absolutely desolate? Or are you caught up in the spin cycle of an old reel in conditioned response? Absolutely feel what you are feeling...while also giving yourself the respect of compassionate observation - you deserve it.

May you feel the magical power of surrender as you choose another way - as you choose Good Grief.

good grief workbook

Tools to Help Integrate the Experience of Good Grief

#1 CHOOSE TO HONOUR LOVE

If you are consciously making the decision to experience grief differently, then you are declaring to Love yourself as you have never done before. It is not a question about Loving that which you are grieving. That's a given - that love is real. This is about you loving yourself more, rather than focusing on that which is gone. It's about permitting yourself to feel whatever comes up, without judgment and without succumbing to difficult emotions. You are in a healing process and you can choose to do it with LOVE.

Declaration of Self Love "I _____, Hereby Choose to Honour Love"

Describe how will you love yourself even more during this time?

_____

_____

_____

In the energy of lovingly caring for yourself, what do you need to do for YOU?

For example...

Face your fears in order to alleviate them

If you are fearing a pending, probable, or possible outcome; make a simple checklist of steps that you'll be required to do, not necessarily right away, but eventually, when and if your fear becomes reality. This is not about feeding fears or focusing on lower energy. It is simply to acknowledge and plan for what may be coming and might inhibit your clarity and ability to give yourself loving care. Worrying drains a lot of energy. Make the list so that your energy is available for the experience at the moment instead of dreading what might become.

For me, in the experience of a passing loved one, this meant making a checklist of what I would need to do when they passed away. It was a simple list: Remember to Breathe. Call a pre-designated person for support. Make celebration of life arrangements and so on. Once I made the list, it relieved the panic of what to do when it happened.

Which fears are overwhelming this grief experience?

_____

_____

Make a checklist of steps or to-dos that alleviates the fears that are draining you.

_____

_____

#2 CONSIDER THE LIBERATIONS

This is a touchy concept especially when the loss, whatever it is, is causing so much turmoil. You may think, how dare I feel liberated by loss? But this exercise, sent from my Guides, literally channelled through me and I was so grateful to have it after the fact. This was a list of possibilities that were newly available in the reality where I felt such great loss. This included things such as: Bringing live plants into the home, travelling, sleeping through the night, experiencing new people, and utilizing other gifts. I remember when the pen took over and an extensive list was created, I felt mortified that the page reflected I celebrate, in so many ways, something that I was feeling such a tremendous loss over. And then something truly unexpected happened; I also felt the morsel of hope that I would indeed enjoy these aspects of life.

Which liberations are you willing to acknowledge?

Make a list of Liberations.

_____

_____

_____

#3 CEREMONY

Ceremony honours and celebrates the connection and/or experience. The key note here is that this ceremony is not necessary for anyone else but YOU. A Ceremony to acknowledge, accept, honour and embrace what was, what is and what will be.

Whether it is the end of a relationship, being liberated from a job, lost possessions of any kind, a loved one passing away, or even the etheric death of an outdated version of yourself; they were all part of your life for reasons that are now complete and therefore worthy of celebration.

What did you learn from the connection or experience?

_____

_____

_____

What are you grateful for? From the connection or experience?

_____

_____

_____

#4 FEEL IT

A perception fuels a thought, which triggers an emotional response, which creates a physical reaction/behaviour and if necessary, a release to get the energy out of the body. Acknowledge them all and feel them all, as deeply and as often as they surface. Whether it is a thought, an emotion or a physical reaction; the energy is in your awareness because it wants to leave your body. It is all coming out of your energy field and making room for new and magical alignments!

Be honest with yourself.

Are you comparing your current experience to a previous one? (You are - because that is how conditioning works - until you change it)

_____

_____

_____

Are you willing to acknowledge and accept that you are, fundamentally LOVE, and in this moment, you are still Love; you are still you; you are okay no matter what?

_____

How are you really feeling?

Another fascinating revelation around conditioned response occurred when I realized that once the collective around you has moved past the initial experience, it can feel like everyone has forgotten that you are still experiencing much grief. This can then be felt as though you are expected to be over it by now. Yet the reality is very different; the releasing action of grieving energies don not go away, just because you are choosing to love yourself. You may still feel the sadness and you may still miss whatever or whoever is now gone. No one is going to feel your grief like you do, and that is amazing. It is your personal experience, which is why it is also your choice to acknowledge love while experiencing the roller coaster, no matter how long that takes. The point of loving yourself more is to permit yourself to feel the way you feel, so celebrate even that while you allow the grieving energy to leave your body.

Choose a few release techniques that you can easily do on your own. Some personal faves for me; literally allowing a good cry at any moment it comes up, writing, screaming into a pillow, dancing, shaking out parts of the body, deep breathing exercises, singing loudly and with emotional emphasis...the list can go on and on!

What are your Release Techniques?

#5 SHIFTERS

These are used to help anchor in more Light, as you release the denser energies of grief. They also help to re-train your brain so that your transformed automatic response after allowing the denser energies to release, is to do something positive for yourself and celebrate how awesome you are!

What gives you warm fuzzies? What helps you feel even just a little bit better, lighter or hopeful?

These are Shifters and by consciously bringing them into your life, you are telling the Universe, "I want to feel good" regardless of what is going on in your life. Some examples include; seeing mountains, birds chirping, sunsets, certain smells, like vanilla or roses, babies laughing, dogs, cats, monkeys or any animal, favourite colours, giving hugs, smiling at a stranger, bubble baths, and so on. Consider all of your senses and the possibilities are infinite!

My Shifters List

_____

_____

_____

#6 ASK

Ask for help: We are in this life together and meant to help one another. Whether it is reaching out to receive support from loved ones or seeking assistance from professionals, it is a strength to honour what you are feeling. Be authentic and ask for help when you feel you need it.

There are also oodles of Angels ready to assist you and all you need to do is ask.

Who can I ask for help?

_____

_____

_____

Ask for Signs: Receiving signs from the Universe is a beautiful way to affirm that we are exactly where we are meant to be, regardless of what is going on. Whether it's asking your Guides or chatting with loved ones who are in Spirit, remember all you have to do is ASK and then pay attention. The more often you are in the Self-Love vibration, the easier it is to recognize the signs that are constantly being given to you.

#7 ACCEPT THE INVITATION

Sometimes we need a reminder that we do live in a realm of free will, free spirit and free choice. So as affirmative nudges are necessary, to look in the mirror and say...

You are going through a tremendous change as a Human Being. Despite it all, you are still here! You are free to continue on your journey. You are free to choose differently in every moment of every day. You are free to be grateful for everything that happens as a way of helping to clear your energy.

You are free to choose the Truth of LOVE. You are free to share that LOVE with everyone around you. You are free to be brave. You are free to express what you feel. You are also free to repeat any story or limiting belief that keeps you struggling. It is all freedom. Accept this freedom as a choice so that you can experience it as your way of Being Human.

Additional Notes to Self:

_____

_____

_____

_____

_____

_____

_____

_____

_____

_____

_____

_____

_____

_____

_____

_____

_____

_____

CPSIA information can be obtained
at www.ICGtesting.com
Printed in the USA
BVHW091950250222
630113BV00001B/1/J